The Green Business Guide

A One Stop Resource
for Businesses of All
Shapes and Sizes to
Implement
Eco-Friendly Policies,
Programs, and Practices

GLENN BACHMAN

CAREER
PRESS
Franklin Lakes, NJ

Mixed Sources

Product group from well-managed forests, controlled sources and recycled wood or fibre

www.fsc.org   Cert no. SW-COC-002985
© 1996 Forest Stewardship Council

THE GREEN BUSINESS GUIDE
EDITED BY JODI BRANDON / TYPESET BY EILEEN MUNSON
Cover design by Howard Grossman/12E Design
The Career Press, Inc., 3 Tice Road, PO Box 687, Franklin Lakes, NJ 07417
www.careerpress.com

Library of Congress Cataloging-in-Publication Data

Bachman, Glenn.
    The green business guide : a one stop resource for business of all shapes and sizes to implement eco-friendly policies, programs, and practices / by Glenn Bachman.
        p. cm.
    Includes bibliographical references and index.
    ISBN 978-1-60163-048-3
        1. Management—Environmental aspects. 2. Business enterprises—Environmental aspects. 3. Industries—Environmental aspects. I. Title.

HD30.255B33 2009
658.4′083—dc22

2008053949

Acknowledgments

Thanks to Amory Lovins, an inspirational scientist with the Rocky Mountain Institute, who first introduced me to energy efficiency and effectiveness; to the Odoms, who introduced me to systems thinking and ecology; to Herman Daly, who spoke of sustainability through the lens of a steady-state economy; to Al Gore, who publicized the inconvenient truth of climate change; and to Joel Makower, whose writings on business and sustainability provoke thought and response.

Special thanks to Michael Weinstein, a mentor, who taught me about ordered problem-solving in complex worlds.

Thanks go to the many clients who helped me create the framework by asking the right questions and reinforcing the value of checklists and keeping things simple.

Thanks to Michael Pye, Kirsten Dalley, and Jodi Brandon, all of Career Press, who patiently believed in the concept of the guide. Thanks to my agent, the steady Neil Salkind of the Salkind Agency, who found me through the thoughtful Ted McGuire (thank you, Ted!).

Thanks to many people who directly and indirectly influenced the content and shaping of this book: Craig Lindell of AquaPoint, with constant reminders to seek the deep drivers; John Bullard, who opens both minds and doors; Katherine O'Dea, with a sharpened pencil and the reasoned response mantra of "it all depends"; Robert Leaver and the good folks at New Commons, who assemble and facilitate sustainability conversations at their cafés; Chris Jones with the University of California at Berkeley; Jane Bare, Abby Swaine, and James Critchfield of the EPA; and Joelle Michaels and Eugene Burns of the EIA. Many thanks to the many representatives of certifying organizations who worked with me in assembling data for chapters 28 and 29.

Special thanks to Jeff Thurlow of Wood Specialties of Seattle: show me; to Gerritt Rosenthal, my favorite contrarian; to Bill Jacobson, who seamlessly brings sustainability back to deep ecology roots; to B & Dave, who are my most enthusiastic supporters; to Terry and Jerri, who remind me to pursue craftsmanship; and, most importantly, to Shannon, whose heart, light, and ongoing encouragement bring joy...forever.

Contents

Chapter 1

Introduction

We live in an extraordinary time—a time that is being defined by a perfect storm of depleting natural resources, imperfect economics, and climate change. Our institutions are challenged by the trends that make up the storm.

One trend is a growing population of worldwide consumers; however, there also are more than a billion people who lack clean water and sanitation, who go to sleep hungry, and who have inadequate healthcare.

A second trend is a global economy that is defined by a relatively free exchange of goods. Production of these goods is dependent on a dwindling reserve of natural resources. And as we remember, the law of supply and demand tells us that as the availability of a commodity goes down, its price goes up. Furthermore, we have priced many of these goods and services without capturing the full costs associated with their manufacture, use, and disposal.[1]

The final trend is a change in the health of the planet. We've cut down forests, and allowed toxic chemicals to enter oceans, rivers, and lakes, and we're pumping large quantities of pollutants into the atmosphere, causing climate change, the magnitude and consequences of which have only recently been acknowledged.

The intent of this guide is not to describe these trends in detail; others already have done that successfully. The objective is to provide tools and resources that enable organizations to weather the storm by becoming more ecologically responsible. Even so, it is useful to provide an overview of these trends in order to create a workable foundation for the reader.

Population

More than 6.7 billion people inhabit the planet, a figure that has more than doubled since 1960 and will surpass 8 billion in the next 20 years. The United States is home to slightly more than 300 million residents, or about 4.5 percent of the world population.[2] The U.S. Census Bureau projects that the population will cross the 400 million mark in approximately 30 years.[3]

Natural Resources

The growing population places tremendous burdens on global natural resources. Known reserves of mineral resources, such as lead, copper, silver, and zinc, are projected to last a couple of decades.[4] Forests have been harvested; some converted to crops. Productive agricultural soils are devalued by erosion and require vast quantities of fertilizers. Many of these same fertilizers wash into streams and rivers, and are then deposited into ponds, lakes, and our oceans, where plant life is stimulated, but at the expense of fisheries and aquatic mammals.

Energy fuels the global economic boom, with 87 percent of the worldwide energy produced from non-renewable reserves of petroleum, natural gas, and coal. U.S. oil production peaked in the early 1970s and has declined since, making the country reliant on foreign sources of oil—and vulnerable to disruption in oil supplies. Global petroleum production is hitting its peak now and will continue to decline over the next decades. There is some scientific disagreement over the timing of the peak of oil production. However, it is just that—a question of timing. Supplies of oil will be largely depleted in the next generation or two. The United States is rich in coal deposits; however, mining coal devastates land and burning coal results in greenhouse gas emissions (as does burning all fossil fuels).

Greenhouse Gases and Climate Change

Greenhouse gas emissions have been increasing for more than a century. The repercussions of these emissions has been little understood until the last couple of decades, when the scientific community has observed that increasing concentrations of greenhouse gases is resulting in climate change.

The average global temperature already has increased by 2 degrees Fahrenheit over land areas.[5] This increase seems innocuous in the context of day-to-day fluctuations. The term global warming sounds warm and fuzzy. However, climate change is anything but that. It is moving relatively stable natural systems into flux and chaos, resulting in a series of ecological impacts that are exceeding the initial projected rate of occurrence and promising to become more acute:

- As air temperatures rise, glaciers are melting, changing runoff patterns and the availability of water.
- The extent of sea ice is diminishing: 2007 had 25 percent less Arctic sea ice than ever before, and 2008 was the first time in modern history that a Northwest Passage allowed circumnavigation.
- Less glacier, snow, and ice coverage means less solar radiation reflectance and more absorption, accelerating the warming of soils, the air, and high latitude waters.
- The oceans are becoming warmer, fueling tropical storms.
- Regions are becoming warmer, reducing winter and increasing summer temperatures.
- Storm events are becoming more intense, increasing the intensity of runoff and reducing the water content of soils and groundwater recharge.
- As water, air, and soil temperatures change, aquatic and terrestrial habitats are being altered, in some cases more rapidly than plants and animals can adapt; in other cases supporting invasive species.
- As ocean temperatures rise, and as ice caps and glaciers melt, sea levels are rising, at first causing subtle reductions of beach, but over the next century inundating low-elevation coastal communities. It was previously thought that the rise would be 1.5–2 feet before 2100. Global sea level rise before 2100 is now projected to be closer to 7 feet.[6]

▶ Changes in weather patterns will alter human health as new regions are exposed to infectious diseases that thrive in the altered climate patterns, and individuals are exposed to debilitating temperatures.

James Hansen, director of NASA's Goddard Institute for Space Studies and the United State's leading climatologist, believes that a safe level of carbon dioxide concentration is no more than 350 parts per million (ppm). Yet, current levels already exceed 385 ppm and are rising at 2 ppm per year. Without a dramatic, immediate shift (that is, stabilizing emissions by 2012), the planet will reach a tipping point, and civilization, as we know it, will no longer be possible.

There are many excellent, thorough resources that describe these trends in detail. A collection of readings is listed in the Bibliography for individuals interested in exploring topics in greater depth.

Climate Change and Enterprise

The perfect storm represents a collision between a growing global population, quality of life expectations, and the capacity of our resources to accommodate that demand. The United Nations' *Millennium Ecological Assessment Report* summarizes it: "Human activity is putting such strain on the natural functions of the Earth that the ability of the planet's ecosystems to sustain future generations can no longer be taken for granted."[7]

The implications of climate change are listed not to evoke fear or dismay but instead to point out that business—and all our institutions—face change and risks associated with that change. For enterprises we can expect that:

▶ The supply and costs of materials and supplies will increase.
▶ Operational costs will increase.
▶ Risks abound from physical changes to the natural environment, and from demands for capital needed to contend with these changes.
▶ "Business as usual" is not a possibility.

These challenges also will be faced by households, schools, places of worship, organizations, and governmental agencies. It will not be one sector or one institution that will lead through the storm. It will be many leaders from many sectors.

Green Enterprise, Opportunity, and Leadership

If the sense of enterprise is that the perfect storm jeopardizes the license to operate, then it also should appreciate that the storm conditions reveal extraordinary opportunity. The opportunity lies in correctly identifying the risks to the organization, determining how best to allocate resources to blunt the most destructive risks, and positioning the enterprise to thrive in a period of oil and natural resource depletion, and climate change.

Organizations planning to thrive will do so by earning market trust, recognition, and respect; leading their industries; and collaborating with fellow stakeholders caught in the storm. *The Green Business Guide* is a resource for an organization that is considering or is in the process of transforming itself, with narrative and charts to explain, ideas to provoke thought, and templates and checklists to simplify taking action.

Enjoy the journey. Celebrate your successes along the way.

Chapter 2

Attributes of a Green Enterprise

Green organizations recycle. They install faucet flow restrictors to conserve water and compact fluorescent lamps to conserve electricity. They reduce the packaging materials that enclose their products. They use hybrid cars and encourage their workers to take public transportation to work. They do all of those and so much more: They aren't just efficient; they are effective.

Green organizations have the ability to see the world objectively and to develop and take actions that will improve the ecological footprint of the enterprise and, by extension, the global environment. Seven organizational qualities distinguish the green enterprise.

▶ **Awareness**

The green organization is an observant participant in the community, region, industry, and global environment. The enterprise is knowledgeable of ecological, economic, and cultural trends and forecasts, and it understands its own strengths and weaknesses. This awareness is used by the green enterprise to proactively manage risks—developing responses to mitigate threats and creating programs to capitalize on opportunities.

▶ **Resource Efficiency and Effectiveness**

Green enterprises understand that the delivery of their products and services results in the consumption of fossil fuels, minerals, water, and other natural resources, which in turn results in the loss of natural capital.

By conducting audits, the enterprise is aware of its own consumption of natural resources and establishes a baseline for reducing its consumption footprint. But it considers consumption beyond its own operations: acknowledging how its suppliers' and customers' consumption, with respect to the product and service, is—by extension—a part of its own.

Green enterprises typically take the first step on the path of resource effectiveness by incorporating efficiency strategies to eliminate resource waste, embracing the mantra of "avoid, reduce, reuse, and recycle." Green organizations look to substitute abundant materials for those that are scarce and to substitute degradable materials for those that persist in nature.

Green organizations continue on the path toward resource effectiveness by relying on renewable resources drawn from sustainable sources. They practice industrial ecology, searching for symbiotic relationships with other enterprises, and use innovation to their competitive advantage.

▶ **Customer Focus**

Green organizations demonstrate an understanding of customer needs. They embrace ecodesign principles and take responsibility for the consequences of manufacture, use, and final disposition of their products and services. Low life-cycle costs are a hallmark of their products, and their labels clearly communicate the attributes of their product. For the green organization, fair pricing, accurate marketing claims, and honored relationships with customers are the norm.

▶ **Worker-Centric Focus**

Green organizations view their staff as crucial partners in achieving and sustaining ecological goals for the enterprise. Foremost is a commitment to the safety and health of workers. The physical well-being extends to a working culture that supports lifelong learning and encourages contributions that help individuals achieve their potential. These contributions are magnified through teamwork that builds collective problem-solving and decision-making, distributes leadership, and achieves a culture of innovation. Staff are compensated fairly for satisfying work, expected to balance work with a fulfilling life outside of work, and are encouraged to be ambassadors to the community.

▶ **Community Partner**

Green enterprises are active and engaged in the community. They recognize their responsibility to improve the ecological, economic, and social health of the neighborhoods, towns, and regions in which they conduct business. They conduct their organization in a transparent manner and accurately communicate the results of their green initiatives to stakeholders.

As responsible corporate citizens, green organizations work to minimize, if not eliminate, the adverse effects of their operations.

▶ **Responsibility**

In acknowledging ecological conditions and trends, green enterprises recognize that "conducting business in the same old way" is not an acceptable course of action. If climate change is to be halted (let alone reversed); if natural treasures are to be protected for future generations; if our oceans, seas, rivers, and lakes are to be vital; and if our resources are not to be depleted, then intervention is needed.

Ecologically friendly enterprises recognize that corrective action isn't the sole purview of government, or schools, or individuals, or nonprofits, or places of worship or industry. It will only be through *all* stakeholders taking action that deteriorating ecological conditions can be reversed.

Though we have limited ability to affect other entities, we do have the power to take ecological initiatives in our places of business. Green enterprises acknowledge that capability and accept their responsibility to transform their businesses.

▶ **Leadership**

Accepting responsibility to minimize the ecological impact of the organization is a statement of leadership that demonstrates alignment between the mission of the enterprise and a set of core values that transcend profitability.

The statement of leadership is an acknowledgment of a greater responsibility that extends to stakeholders, not just shareholders. The leadership that is demonstrated is one that transcends leading the business: It extends to the industry, to the regulating agencies, to the community, to our children, and to their children.

Chapter 3

Benefits of Being a Green Enterprise

There are many benefits to becoming a green enterprise. Some of the advantages are readily apparent; others may be less obvious. Not all benefits apply to all businesses. Creating a business case enables organizations to understand the specific benefits that could accrue from a program to green the enterprise. The following are a dozen ways that a green enterprise can benefit.

Ecological Benefits

Direct ecological benefits include reduction in the consumption of fossil fuels, water use, and treatment; minimizing the amount of resources depleted in producing goods and services; and reducing the volume of waste products that are incinerated or disposed of in landfills.

The benefits extend "upstream" of the organization to reduced ecological impact in the harvesting of raw materials and resources used as inputs to the organization, and "downstream" of the organization as finished goods are transported to the customer, used by the customer, and attended to at the end of their usable life.

If fossil fuel demand is lessened, then there are fewer unhealthy emissions, less mountaintop removal, diminished vulnerability to disruptions of imported petroleum supplies, and associated impacts to water, habitat, and ecosystems. These direct benefits also translate into reductions in emissions that contribute to health problems and climate change.

If the use of natural resources is reduced, then forest resources, water resources, and supplies of ores remain viable longer—available for the enjoyment and use of future generations.

Most importantly, taking steps to green organizations contributes to the ability to halt, if not reverse, climate change.

As enterprises become more efficient in their use of resources, they can extend their capability to effectiveness, thus creating new products and services in a symbiotic way and restoring natural systems whose functionality have been compromised by unsustainable development.

Direct Cost Savings

Reducing energy use saves the organization money. Reducing water consumption lessens supply needs and reduces wastewater treatment requirements, thereby reducing costs, whether there is public supply and treatment, or private wells and on-site treatment of effluent.

As material inputs are reduced and material outputs are managed, there is a reduction in the cost of goods sold and savings associated with waste disposal. In some instances, material outputs can become a profit center by selling waste materials for the beneficial use and reuse by others.

Managed Risks

Organizations face a number of known risks and are vulnerable to uncertainties that may impact their ability to conduct business. The most obvious ecological risks are those that result from disruptions in energy and commodity supplies, and projected increases in the prices of those resources. However, in addition to those real concerns, there are risks associated with regulatory changes and the landscape of consumer preferences.

U.S. laws pertaining to the environment are not as stringent as those in other parts of the world, particularly in Europe and New Zealand. The country has been reluctant to take a leadership role in curbing greenhouse gas emissions. As climate change becomes more acknowledged as a threat to global ecological, economic, and political stability, greater regulation is likely to be passed. It's not a question of *if* so much as it is a question of *when* regulations that are more restrictive will become law. These regulations are likely to take the form of carbon taxes, phaseouts and prohibitions on the use of hazardous chemicals for which there are safe alternatives, ecological performance labels for products, requirements to demonstrate the safety of products, mandatory takebacks, and reporting of the ecological footprints of organizations. Look to California—one of the bellwether states—to see some of these requirements in place or proposed.

Confirmation of the risk is evidenced by stockholder groups lobbying for publically traded companies to disclose their greenhouse gas emissions, which are deemed a financial risk to investors.

Competitors also pose a risk if they embrace ecological responsibility as a way to differentiate their offerings. *They* define the marketplace. If customers prefer to do business with (let alone demand) ecologically responsible enterprises, then falling below the ecological performance bar set by a competitor can depress sales and market share.

Other risks come from the consumer sector. Consumers see plastics in food and lead in toys, and protest that companies are unwilling to protect their customers. The Internet accelerates the ability to mobilize consumer boycotts or disseminate information on organizations—whether that information is true or not.

A growing number of companies view supplier impacts as part of their own life cycle impact. These organizations insist on reducing product ecological impacts and on supplier disclosure as components of their own ecological reporting. Many agencies will only conduct business with those vendors that demonstrate ecological responsibility.

Efficient Operations

The process of scrutinizing business processes in order to identify potential eco-friendly practices often results in improvements to production efficiency.

The examination may focus on reducing environmental impact; however, one of the strategies for accomplishing that objective is to eliminate the causes of product and service rejections. The effect is to reduce disruption in the production of goods and services.

Quality Product

The added benefit of improving production efficiency results from the focus on defining quality and answering the question "what needs to be accomplished to achieve a quality product or service?" By defining quality in objective terms, production expectations are defined clearly. As expectations are met or exceeded, quality improves, reinforcing the validity of the management adage that "the things that get measured are the things that get done."

Better quality translates into greater customer satisfaction.

Attracted and Retained Customers

Creating quality products and services is the minimum effort needed to retain customers. Loyal customers are delighted customers. These are buyers whose expectations are met, if not exceeded. Increasingly, all other considerations being equal (for example, price and quality), buyers take the ecological performance of suppliers into account when making the decision to purchase from one enterprise or from its competitor. Enterprises that successfully communicate their positive ecological performance can tap into this growing consumer preference.

Enhanced Brand Value and Reputation

The benefit extends beyond product reporting to inform customers as they are making their purchasing decisions. The savvy enterprise does not use reporting only as a sales advantage; it tells the eco-friendly story to build the reputation of the organization.

This marketing message enhances the reputation of the organization to customers as well as suppliers, regulators, the industry, and the community. It builds the value of the brand among those who place a premium on ecological responsibility.

High Worker Morale

The characteristics of an eco-friendly enterprise—congruency between values and actions, responsibility and accountability, and the other attributes described in Chapter 2—coupled with the inclusive engagement of staff in developing ecological programs, make green businesses exciting places to work. Workers are challenged to contribute to more than the profitability or mission of the organization; they are helping improve the health of the planet. This culture of challenge and ecological innovation builds morale.

Attracted and Retained Talent

Where worker morale is high, it is easier to attract and retain talent. This will become increasingly important to organizations as demographic data point to a shrinking pool of competent workers. Demand for those individuals who can propel the organization will only intensify.

High morale, an emphasis on innovation that leads to quality products, a compelling brand, a strong market position, managed risks, and minimized operating costs make for sound enterprises. These stable and innovating organizations attract talent and usually are successful in retaining capable workers.

Indirect Cost Savings

In addition to direct cost savings, many of the other benefits translate into indirect cost advantages for eco-friendly enterprises. Quality improvements and enhanced productivity also contribute to higher gross profit percentages.

Having reduced turnover and an organization that people want to work for helps to reduce staffing costs.

Similarly, being able to attract new customers and retain loyal customers reduces marketing and sales costs.

Access to capital and the cost of money also can be reduced for eco-friendly enterprises because their financial ratios—especially gross profit and net profit percentages—look favorable when lending institutions compare the financial performance of a green enterprise to competitors that have narrower margins.

Competitive Advantage

Producing goods and services cost-efficiently, cultivating an innovative environment, establishing brand qualities that resonate for a growing customer base, and attracting and retaining talent all contribute to a competitive advantage.

This advantage is only magnified when an organization incorporates eco-friendly policies and programs earlier than its competitors, becoming a recognized leader in its industry.

Increased Profitability

All of these benefits contribute to a more robust bottom line. Cost-effectiveness, market leadership, and a motivated pool of talented workers all make the organization more profitable.

Even eco-friendly governmental agencies, non-profits, and other not-for-profit organizations enjoy the equivalent of enhanced net profit by having more resources available for the delivery of programs.

An advantage of enhanced profitability is the additional leverage that financial security provides for an organization. Having greater net profit provides the organization with greater resources with which to make strategic choices and pursue opportunities. It can maintain higher cash reserves, distribute rewards to owners and staff, invest in innovation, and be wildly philanthropic. There's usually little difficulty in identifying ways to allocate excess profits. *(Gotta love that term.)*

Chapter 4

Becoming a Green Enterprise

This chapter describes a road map for transforming an organization into a green enterprise. The process is appropriate for medium-sized enterprises and for those organizations whose ecological footprint sinks deep into the sand.

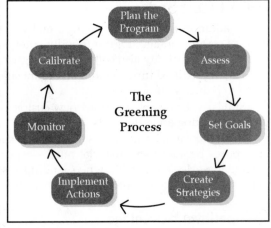

Figure 4.1

The general process for becoming a green enterprise is illustrated in Figure 4.1.

Plan the Program

Not all organizations will need to accomplish all of the planning steps. However, even one-person shops, mom and pops, and enterprises with a handful of workers can benefit from an understanding of the process.

Smaller enterprises plan greening programs with limited elements, such as:

- Items that will be addressed (such as energy, water, and paper).
- The boundary of the evaluation (for example, the operations of the organization; limited source analysis).
- Acknowledgment of ecological risks to the organization (such as energy price or availability of raw materials).
- Tools used to identify and evaluate options (for example, simple payback calculations).
- People involved and date of plan completion.

Larger businesses often will prepare a business case in order to assess the value of "going green." The business case supports the decision-making process by documenting the who-what-where-when-why-how of pursuing a green program:

- A description of what going green means for the enterprise.
- A description of the boundary of the problem (what will be examined as part of the proposed program and what won't—for example, will supplier practices be addressed?).

- ▶ A list of individuals who will participate, including their roles and responsibilities.
- ▶ An identification of stakeholders who may be affected by the program.
- ▶ A definition of the program duration and milestones.
- ▶ Resource requirements.
- ▶ An assessment of the compatibility of a green program with other strategies and programs.
- ▶ An assessment of options to address the program.
- ▶ Internal and external program impacts.
- ▶ A determination of potential program risks.
- ▶ A cost/benefit analysis.
- ▶ Recommendation and summary of rationale.

A completed and approved business case becomes a planning document that can guide the development of an action plan for greening the organization.

Leadership Commitment

Programs to green enterprises, like other change initiatives in organizations, must have the steadfast backing of leadership to be successful.

Workers are exposed to a lot of change initiatives—some of which seem like management's idea du jour. (They are heard about, are introduced, and then simply fade away.) Don't mislead people about the commitment of the organization to going green. Workers look to leadership to walk the talk: If transportation energy efficiency is an enterprise policy, then there shouldn't be any gas-guzzlers in the corporate vehicle fleet.

Leadership can demonstrate the commitment of the organization by taking specific actions that underscore the importance of the initiative to the enterprise. The commitment can be exhibited and confirmed in the following ways:

- ▶ Resolution passed by the board of directors.
- ▶ Written statement from the president, executive director, or general manager of the organization.
- ▶ Statement of the eco-policy of the organization.
- ▶ Public designation of individual(s) with green responsibility and their granted authority.
- ▶ Formal launch of the greening program.
- ▶ Regular monitoring and reporting of progress toward goals.
- ▶ Regular evaluation of green strategies and programs.
- ▶ Integration of green initiatives throughout the enterprise.
- ▶ Allocation of sufficient resources (people, time, money).
- ▶ Performance evaluation, compensation, and reward programs based on green goals (enterprise-wide, departmental, and individual).

The commitment cannot be a single action. It must be reiterated and reinforced by describing programs and results. Over time, this repetition allows eco-friendly practices to become a part of the culture of the organization.

Stakeholder Identification, Assessment, and Engagement

Stakeholders are those organizations and individuals that have an interest in the enterprise. Examples of potential stakeholders that are likely to have an interest in a greening program are listed in Figure 4.2.

Stakeholders can be in the position of holding the organization accountable for its ecological, financial, and other impacts. Stakeholders can be champions for the organization, slow the progress of the organization, or choose not to be involved. Figure 4.3 describes some of the risks posed by stakeholder groups.

Figure 4.4 on page 20 outlines some of the ways by which stakeholders can enrich a greening process.

Engaging stakeholders involves more than scheduling a conversation or delivering a report. Effective engagement starts during the planning phase by asking the question "how can our organization's green program be enriched by involving

Examples of Internal and External Stakeholders		
Internal	External	
Owners/Investors	Customers	Wholesalers
Board		Retailers
Management		End users
Staff	Suppliers	Vendors
		Banks, insurers
	Industry associations	
	Competitors	
	Media	
	Environmental organizations	
	Governmental agencies	
	Educational institutions	
	Local community	
	Employee families and friends	
	General public	

Figure 4.2

stakeholders?" The answer to that question then informs the identification of actions needed to maximize that enhancement.

Planning for involvement is based on the following steps:

- ► Assessing the importance of critical stakeholder groups (as well as single stakeholder organizations and individuals within the identified groups).
- ► Determining opportunities for engagement.
- ► Scheduling communication efforts to complement the stages of the greening efforts of the organization. (See Chapter 30.)

Any stakeholder has the potential to affect the operations of an organization. It's desirable to interact with all stakeholders; however, in-depth communications with all stakeholders can demand extraordinary resources that simply aren't available. Therefore, it's essential that the enterprise focus its engagement efforts on those stakeholder groups whose issues, opinions, and impact on the business are potentially the greatest. A straightforward assessment of significance can be based on two considerations:

1. What is the potential for the stakeholder to enrich the greening efforts of the organization?
2. What is the potential for the stakeholder to damage the greening effort?

Examples of Direct and Indirect Risks Associated With Various Stakeholders			
	Stakeholder		Potential Risks
Internal	Owners/Investors		Shareholder suits related to ecological performance Requested disclosure of ecological performance and risks SEC regulations or fund managers requiring carbon or other ecological disclosure
	Board		Unexpected policy direction with ecological consequences
	Management		Inability to integrate green strategies, program
	Staff		Lack of program support if uninvolved, unengaged Availability of capable workers versed in ecological issues Next generations' desire to work for eco-friendly, principled organizations Difficulty in acquiring, retaining, compensating talent Worker concern over exposure to toxic materials Healthcare costs
External	Customers	Wholesalers Retailers End users	Green purchasing requirements Demand for environmental performance: take-back programs Requirement to report ecological performance: product declarations, warning labels, eco-labels
	Suppliers	Vendors	Increased cost of energy, water, materials Inability or unwillingness to cooperate in enhancing eco-performance
		Banks, insurers	Unwillingness to support ecological initiatives
	Industry associations		Product guidelines Campaigns to enhance industry eco-performance (that the enterprise is unprepared for)
	Competitors		Excellence in ecological performance Poor ecological performance degrades industry image
	Media		Publicity of poor or unknown performance Performance comparison to others—whether legitimate or not
	Environmental organizations		Demand for environmental performance information Publicity of poor or unknown performance
	Governmental agencies		Material bans, phase-outs Regulations stipulate ecological performance Expanded requirements for ecological reporting, permitting Taxation: carbon tax, climate change initiatives
	Educational institutions		Inability to provide sufficient numbers of eco-skilled workers
	Local community		Demand for environmental performance information Concern about economic performance
	Employee families and friends		Pressure to work for eco-friendly organization Concern about license to continue operation
	General public		Publicity of poor or unknown performance, whether factual or not Orchestration of boycotts

Figure 4.3

Examples of Beneficial Outcomes From Effective Communication With Stakeholders		
Stakeholder		Communication Outcomes—Examples
Internal	Owners/Investors	Understanding of green's economic benefits Support for green goals, strategies, and programs
	Board	Understanding of benefits Eco-friendly policy approval Acceptance of strategies Approval of resources Recognition of results
	Management	Understanding of benefits Engaged participation/leadership Greening integrated into strategic plan Action plan Monitored results Recognition of contributors
	Staff	Understanding of benefits Engaged participation/leadership Product/process innovations Acknowledgment of results
External	Customers — Wholesalers / Retailers / End users	Engaged partner Product/process innovations Enhanced image, brand
	Suppliers — Vendors	Understanding of mutual benefits Product/process innovations Procurement collaborator
	Suppliers — Banks, insurers	Understanding of direct and indirect financial benefits, including management of risks Preferential financial treatment
	Industry associations	Effectiveness as thought leader Enhancing reputation of industry
	Competitors	Identification of issues of mutual concern Collaborative programs for industry improvements
	Media	Preferred source for industry information Reinforcement of positive reputation
	Environmental organizations	Program development Product/process innovations
	Governmental agencies	Program development Recognition for best practices Influence in refining regulations
	Educational institutions	Educational partner Workforce trained in ecological and 21st-century skills
	Local community	Familiarity with green programs and results Rapport for collaborating on issues of mutual concern Recognized as community leader
	Employee families and friends	Recognized as preferred employer Support for employees' personal green programs
	General public	Communication channels acknowledged Ability to access information

Figure 4.4

Each stakeholder (whether considered as a category, individual organization, and/or individual) can be rated as low, medium, or high for both considerations. Applying the "greater" rating to the pair of scores can unify the individual ratings. For example, if a stakeholder is given a high rating for potential enrichment, and a medium rating for potential damage, then the combined rating would be high. Figure 4.5 presents a framework for reporting the assessment.

Effective stakeholder management follows this initial assessment of significance by determining the level of engagement at each step of the greening process. Figure 4.5 provides a structure for planning the level of engagement and provides an example of how one might plan for board of director involvement.

Framework for Planning Stakeholder Engagement									
Stakeholders	Plan Contribution			Planning Stage Involvement					
	Enrich	Damage	Overall	Audit	Goals	Strategic	Action	Monitor	Calibrate
Owners/Investors									
Board	H	L	H	*Inform audit results*	*Establish goals*	*Confirm strategies*	*Approve action plan*	*Review monitoring results*	*Approve changes in goal, strategies and action plan*
Management									
Staff									
Customers — Wholesalers									
Customers — Retailers									
Customers — End users									
Suppliers — Vendors									
Suppliers — Banks, insurers									
Industry associations									
Competitors									
Media									
Environmental organizations									
Governmental agencies									
Educational institutions									
Local community									
Employee families and friends									
General public									

Figure 4.5

The most critical stakeholders are staff. Organizations have the greatest success with initiatives when they involve workers. For large or complex enterprises, this may mean the establishment of cross-functional teams whose members represent the perspectives of different departments:

▶ Operational staff who are familiar with the equipment and day-to-day process activities and maintenance.

▶ Financial staff who are familiar with financial evaluations, return on investment, and competition for resources.

- ▶ Marketing/sales staff who can address customer expectations and how customers can be involved.
- ▶ Human resources staff who can orchestrate needed training or ensure that hiring, evaluation, and compensation programs support the eco-efficiency goals.
- ▶ Purchasing.
- ▶ Research and development staff who have the responsibility of combining energy efficiency into product and service functions.

(Chapter 30 describes a method for orchestrating communications as part of stakeholder engagement.)

Assess Ecological Performance

Before an organization sets out on a path to green the business, it needs to understand its ecological performance. This provides a baseline against which goals and improvement options can be developed and evaluated. The assessment process incorporates the following steps:

- ▶ Determining the boundaries of the assessment.
- ▶ Assembling data.
- ▶ Establishing baselines.
- ▶ Benchmarking baseline performance.
- ▶ Using audits to identify improvement options.

Determining Boundaries

The first step is to determine the boundaries of the analysis in terms of:

- ▶ The degree to which performance assessment extends outside the organization.
- ▶ The ecological categories that will be assessed.

The context of the organizational boundary is derived from an understanding of the life cycle of the products and services of the enterprise (a topic addressed more fully in Chapter 5). Essentially, a life cycle is an expanded view of the existence of a product, as illustrated in Figure 4.6.

Typical Product Life Cycle

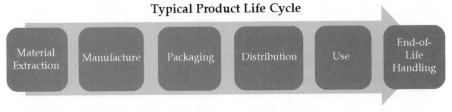

Figure 4.6

A manufacturer's assessment may extend throughout the entire life cycle. A retailer's primary focus may extend from packaging through the end of life phase; however, the retailer may extend that boundary if it wishes to sell products that have been manufactured using clean production techniques or that contain materials with minimal ecological impact. Some organizations may wish to limit their initial performance assessment to a smaller set of life cycle stages. After initial ecological performance goals are achieved, it can expand the boundary of assessment and performance improvement.

Ecological performance categories are based on a determination of resource inputs to the organization, outputs from the organization, and the consequences of those outputs. Figure 4.7 illustrates how these categories interact with life cycles.

A review of the inputs, outputs, and potential consequences for their likely significance determines the life cycle stages to profile and dictates which data are important to assemble.

Life Cycle Stage Relation to Resource Inputs, Outputs, and Their Consequences

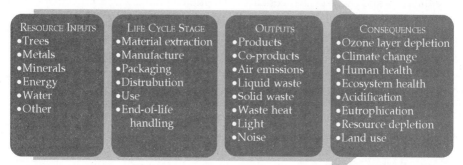

Resource Inputs	Life Cycle Stage	Outputs	Consequences
•Trees	•Material extraction	•Products	•Ozone layer depletion
•Metals	•Manufacture	•Co-products	•Climate change
•Minerals	•Packaging	•Air emissions	•Human health
•Energy	•Distrubution	•Liquid waste	•Ecosystem health
•Water	•Use	•Solid waste	•Acidification
•Other	•End-of-life	•Waste heat	•Eutrophication
	handling	•Light	•Resource depletion
		•Noise	•Land use

Figure 4.7

Assembling Data

Data should be assembled for the life stages that have been determined to be significant. Use data will come from a variety of sources: utility statements, waste haulers, observations, calculations inferred from industry information, and vendors.

Processes and forms for recording data are described throughout this guide. (Blank worksheets are contained in the Appendix.)

Additional data also are collected on facility area, conditioned area, operating hours, gross revenues, production rates, and weather. These data are used to normalize the data acquired through audit.

Establishing Baseline Performance Profiles

In assembling and organizing raw data, variations in inputs and outputs over time may be noticed. These variations are attributable to such factors as production rates, acquisition of equipment, weather, and hours and days of operation. Where there are "meaningful" variations, the performance profiles should be adjusted. The adjusted profiles reflect typical performance, such as BTU/square foot per year, or gallons/widget produced.

Benchmarking Baseline Performance

Benchmarking is used to analyze data relative to like organizations in order to determine whether the performance of the organization is similar to, better than, or worse than the comparables. A performance metric may be compared against:

- ▶ Average (median) performers in the industry.
- ▶ Best in class (highest) performers in the industry.
- ▶ Best practices, representing state-of-the-knowledge base in the industry.

Using Audits

Audits are detailed technical assessments that examine the ecological performance of the organization. The objective of the audit is to discover and characterize options that can improve performance.

Reports that summarize audited activities should identify specific options for improvement, describe the steps needed to accomplish the improvement, and identify the costs and the expected benefits from implementing the improvement.

Audits should initially focus on those areas in which the level of adverse impact or risk is greatest and where the performance is poor relative to best practices levels. As the functioning of poor-performing areas improve, the remedial efforts of an organization can shift to the next under-performing areas.

Goals and Strategy

Ecological performance goals can be expressed in a variety of ways:
- ▶ Organization-wide goals (example: reduce enterprise's carbon footprint by 30 percent within three years).
- ▶ Facility-, department-, or profit-area goals (example: reduce the normalized life cycle impact of a widget by 25 percent within two years).
- ▶ Process or equipment goals (example: reduce energy-intensity of compressors by 15 percent within one year).
- ▶ Benchmarked goals (example: meet or exceed median performance with respect to a parameter).
- ▶ Efficiency improvement goals (example: reduce energy for lighting by 20 percent).
- ▶ Threshold performance goals (example: reduce manufacturing quality rejects so as not to exceed 0.05 percent).
- ▶ Environmental enhancement goals (example: reduce weight of solid wastes by 60 percent).
- ▶ Time period goals: (for example, a series of goals to be accomplished in one year, and other goals in two years).

Effective goals have recognized attributes: They are specific, measureable, attainable, and scheduled to occur by a defined time.

Goals are developed from an understanding of the performance improvement levels that are possible. These technical improvement possibilities should be considered against theoretical improvement potentials as suggested by best practices and best-in-class performance information.

Strategy represents the "how" of goal achievement. It operates at a higher level than the individual actions that make up the ecological improvement plan. Some of the strategic questions that organizations typically deal with include:

▶ Is greening an organizational strategy designed to differentiate from the competition?

▶ Should the organization first pursue cost-effective options or instead engage in options to increase the eco-performance in a particular impact category (energy, for example)?

▶ Should staff implement improvements or should contractors be used?

▶ How much financial support should the initiative be given relative to funding competing strategic programs?

▶ Should there be an initial capitalization with cost savings from those improvements allocated to funding future improvements?

▶ How do we address options with low capital cost but high staff involvement?

Responding to these questions aids the enterprise in aligning the action plan with overall strategy.

The Action Plan

The action plan is a summary document that identifies the improvement measures that are to be implemented, their scheduling, and the people who are responsible for accomplishing the actions. Background information, such as monitoring data, measurements, evaluation calculations, and related support material, should be incorporated into the document for easy reference.

Identifying Potential Actions

Chapters 5 through 26 of this guide identify potential measures that can be considered by an enterprise in order to improve its ecological performance. Not all measures apply to all organizations. These measures are not intended to be all-inclusive, but rather to highlight possibilities and to stimulate the identification of potential actions.

Evaluating Potential Actions

Potential actions can be evaluated against a number of variables, such as:

▶ Ecological performance enhancement.

▶ Ecological performance goals.

▶ Support of other enterprise initiatives.

▶ Financial criteria.

The following discussion relates to the evaluation of the actions' financial performance: focusing on simple payback, cash flow, internal rate of return, and net present value.

Simple Payback

A simple payback of a measure is calculated using the following formula:
Payback period =

(Measure's Effective Cost) ÷ ((annual resource savings) × resource price)

Where: Measure's Effective Cost = Capital cost + installation cost − rebate

Annual resource savings = the forecast amount of resource saved

Example: A programmable thermostat is proposed for a small business that pays $0.12/kWh for electric heat for 6 months and air conditioning for 2. If the thermostat costs $100, $20 to install and is eligible for a $25 rebate, and it is assumed that the thermostat results in savings of 125 kWh a month, then simple payback is calculated as follows:

Payback period =

$$(\$100 + \$20 - \$25) \div ((125 \text{ kWh/mo}) + (6 + 2 \text{ months}) \times \$0.12) = 0.79 \text{ year}$$

Cash Flow Analysis

A cash flow analysis indicates the flow of moneys resulting from an investment. It is a statement of the costs and the economic benefits that accrue over defined time periods (typically annually over a 10-year period).

Internal Rate of Return

The internal rate of return (IRR) analysis is an interest rate equivalent that indicates the current value of the initial cost of an investment compared to the expected future value of that investment. An IRR analysis can be performed using commonly used spreadsheet tools, such as Excel, Lotus 1-2-3, and Quattro Pro, as well as financial analyses incorporated into accounting software packages.

Net Present Value

The net present value of an investment indicates the current value of future cash flows relative to the initial cost outlay of the investment. Effectively, it's a financial indicator that adjusts for inflation.

Figure 4.8 represents a simplified cash flow for a hypothetical upgrade of a lighting system. In this example, a central timer represents a better value from a

	Hypothetical Financial Comparison of Two Lighting Improvement Options[1]			
Year	Option A: Central Timer		Option B: Occupancy Sensors	
	Effective cost	Savings generated	Effective cost	Savings generated
0	$9,000	0	$42,000	0
1	0	$3,500	0	$12,200
2	0	$3,500	0	$12,200
3	0	$3,500	0	$12,200
4	0	$3,500	0	$12,200
5	0	$3,500	0	$12,200
6	0	$3,500	0	$12,200
7	0	$3,500	0	$12,200
8	0	$3,500	0	$12,200
9	0	$3,500	0	$12,200
10	0	$3,500	0	$12,200
Cumulative savings	$35,500		$122,000	
Simple payback	2.5 years		3.4 years	
Internal Rate of Return	38%		26%	
Net Present Value	$4,903		$7,623	

Figure 4.8

payback and rate of return. However, energy savings and net cash value to the organization are greater with the occupancy sensor option.

Selecting Potential Actions

There are two versions of the worksheet, representing two levels of analysis. An example of a simplified version of the worksheet is presented in Figure 4.9. (An expanded template, *Green Measures Summary Worksheet*, is appended.)

A more comprehensive worksheet (see Figure 4.10) uses initial costs, simple payback, NPV, and IRR to facilitate the economic comparison of measures. (That worksheet, *Green Measures Economic Summary Worksheet*, is also appended.)

Typically, the action plan preparer makes choices about dozens if not hundreds of improvement options. Regardless of the number of options, there must be a method for prioritizing: evaluating, selecting, and then arranging their implementation.

A straightforward technique for prioritization of options is based on an assessment of two variables: performance and cost. Options are evaluated based on a determination that a performance improvement is low, medium, or high, and that its cost is low, medium, or high. The determination can be based on quantitative data or, less accurately, qualitative information. Figure 4.11 illustrates the application: Options that fall into the darkest gray cells are high priority, light gray cells are medium priority, and white cells are lowest priority. This technique can be further simplified using only low-high assessments.

Green Measures—Example of Simplified Summary[2]		
Measure	Performance Improvement [energy savings] (L, M, H)	Resource Cost (L, M, H)
Install lighting timer	L	M
Install lighting occupancy sensors	H	H
Install LED exit signs	L	L
Improve corridor lighting	L	M
Improve office lighting	H	H
Upgrade task lighting	L	M
Install daylighting controls	M	H

Figure 4.9

Energy Efficiency Measures—Example of Detailed Summary[3]					
Measure	Effective Initial Cost	Annual Net Cash Flow	Simple Payback (years)	Net Present Value	Internal Rate of Return
Install lighting timer	$9,000	$3,550	2.5	$4,902	38%
Install lighting occupancy sensors	$42,000	$12,200	3.4	$7,623	26%
Install LED exit signs	$3,250	$2,380	1.4	$5,606	73%
Improve corridor lighting	$9,490	$3,725	2.5	$5,106	38%
Improve office lighting	$57,605	$15,100	3.8	$4,751	23%
Upgrade task lighting	$9,500	$2,000	4.8	($929)	16%
Install daylighting controls	$59,080	$6,500	9.1	($26,524)	2%

Figure 4.10

Framework for Option Comparison and Selection			
Performance — low			
Performance — medium			
Performance — high			
	low	medium	high
		Cost	

Figure 4.11

More sophisticated prioritization uses evaluation criteria, such as:

- Amount of ecological improvement (for example, a lighting improvements action may result in energy electricity savings of 20,000 kWh per year).
- Amount of associated savings (for example, the use of compact fluorescent lamps is estimated to result in a reduction of 4 hours of maintenance labor per year, due to less frequent bulb replacement).
- Other benefits (for example, the reduced electricity consumption also results in 17.5 fewer tons of greenhouse gases being emitted annually, due to reduced fossil fuel burning at electricity generating plants).
- Installation cost (including capital cost, labor costs, and production downtime).
- Cash flow analysis.
- Calculated payback.
- Internal rate of return.
- Net present value of the investment.

> The following perspective contains excellent advice for the planner: "While we often think of upgrade projects in terms of how quickly the investment is paid off through the savings, we don't usually recognize the other side of this equation. For each month or year that you delay your upgrade projects, you completely lose that potential savings forever."[4]

Figure 4.12 illustrates my preferred format for presenting the Action Plan once the prioritization of action items has been finalized.

Action Plan Format								
Date	Lead Person	Action	Goal Area	Cost	Estimated Performance Improvement	Staff Time	Resources	Other
August 15, 2009	Bob	Replace incandescent lamps w CFLs	Energy, air quality	$800	18% reduction in electricity used for lighting	4 hours	None	NA
September 15, 2009	Sarah	Replace printers with duplexing, energy-efficient capability	Energy, paper	$1,200	15% reduction in printing electricity; 24 reams of paper saved annually	6 hours	Coordinate with Procurement	Life cycle cost analysis of printer options

Figure 4.12

Implementing the Action Plan

Implementation of the plan should be methodical, following the scheduling of the milestones. Particularly complicated actions (such as redesign of product packaging) may require their own plans that define and describe the execution of individual tasks that make up the overall action.

Organizations that undertake successful change initiatives manage the change process in part by careful planning, but also through effective implementation:

- Involve affected parties in planning and implementing change. Let it be *their* program.
- Describe the change in detail.
- Describe the reason for change.
- Describe what the change will mean for workers and other stakeholders, objectively explaining both positive and negative effects.
- Assure workers, recognizing that individuals have different tolerances and capacities for change.
- Anticipate and welcome resistance. It's not only natural; it's valuable in revealing faults that, once corrected, improve the outcome. Be empathetic.
- Describe goals and expectations for the individual: It establishes the linkage between the individual and the overall goals of the organization.
- Provide training that may be needed.
- Encourage prudent risk-taking; invite suggestions and exploration.
- Communicate.
- Report.
- Recognize achievements and celebrate successes.

Monitor Progress

There should be regular measuring of the expected outcomes to determine whether projected performance improvements are coming to fruition.

Periodic reviews should be conducted in order to explain why projections are being surpassed or why they are not being met. Mid-course projections may be needed to improve the performance of actions falling short of their expected results. Similarly, lessons from wildly successful actions may be candidates for replication in other action items.

Calibrate the Plan

A review of the work plan should be done at least every two years—preferably annually. The update process should:

- ▶ Revisit ecological, industry, and technology conditions.
- ▶ Examine the performance of the enterprise in light of updated data on best practices and industry benchmarks.
- ▶ Reassess risks.
- ▶ Evaluate the suitability and productivity of stakeholder engagements.
- ▶ Forge new goals with an updated Action Plan to achieve those goals.

Chapter 5

Ecodesign

Ecological design (also referred to as ecodesign, design for environment, and green design) is a meld of art and science that creates ecologically benign and economically viable products and services. Ecodesign also includes product re-design to correct ecological harm of existing products.

One way to consider ecodesign is that it builds on the fundamental qualities of industrial design and lies just shy of sustainable design, where industrial design balances usability, aesthetics, engineering, production efficiency, user ergonomics, and marketing, and where sustainable design adds economic viability, ecological benevolence, and social equity.

Although one usually thinks of ecodesigning products, the ecodesign process described in this chapter also can be applied to business practices.

Concepts Guiding Product Ecodesign

Ecodesign integrates holistic product thinking from the perspective of natural systems.

Life Cycle Thinking

Life cycle thinking is a framework for thinking of a product throughout its life: from the initial conception and development of a product, to harvesting and processing the raw materials and components used in its manufacture, to its distribution to the user, to the use of the product, and lastly, to its recovery and disposal. Figure 5.1 illustrates the basic stages in the physical life of a product as it travels from cradle to its end of service.

Each of the stages of the product can be further segmented into activity areas or phases. Figure 5.2 illustrates principal phases within stages of a generic life cycle. These activity areas more fully capture the points at which the designer can affect the ecological impact of a product.

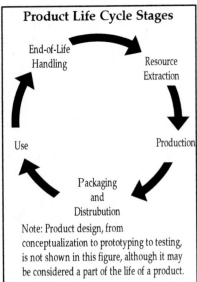

Product Life Cycle Stages

End-of-Life Handling

Resource Extraction

Production

Packaging and Distrubution

Use

Note: Product design, from conceptualization to prototyping to testing, is not shown in this figure, although it may be considered a part of the life of a product.

Figure 5.1

Product Physical Life Cycle Stages and Phases		
Stage	Phase	
Resource extraction	Resource selection Raw material extraction and transport Recycled material processing Material processing and transport	
Production	Parts fabrication Component assembly Product assembly Quality control	
Packaging and distribution	Product packaging manufacture Transport packaging manufacture Transport to consumer	
Use	Installation Operation Maintenance Repair Upgrade	
End-of-life handling	Reuse and recycle	Product reuse Disassembly Component reuse Material recycling
	Residual waste disposal	Landfill Incineration

Figure 5.2

Ecological Impacts of Products

At various stages of the life of a product, there is an inflow of resource materials, energy, and water, and an outflow of product and waste, as depicted in Figure 5.3.

The types and volumes of resource inputs and desired and undesired outputs vary with the type of product being considered. For example, kitchen cabinets that are manufactured from hardwood veneers have less of an impact on native forests than solid hardwood cabinets. However, the veneered cabinets are constructed from veneers glued to a type of particleboard, which also is held together by glue slurry. These glues become airborne during their manufacture and application, during the milling and assembly of the veneered particleboard, and they may release vapors (outgas) after installation. Thus, there is an ecological tradeoff between manufacturing kitchen cabinets from solid hardwoods or from veneers.

It is the ecodesigner's responsibility to identify the ecological impacts of a product throughout its life cycle and to develop design options that will eliminate or minimize the effects.

The Concept of Resource Inputs and Product and Waste Outputs Throughout the Life Cycle of a Product

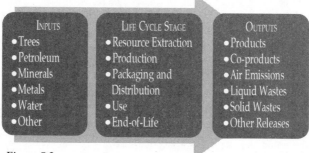

Figure 5.3

There are many different tools for environmental assessment of products (and they are described later in this chapter). However, most of the assessment tools share a focus on evaluating a common set of environmental impacts, which are listed in Figure 5.4.

Key Environmental Impacts, Their Causes, Pathways, and Principal Effects[1]

Ecological Indicator	Manmade Cause/Pathway	Principal Effects
Ozone layer depletion	Ozone-depleting substances (e.g. chlorofluorocarbon [CFC, Freon] and bromoofluorocarbon [Halon]) compounds used as refrigerants, propellants, fire retardants, and solvents	Increased ultraviolet penetration is suspected to increase incidence of skin cancer Plant damage
Climate change	Greenhouse gases (carbon dioxide, methane, ozone, nitrous oxide, CFCs, water vapor) due to burning of fossil fuels, deforestation, livestock, and use of CFCs	Air and water temperature warming Glacial melting Reduction in sea ice extent Sea level rise Dramatic storm events Habitat change
Toxicity to humans	Hazardous substances that enter water, soils, and atmosphere, and/or that may be absorbed through the skin*	Injury Illness Mortality
Photochemical smog	Emissions of nitrogen oxides (NOx), volatile organic compounds, and other substances released into atmosphere from combustion engines and industrial processes	Respiratory illness Lung disease Plant productivity loss
Acidification	Sulfur and nitrogen compounds emitted from combustion engines react in the atmosphere to create acids	Increase acid deposition in receiving waters and soils, and on surfaces results in changes to terrestrial and aquatic ecosystems, manmade resources, and health
Eutrophication	Agriculture and landscape practices that produce runoff laden with nitrogen and phosphorous	Excessive plant growth and decay (algae blooms) reduce oxygen availability and degrades habitat for fish and other aquatic creatures
Toxicity to plants and animals	Contaminants that enter water, soils, and atmosphere**	Injury Illness Mortality
Habitat extent and quality	Development and land use resulting in physical encroachment, climate change, emissions, spread of invasive species	Reduced wildlife and extinction. Loss of biodiversity. Loss of secondary benefits from various biosystems (e.g., wetlands, forests, fishery)
Natural resource depletion and degradation	Non-renewable (or lower functional) use of tangible resources (e.g., water, forests, soils, mined materials, fisheries, petroleum) for human benefit. Intangible losses, such as degradation of views.	Loss of resource supplies Diminished resource quality
Waste	Poor system, product, or service design. Disposal of usable resources.	Loss of resource supplies
Noise	Equipment, vehicles, rail, airplanes	Stress, sleep disturbance

*The *Cradle to Cradle Design Protocol* applies the following criteria in evaluating a substance's effect on human health: carcinogenicity, teratogenicity, reproductive toxicity, mutagenicity, endocrine disruption, acute or chronic toxicity, irritation of skin or mucous membranes, sensitization, carrier function.

**The *Cradle to Cradle Design Protocol* applies the following criteria in evaluating a substance's effect on ecological health: algae toxicity, bioaccumulation, halogenated organic compounds content, daphnia toxicity, fish toxicity, heavy metal content, persistence, toxicity to soil organisms [as well as climate change and ozone depletion potential].[2]

Figure 5.4

A secondary set of impact areas includes:

- Odor.
- Land use.
- Waste heat.
- Accidents.

- Radiation.
- Erosion.
- Light pollution.
- Use of genetically modified organisms (GMOs).

Extended Producer Responsibility, Product Stewardship

Ecodesign reflects the acknowledgment of manufacturers that they have a responsibility to consider the implications of producing a product or service that extends beyond the manufacture or delivery. This extended producer responsibility looks "upstream" to the selection of natural resources and components that are incorporated into the product, as well as "downstream" to the use of a product and (post-consumer) end-of-life handling.

Eco-Effectiveness—Not Just Eco-Efficiency

Bill McDonough and Michael Braungart in their seminal book *Cradle to Cradle* observed that the prevailing form of industrial production combined with unchecked consumerism in the developing world have resulted in environmental degradation and destruction. The authors also have observed that the preliminary corrective response to this unsatisfactory form of production has been partial remedial strategy that can be termed as "do less bad," or eco-efficiency, which is characterized by:

- Releasing *fewer* toxic wastes into the air, soil, and water.
- Generating *smaller* quantities of waste.
- Producing *less* toxic material that will need safe isolation from air, water, and soil pathways to the biosphere.
- Landfilling *reduced* resources that cannot be economically retrieved.

McDonough and Braungart make the compelling argument that efficiency has been applied in narrow niches with little or no regard for the larger context. For example, an energy-efficient building that reduces air infiltration also traps unhealthy air pollutants that must be evacuated to maintain air quality for the occupants of the building.

An improvement to design eco-efficiency is eco-effectiveness. Instead of making the wrong things "less bad," eco-effectiveness emphasizes first the creation of the right things, and second the manufacture of those right things efficiently.[3]

Sustainable Thinking

Non-renewable resources cannot form the basis for a sustained economy, because the natural capital is depletable. Substituting renewable resources for non-renewable resources is a principle for sustaining economic growth. When using renewable resources, they must be managed for sustainable harvesting.

Cradle-to-Cradle Lifetime

Instead of looking at a product as a unit with a finite lifetime (cradle to grave), ecodesign considers a cradle-to-cradle viewpoint, in which the components of a product are a part of a continuum of usage of its parts. In order for components to become a useful input, or "food," after their working lifetime, they must be designed for reuse, becoming a part of a closed loop system.

In order to eliminate waste and to design for reuse, biological and technical production inputs cannot be intermingled without being designed to later be separated. Biological nutrients refer to those biodegradable elements that can be returned to the biological world and be consumed by animals and microorganisms found in the soil. Peat containers for nursery plants are an example of biological packaging. Technical nutrients are those components that can be reused in the industrial cycle. For example, a toner cartridge can be returned to the manufacturer for refilling and resale.

Emulate Natural Systems

Multiple plant and animal niches respond to a complex system of solar income, temperature variations, soil types, and water characteristics. This biodiversity establishes a web of complementary relationships, which results in healthy ecosystems that cycle resources and nutrients and provide a buffer against environmental stressors.

Biomimicry refers to product and process design drawing inspiration from nature. Concentrating solar collector mirrors that follow the path of the sun across the sky, for example, mimic the response of the sunflower to the sun.

Current solar income refers to the use of incoming solar energy to fuel all natural and human systems. In effect, it avoids non-renewable energy sources (coal, petroleum, natural gas) and embraces renewable sources, such as solar, wind, hydro, geothermal, and biomass.

"Waste equals food" ("zero waste") refers to each organism in a living system contributing waste that is "food" that benefits another living creature. The earthworm is nature's perfect example: digesting compostable material into nutrient-rich soil for plant growth.

Dematerialization

Dematerialization refers to a reduction in the amount of materials and energy used in meeting the consumer's objective for the use of a product. Voice mail, for example, takes the place of an answering machine.

Product as Service

One way to facilitate the reuse of technical components is to design for ease of product disassembly. Product service systems are a way to offer consumers the use of a product while the manufacturer retains ownership. This arrangement facilitates the reuse of individual components by establishing the ability to change out parts.

Interface Carpets, for example, installs carpet the consumer specifies. If the consumer wants a change in the carpet design, Interface reuses the fabric backing and recycles the old carpet fibers into new carpet.

Green Chemistry

In order for a product to avoid the possibility of harm, it must not generate toxins in its creation, use, or disposal. Toxins include both those substances that are harmful to humans as well as those that create ecological harm.

Obviously, substances that are inherently toxic must be avoided. However, avoidance extends to harmful byproducts that could be generated during the processing, manufacturing, distribution, use, and dismantling of products after their lifetime.

Chemical risk assessment is the process of identifying the chemicals and their concentrations, pathways, and exposures that could impact human health and the environment.

The U.S. Environmental Protection Agency has had chemical surveys prepared for hundreds of chemicals that are of very high concern and enables chemical profiles to be accessed through the Integrated Risk Information System (IRIS). Specific information on approximately 5,000 chemicals is available through the TOXNET database. (However, not all known chemicals are included; see the Resources for access information for TOXNET and other health-related databases.)

The European Union strictly regulates substances that are of very high concern through the Registration, Evaluation, Authorisation and restriction of Chemicals (REACH) program, administered by the European Chemicals Agency (ECHA). The *Navigator* software program describes risks and European regulations associated with various chemicals.

Green chemistry is dedicated to the reduction and elimination of the use and generation of hazardous substances. The 12 principles of green chemistry are:

1. **Prevent waste:** It is easier to prevent waste than to treat it once it already has been created.

2. **Develop safer chemicals:** Chemical products should achieve their intended function while minimizing their toxicity.

3. **Design for less-hazardous chemical syntheses:** Synthetic methods should produce substances with little or no toxicity to humans and the environment.

4. **Use renewable feedstocks:** Raw materials and feedstocks should be from renewable, rather than depleting, resources.

5. **Use catalysts, not stoichiometric reagents:** Reduce waste by using catalytic reactions, which can be accomplished with catalysts used multiple times, unlike stoichiometric reagents, which are used once.

6. **Avoid chemical derivatives:** When possible, avoid using blocking or protecting/deprotection or any temporary modifications of physical and/or chemical processes, which require additional reagents and generate waste.

7. **Maximize atom economy:** Synthetic end products should incorporate all of the materials used in their manufacture.

8. **Use safer solvents and auxiliaries:** Avoid solvents, separation agents, or other auxiliary chemicals. If these chemicals are needed, use innocuous chemicals.

9. **Increase energy efficiency:** Whenever possible, run chemical reactions at ambient temperature and pressure in order to reduce energy impacts.

10. **Design for degradation:** Design chemical products to decompose into innocuous substances after their use so that they do not persist in the physical environment.
11. **Analyze in real time to prevent pollution:** Incorporate real-time, in-process monitoring and control of chemical processes to prevent the creation of hazardous substances.
12. **Minimize the potential for accidents:** Design chemical processes to minimize the potential for chemical accidents including explosions, fires, and releases to the environment.[4]

Precautionary principle

The precautionary principle states that when an activity poses a potential threat to human health or the environment, it is the proponent's responsibility to establish the impacts of the activity in a manner that is transparent, is democratic, and involves potentially affected parties.

Cleaner Production

Cleaner production seeks to prevent environmental damages by improving production process efficiencies. This approach often results in cost savings and reduced risks to human health.

Eco-Effective Product Design

Eco-effective design is not an entirely new process; rather it is a variation on an existing approach to designing and redesigning products.[5] Figure 5.5 illustrates the major stages in an ecodesign project.

Ecodesign in the Product Development Process

Figure 5.5

An ecodesign approach affects the earlier stages of product design: The latter stages mirror standard industrial design processes. Figure 5.6 on page 37 illustrates outcomes (output) for each of three principal ecodesign stages and identifies sources of information and tools that can assist the design team in achieving its project goal.

Ecodesign project planning

Effective ecodesign processes require that the project manager has the support of the management of the enterprise, including the involvement of a team that represents necessary competencies in production processes, materials science, environmental assessment, marketing, and consumer knowledge.

During the planning stage, the design team should understand the internal and external factors that are driving the design or redesign process.[6] That knowledge provides a basis for examining product features and tradeoffs.

Inputs, Tools, and Outputs in Ecodesign Steps Leading to Prototype Development

Ecodesign Steps

	Step 1 — Planning; product and system definition	Step 2 — Environmental Assessment — LCA (Life cycle assessment) perspective	Step 2 — Environmental Assessment — Stakeholder perspective	Options	Step 2 — Environmental Assessment — Assessment	Selection
Input and Tools	Current product specifications; Supply chain interviews; Matrix LCA; Overall enterprise strategy; Enterprise environmental strategy	Screening LCA (MET, MECO, ERPA); Ecodesign checklists; SimaPro Ecoindicator	Benchmarking assessment; Regulatory requirements; Consumer preferences (e.g. Quality Function Deployment (QFD))	Brainstorming, lateral thinking, mind mapping, TRIZ, ecodesign checklists; Product ideas tree diagram	Screening LCA or full LCA; Production process analysis; Technical, financial, market feasibility analysis	Selection criteria; LiDS Wheel; EcoCompass
Output	Product profile; Life cycle stages; Materials and components profile; Production process profile; New product (redesign) objectives	Ecological profile throughout product's life cycle	Competitor products' profiles; Regulatory compliance determination; Market-based functions and features statements	Alternate products, processed, materials, and technologies; Product improvement options and variants related to design objectives	Environmental impact(s) of product improvement options; Feasibility of improvement options	Prototype specification; Procurement requirements

Design objectives based on environmental, regulatory, and customer factors

Figure 5.6

Internal Drivers
- Enhance quality.
- Cost-savings.
- Desire to innovate.
- Ecological responsibility.
- Establish an advantage over competitors.
- Improve business image.
- Risk reduction.
- Other.

External Drivers
- Regulations.
- Trade organization activities.
- Competitor activities.
- Customer demands.
- Market demands from customers.
- Technical innovations by suppliers.
- Risk reduction.
- Other.

The team also should be aware of what internal obstacles to ecodesign they might be confronted with during the design process, and develop responses to blunt their potential effect. (See Chapter 30.)

The team should assemble detailed records of the product, including:

- ▶ Product specifications.
- ▶ Component manufacturers.
- ▶ Source, material, and weight of all materials.
- ▶ Production processes for all stages of fabrication, including resource inputs, quality issues, and waste materials (including emissions).
- ▶ Use profile, including product lifetime, usage patterns and reliability, repair patterns, resource consumption, and emissions.

Additionally, information on user (feature) preferences, and competitors and their products should be assembled.

The project team defines the scope of the project based on a preliminary consideration of the ecological impacts in life cycle stages and the availability of data.

Product Ecological Assessment

The objective of the product environmental assessment is to understand the greatest environmental impacts of a product in order to focus ecodesign efforts on those significant impacts.

There are three increasingly detailed levels of LCA tools:

1. Matrix LCA—qualitative or quantitative.
2. Screening LCA—quantitative, using readily available data.
3. Full LCA—quantitative, including product-specific data

These three levels are appropriate for different product design projects. The Matrix LCA is suitable for creating an overview of the impact of a product throughout its life cycle, and can be an effective screening tool for defining the scope of an ecodesign project.

The MET-Matrix is a simple tool for identifying three categories of impact: Materials, Energy, and Toxic emissions. It's suitable for enterprises that are manufacturing uncomplicated products or are seeking a quick qualitative snapshot of the ecological effect of the product. Figure 5.7 illustrates the basic form of the MET-Matrix. It is completed with an identification of inputs and outputs but doesn't necessarily involve the quantification of those flows.

Similar to the MET-Matrix, MECO is another matrix-level LCA tool that can be used to identify environmental impacts in four major categories (Materials, Energy, Chemicals, Other) throughout the life cycle of a product. (See Figure 5.8.)

The Environmentally Responsible Product Assessment (ERPA) Matrix generates a quantitative result from qualitative assessment. For each life cycle stage an evaluation of five criteria is made using scores ranging from 0 (highest impact) to 4 (lowest impact). A 0, for example, may be awarded for a product that releases toxic fumes, or a 4 for no release of gases. Figure 5.9 illustrates the reporting array.

For more detailed environmental assessments quantifying the flows (input resources and outputs) is the easier part of the process. Figure 5.10 on page 40 offers a template for reporting environmental impacts (using the main ecological impact categories in Figure 5.4) throughout the life of a product (using the life cycle stages in Figure 5.2). Figure 5.10 suggests quantification units that can be used to characterize the ecological impact.

Once impacts have been identified and quantified, the product designer can address the significance of the environmental impact of a product. There are three factors

MET-Matrix Template

Life cycle stage		Impact Category		
		Material cycle (input/output)	Energy use (input/output)	Toxic emissions (output)
Materials and component production				
Manufacturing				
Distribution				
Use	Operation			
	Service			
End-of-life	Recovery			
	Disposal			

Figure 5.7

MECO-Matrix Template

Life cycle stage	Impact Category			
	Material*	Energy**	Chemicals***	Other
Material supply				
Manufacture				
Use				
Disposal				
Transport				

*   All material needed to produce and use the product.
**   All energy used in each life cycle, including both primary and oil resources.
***   All chemicals categorized by hazard level:
        1—very problematic; 2—problematic; 3—less problematic.[7]

Figure 5.8

Environmentally Responsible Product Assessment (ERPA)-Matrix Template

Life cycle stage	Impact Category				
	Material choice	Energy use	Solid residues	Liquid residues	Gaseous residues
Pre-manufacturing					
Product manufacture					
Product delivery					
Product use					
Refurbishment, recycling, disposal					

Figure 5.9

Ecological Impact by Life Cycle Stages and Phases
Inventory Recording Template

Life Cycle Stages and Phases	Ozone layer depletion (CFC-11 eq. emissions)	Climate change (CO$_2$ eq.)	Human health (Injuries; illnesses from hazardous emissions)	Photochemical smog (NO$_x$ eq.)	Acidification (H+ eq. related to receiving airshed, water bodies, and soils)	Eutrophication (N eq. related to receiving waters	Plant and animal toxicity (Injuries; illnesses from emissions)	Habitat impact (Area loss, degradation)	Resource depletion and degradation (Consumption by type)	Waste (Volume by type)	Noise (Change in dB related to ambient)
						Ecological Impact					
Raw material extraction and transport											
Recycled material processing											
Material processing and transport											
Parts fabrication											
Component assemble											
Product assemble											
Quality control											
Product packaging manufacture											
Transport packaging manufacture											
Transport to consumer											
Installation											
Operation											
Maintenance											
Repair											
Upgrade											
Product reuse											
Disassembly											
Component reuse											
Landfill											
Incineration											

Figure 5.10

that affect the determination of significance: the availability of reliable data, the magnitude of the impact, and the context of its impact.

The difficulty in obtaining primary information can make the reporting of ecological impact difficult. (Although an impact may be significant, even if there is no reliable data to support the determination.) A growing number and robustness of databases are useful in simplifying the calculation of environmental impact. (A partial list of software tools—several of which may be downloaded for free for trial purposes—is included in the Resources.)

From an eco-efficiency or eco-effectiveness perspective the magnitude is a straightforward concept: it is the amount of resource consumed or the contaminant released.

However, from the two perspectives there is a divergence in assessing what constitutes significance. Because the objective of eco-effectiveness is to eliminate criteria impacts, any impact on non-renewable resources and *any* releases of contaminants would be judged to be significant.

The less-rigid eco-efficiency perspective considers the context of a release or of resource consumption. This approach first identifies the geographic scale at which the impact occurs and then makes a determination of the underlying conditions of the affected environment. The geographic scale may be considered on local, regional, or global basis. The affected environment is the condition of the specific resource. For example, the manufacturing process of a product could require substantial amounts of energy. If that energy is generated from a coal plant, then air emissions are released from the coal plant. These emissions may meet the regulatory requirements for contaminant concentrations being released. This suggests there is an "allowable" residual impact: Greenhouse gases, acidifying gases, and minute quantities of metals, such as mercury, are released into the atmosphere, where they create secondary impacts, such as respiratory ailments, acid rain, global warming, and the deposition of mercury into soil, and water bodies that can enter the food chain. On their own, these impacts are arguably minute and within tolerance (regulatory) levels; however, combined with other sources, the impacts accumulate and can contribute to significant impact.

Okala Normalization, Unit and [W]eighting of 10 TRACI Impact Categories[8]			
TRACI Impact Category	Normalization	Unit	Weight
Climate change	24,500	Tons CO2 equiv/yr/capita	35.4
Fossil fuel depletion	0.0408	Megajoule/yr/capita	11.7
Human respiratory	76.3	PM2.5 equiv/yr/capita	10.6
Human cancer	0.258	Benzene equiv/yr/capita	9.2
Ecotoxicity	73.8	2,4-D equiv/yr/capita	9.1
Water eutrophication	18	N equiv/yr/capita	7.5
Human toxicity	1470	Toluene equiv/yr/capita	6.3
Photochemical smog	121	NOx equiv/yr/capita	4.2
Acidification	7440	H+ equiv/yr/capita	3.6
Ozone layer depletion	0.311	CFC-11 equiv/yr/capita	2.4

Figure 5.11

One difficulty in assessing impact occurs when making a determination of what impact is preferable when there are two different types of impact, such as greenhouse gas emissions from a coal plant and radioactive waste storage issues associated with a nuclear generating station. The Okala Impact Factors and Eco-Indicator 99 databases are two databases that normalize impacts (to a single reference unit) and weight impact areas in order to facilitate comparison of different types of materials and processes. Figure 5.11 illustrates the normalization factor, unit, and weighting for 10 TRACI impact categories that have been developed by the Okala Team. Although the data have been developed for global and national scales, the TRACI model does analyses on a regional level.

In comparing the TRACI impact categories to the impact category table (Figure 5.4) there are environmental impact categories that are not captured currently, although in the future the model may be expanded to include additional impact categories.[9] Even so, these Okala factors facilitate comparison of product option impacts.

In addition to ecological impact the environmental assessment should consider regulatory requirements, emerging trends in technology, especially materials science, and how customer expectations may change over time. The combination of environmental, market, and regulatory factors form the basis for crafting design objectives that can be used by the design team.

Quality Function Deployment (QFD) is a tool used to capture consumer needs and wants, and then translates these preferences into product specifications.

Developing and Evaluating Design Options

The third step of ecodesign takes the product objectives that are the outcome from Step 2 and identifies design options to satisfy the objectives, evaluates the options, and then selects one or more of the options on which to base the product design.

At the outset of the ecodesign step the design team should be clear about the extent to which they will be addressing the product or service. The following are increasingly effective approaches:

- **Optimizing the existing system** is an incremental approach that is consistent with eco-efficiency (having an existing product be "less bad").

- **Re-engineering the system** is a holistic approach that begins to address the eco-effectiveness of the product or service.

- **Redefining the problem** is an even broader approach that examines options for delivering the result of a product or service.

> "You never change things by fighting the existing reality. To change something, build a new model that makes the existing model obsolete."
> —Buckminster Fuller

It is important that the ecodesign team extend their thinking beyond identifying "good" and "bad" impacts, and brainstorm benefits by creating new systems.

Option generation can be accomplished through brainstorming, mind mapping, TRIZ, ecodesign checklists (see the following section), and other problem-solving tools. Innovation also can be accomplished by applying structured analyses that help reveal design opportunities. The Product Ideas Tree (PIT) diagramming system (not shown) helps to structure idea generation among multiple disciplines.

The generated options will include alternate materials, product delivery models, product features, production processes, and technologies.

The individual brainstormed options that have been identified then can be evaluated in terms of their expected ecological improvement and their technical, financial, and market feasibility. The options then can be categorized into four groups:[10]

Category 1: Options likely to achieve significant environmental gains and that are feasible.

Category 2: Options likely to offer limited environmental gains and that are feasible.

Category 3: Options likely to achieve significant environmental gains. However, their feasibility is questionable.

Category 4: Options with limited environmental gains and questionable feasibility.

Options falling in Category 1 should be advanced into product design. Options falling into Category 2 should generally be advanced, unless the environmental gain is negligible. Category 4 options should be eliminated from consideration (although they should be revisited in future analyses to determine whether any factors (for example, technological innovations) have changed their feasibility). Category 3 options warrant further analysis.

The menu of options that are advanced should be evaluated for conflicts with other options to ensure that an option doesn't fix one problem while creating another. For example, the use of recycled materials in a component may result in greater weight to achieve needed strength, compared to use of virgin material, which has greater structural strength and therefore requires less material.

The LiDS (Lifetime Design Strategies) Wheel is a tool that graphically presents the environmental impacts of one or more product designs. The impacts are illustrated along the seven spokes of the wheel, which represent seven design principles:

- ► Innovate for new concept development (dematerialization, shared use, functional integration).
- ► Select low-impact materials (avoid toxins and ozone-depleting substances; use renewable materials and renewable energy).
- ► Reduce material usage.
- ► Optimize production systems (eliminate production steps, energy efficiency, waste minimization, alternative production processes).
- ► Optimize distribution (packaging, transport, and logistics).
- ► Reduce impact during use (low-energy intensity; ease of maintenance and repair).
- ► Optimize initial lifetime (functionality, durability, reliability, ease of maintenance, and so forth).
- ► Optimize end-of-life handling (reuse, remanufacture, recycle).

It's useful to use LiDS diagrams early in the design process as a way to focus environmental improvement discussions because it effectively illustrates the relative emphases. LiDS also can be used to compare a product against the performance of a competing product. In later design stages LiDS is useful for the evaluation of environmental impacts from potential design options.

Figure 5.12 illustrates a LiDS diagram for a hypothetical product and its proposed improvement objectives.

Similar in concept to the LiDS Wheel, Figure 5.13 shows an Eco-Compass, which uses six axes of impact to capture the environmental characteristics of a product:

- ▶ Material intensity.
- ▶ Health and environmental risk.
- ▶ Energy use.
- ▶ Recoverability.
- ▶ Resource conservation.
- ▶ Service extension.

The concept is particularly useful for comparing two or more products.

Total Cost Accounting (economic costing), Life Cycle Cost Analysis (economic costing in individual life cycle stages), and Full Cost Accounting (quantifying ecological, economic, and social costs) are additional tools that enable designers to investigate more than the environmental assessments of product design options.

Once the options have been selected from the full menu, the design team is in the position to develop a detailed design, produce prototypes, test, and launch.

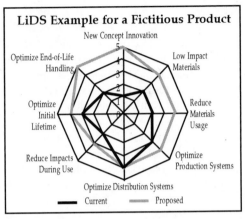

Figure 5.12

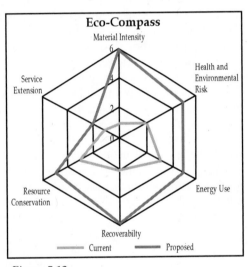

Figure 5.13

Managing the Ecodesign Process

When taking on the first ecodesign project of an enterprise (and in subsequent efforts) the project team should record project successes and obstacles. Such ongoing debriefing will build the ability of the organization to execute ecodesign projects.

Strategies to Reduce Product Impacts

A core set of strategies can be considered to reduce the environmental impact of a product. These strategies are captured in the "6 RE philosophy":

1. Re-think the product and its functions (for example, how the product may be used more effectively).
2. Re-duce the energy and materials used throughout the life cycle of a product.
3. Re-place harmful substances with more environmentally friendly alternatives.
4. Re-cycle. Select materials that can be recycled, and build the product so that it can be easily disassembled for recycling.
5. Re-use. Design the product so that parts can be reused.
6. Re-pair. Make the product easy to repair so that the product does not need to be replaced too soon.[11]

These strategies can be adapted to the life cycle framework discussed previously. The next section of the chapter identifies questions that can be used to evaluate the eco-friendliness of a product during each life cycle stage. These considerations are intended to stimulate thinking about ecodesign: An ecodesign initiative warrants greater depth of analysis to capture nuances.

Ecodesign Considerations for Product Development and Redesign

Whether the enterprise is considering developing a new eco-effective product or redesigning an existing product to be more eco-efficient, the process starts with examining the product from a broader perspective.

- What needs do the product and product system fulfill? What functions does the product perform?
- Can the product be dematerialized?
- Can the essential use of the product be expanded to incorporate functions provided by another product?
- Can multiple users share the product?
- Can the product be designed to accommodate anticipated changes in technology?
- Can the amount of product being manufactured be adjusted to quickly accommodate market demand, minimizing over-production?
- Can the design be based on a typical range of operation so that the product is not over-engineered for exceptional performance?
- If exceptional performance is warranted in some applications, can a premium product be designed in addition to the standard?
- Can product promotion and distribution channels minimize the need for consumers to "see and feel" the product?
- Can the overall design of the product be engineered so that all components have comparable lifetimes? Or be designed for ease of component replacement?
- Can the product achieve necessary rigidity through structural design, such as reinforcement ribs, rather than over-dimensioning for strength?
- Can the product be offered as a service?

- ▣ Can the product be taken back by the manufacturer after the consumer has finished its use? If so, can the distribution system be reconfigured for efficient collection and return?
- ▣ Can the product be given a "timeless" appearance?

Ecodesign Considerations in Materials Selection and Resource Extraction

In resource extraction, the eco-effective design avoids toxic, environmentally damaging, and non-renewable resources that require high energy inputs for processing.

- ▣ What are the current types and weights of metals, glass, ceramics, plastics, and rubber used—and what are their ecological impacts?
- ▣ Can the product use minimal quantity and weight of materials?
- ▣ Can the product incorporate refurbished components from dismantled or recycled material from previously used product?
- ▣ Can the product be manufactured from recycled material?
- ▣ Can the product use materials that minimize the depletion of non-renewable resources?
- ▣ Can the product be manufactured with cleaner materials—without substances that are toxic to humans or to the natural environment, or deplete the ozone layer, or that involve hydrocarbons that cause smog?
- ▣ Can the product materials be manufactured from renewable resources that are made from sustainably managed sources?
- ▣ Can the product be manufactured from materials that can be recycled?
- ▣ Can alternatives to non-ferrous metals (for example, copper, zinc, brass, chromium, and nickel) be used in order to avoid production emissions?
- ▣ Does the location of the material source minimize the need for (energy expenditure in) transport from point of extraction/collection to where the product will be manufactured?

Ecodesign Considerations for Production

Manufacturing the product components and assembling the product uses efficient production systems that minimize waste and energy consumption.

- ▣ Do analyses suggest multiple manufacture facilities and/or product warehousing locations to optimize logistics?
- ▣ Can the selected materials be processed in a more eco-effective manner?
- ▣ Can production waste be minimized?
- ▣ Can the manufacturing waste be used in another product?
- ▣ Can the number and complexity of operational processes and production steps be minimized?
- ▣ Can the energy used in production be minimized with energy-efficient equipment and processes?
- ▣ Can cleaner production processes be specified?
- ▣ Can the operational waste from manufacturing (wastewater, waste heat) be reused or recycled?

▶ Can operational processes be powered by on-site renewable energy sources?

▶ What are the quality control issues?

▶ Can quality controls be designed to minimize product rejects and returns?

▶ If product reuse is part of the intended design, have collection, transport, and production refurbishment been planned for efficiency?

Ecodesign Considerations for Packaging and Distribution

Ecodesign minimizes packaging and is mindful of the energy impacts of transporting the product to the consumer. (See also Chapter 6.)

▶ Can the product be designed to reduce transport volume?

▶ Can product packaging (primary, for product enclosure) be eliminated?

▶ Can the necessary primary packaging be redesigned to minimize impact?

▶ Can reusable packaging be used for primary product and transport (secondary and tertiary) packaging? If so, does a packaging collection system need to be designed?

▶ Can the packaging material be produced from recycled material?

▶ If the reuse of product packaging for additional product transport is not possible, can the consumer be encouraged to reuse or recycle the packaging material?

▶ Can the overall transportation system be designed to use energy-efficient transport modes (such as ship or train, instead of air or truck)?

▶ Can energy-efficient vehicles be specified for distribution and delivery vehicles?

▶ Can the product be stored (warehousing) and displayed (retailing) using a minimal amount of space?

Ecodesign Considerations for Use

Ecodesign means that the product uses minimal resources in its operation.

▶ What problems currently arise in product installation, use, maintenance, and repair?

▶ Can the product be designed to be usable for everyone regardless of physical capabilities or limitations, requiring low physical effort, and be simple and intuitive?

▶ Can the product be installed easily with common hand tools?

▶ Can energy use be minimized in standard operating mode as well as standby conditions (for example, insulation, energy-efficient fans, power-conserving mode, and so forth.)?

▶ Can the product be powered by renewable sources (solar, wind)?

▶ Can the need for batteries be avoided?

▶ Can air, water, and waste emissions (both volumes and contaminants) be minimized?

▶ Can water use be recaptured in the product or its quality be maintained to foster its reuse in another application?

▶ Can the use of consumable supplies be avoided or minimized?

- ▣ Can replenishable consumable supplies be derived from renewable products?
- ▣ Can the access to replenishable supplies and components requiring more frequent replacement be made convenient for the operator?
- ▣ Can access be simplified with minimal fasteners that can be opened and closed by hand, without or with common hand tools?
- ▣ Can the user maintain the product easily?
- ▣ Can the operator perform inspection, cleaning, lubrication, changeout, and other maintenance activities easily?
- ▣ Can self-test and automated fault indicators facilitate troubleshooting, maintenance, and simple repairs by the consumer?
- ▣ Is the product sufficiently durable to withstand wear and tear?
- ▣ Can the product be repaired easily?
- ▣ Can the product be upgraded easily by changing out components, sub-assemblies, or modules?
- ▣ Can the product appearance be designed to be timeless?

Ecodesign Considerations for End-of-Life Handling

Ecodesign means that after its useful life the product can be reused easily, become "food" for another industrial production, or be safely disposed.

- ▣ How is the product currently disposed of?
- ▣ What problems arise at the end of the life of the product?
- ▣ Can the product and/or product components be reused?
- ▣ Can the product be collected easily and safely?
- ▣ Would a "deposit" system facilitate return of product rather than its disposal?
- ▣ Can the product be disassembled easily (for example, using fasteners that can be removed with hand tools instead of adhesives) so that parts and/or component sub-assemblies are not damaged and can be reused?
- ▣ Can adhesives, coatings, and other unnecessary products be eliminated in order to facilitate recycling processing?
- ▣ Can materials be identified clearly?
- ▣ Has the product minimized the mixing of materials and colors, so that recyclable materials can be separated easily for recycling?
- ▣ Can the product be taken back by the manufacturer after the consumer has finished its use?
- ▣ Can hazardous components be manufactured to be easily and safely detachable?
- ▣ Would product incineration release toxic emissions?

Chapter 6

Packaging

Packaging is a system that integrates the design, evaluation, and manufacture of packages and then their fill, use, and discard. The packaging materiel refers to the components that are used in the individual packages, ranging from cardboard, paperboard, plastics, and glass used to enclose the product, as well as the cartonboard, containers, pallets, void filler, and shrink-wrap used in the transport of the product.

The objective of ecological packaging is to ensure that packages fulfill their intended purposes in a manner that does the least harm to the natural environment.

Packaging Purposes

Ecologically friendly packaging requires that environmentally sensitive design be balanced with other packaging functions such as:

- Physical protection. The packaged objects are protected from shock, vibration, crushing, temperature extremes, and so forth.
- Barrier provision. Some packaged items (such as foods and humidity-sensitive electronics) cannot interact with the environment.
- Containment. Liquids, powders, and multiple small items (screws, for example) must be enclosed for efficient transport.
- Security. Certain substances, such as food and pharmaceuticals, must be tamperproof.
- Safety. Some products, such as razor blades, must be packaged to avoid the potential for harm.
- Information. Most product packages convey information to the user (which may include promotional presentation).

Package design also must consider secondary objectives, such as:

- Manufacturing efficiency.
- Product presentation and differentiation.
- Convenience of handling, stacking, use, and reuse.
- Loss prevention.
- Cost effectiveness.

The purpose of packaging may vary depending upon the stage of the movement of the product through the supply chain:

- ▶ **Primary (sales) packaging:** the material that encloses the product at its point of purchase (for example, a milk carton).
- ▶ **Secondary (grouped) packaging:** the enclosure of primary packages usually for transport to its point of sale (such as a plastic case containing milk cartons).
- ▶ **Tertiary (transport) packaging:** the packaging for bulk handling and shipping (for example, a series of tightly packed boxes that are secured by shrink-wrap and supported by a pallet).

Packaging Materials and Types

Most of the packaging used by small and medium sized enterprises falls into one of the following categories: fiberboard, shipping bags, glass, plastic, and metal.

Fiberboard

Fiberboard is a general term for paper-based packaging:

- ▣ **Paperboard** is often used in primary packaging as a backing or as a hanger from which an attached product is displayed. Typically there are two or more layers, with an outer displayed layer having a coated or laminated surface that displays consumer information, such as product name, size, price, UPC marker, intended use, and simple safety data.
- ▣ **Boxboard** is a lightweight paperboard used in packaging boxes and primary cartons, such as cereal boxes.
- ▣ **Cartonboard** is typically a series of four to five paper layers that are formed into solid bleached board or folding boxboard, which is used for luxury items and where there is direct food contact. Unbleached cartonboard, with a coated, bleached pulp top layer, is typically used for secondary packaging. Cartonboard is often made with recycled paper.
- ▣ **Containerboard** is a single layer of corrugated board sandwiched between two sheets of linerboard. Boxes made from containerboard are usually brown; although a coating or white bleached pulp may be added to the exterior for presentation.
- ▣ **Corrugated board** is packaging that is strengthened by incorporating corrugations or flutes between the inner and outer layers of the board. Corrugated board usually contains a high percentage of recycled materials and may be coated, which sometimes renders it non-recyclable.

Flexible Packaging

Flexible packaging includes bags, envelopes, and other pliable containers made from paper, plastic, or a blend of paper and plastic. Flexible packaging can incorporate padding manufactured from polyethylene foam, polyethylene bubble, or macerated newsprint. This packaging is suitable for shipping smaller, soft items, such as clothing, books, and electronic media, directly to customers. Flexible packaging made from unlike materials can be challenging to recycle because of difficulties in separating its component materials.

Glass

Glass is a strong, durable, and chemical-resistant container suited for most liquids. The containers are made from sand (silica) and almost all contain some recycled glass. Glass is a relatively heavy material and can cause increased use of transport fuel and increased greenhouse gas (GHG) emissions during transport.

Plastics

Plastics are a versatile material made from petroleum resources. Plastics have a very high strength-to-weight ratio (making plastic containers an efficient alternative to heavier glass), are durable and smooth, and can be made transparent. Plastic can be resistant to chemicals, and provide thermal and electrical insulation. Common types of plastics used in packaging include:

- Polyethylene terephthalate (PET), used in soda containers and oven-ready meal trays.
- High-density polyethylene (HDPE), used in milk containers and cleaning liquids.
- Polyvinyl chloride (PVC), used in cling film, mineral water bottles, and shampoo containers.
- Low-density polyethylene (LDPE), used in bags and bin liners.
- Polypropylene (PP), used in margarine tubs and microwaveable trays.
- Polystyrene (PS), used in foam trays for meats, egg cartons, vending cups, and protective packaging for electronics.
- Expanded polystyrene (EPS), used in packing peanuts.
- Poly-lactic Acid (PLA), used in containers and bags.

PVC and EPS are environmental concerns because of the potential release of hazardous substances during manufacture, use, and disposal.

Steel and Aluminum

Steel and aluminum are durable and strong, and offer lasting protection for many food and drink products. Packaging manufactured from these materials usually incorporates recycled metal.

Degradable Packaging

Compostable, degradable, biodegradable, and renewable materials are evolving sources of packaging. Some care is needed in understanding their differences, as the three terms are not interchangeable and can be used to confuse a well-intentioned consumer.

Biodegradable plastics are plastics that decompose in the natural environment. However, to stimulate biodegradation these plastics incorporate chemical agents, whose toxicities are not always well known. Compostable materials are a subset of biodegradable materials that readily break down into compost biomass, carbon dioxide, methane, and water. Degradable plastics include biodegradable and compostable plastics, as well as other plastics that degrade as a result of physical and chemical processes.

Paper can be made from trees grown in sustainably managed forests, or be produced from rice, flax, and other renewable materials. (See Chapter 26.)

Molded packaging, such as paper egg cartons, can be made from recycled paper.

Biodegradable laminates and coatings can be made from agricultural products, such as cornstarch and wheat (although not all have a favorable footprint based on LCA).

Ecological Impacts of Packaging

The environmental impacts of packaging are a consequence of the types, quantities, and sources of materials. Packaging materials include fiber (such as paper cardboard and paperboard); plastics; glass; metals; wood; and adhesives, inks, and coatings. Impacts from these materials can include:

- Consumption of non-renewable materials (such as steel and other metals).
- Unsustainable consumption of renewable resources (water and trees, for example).
- Consumption of non-renewable energy resources (for example, oil, gas, and coal).
- Generation or use of hazardous materials (chlorine, heavy metals, and volatile organic compounds, for example).

Packaging Considerations and Their Environmental Significance[1]					
	Key Environmental Concerns				
Attribute	Resource Efficiency	Emissions	Transport Efficiency	Re-usability	Recyclability
Base material	X	X			X
Color	X	X		X	X
Size and shape of container	X	X	X	X	
Grade/thickness of material	X	X	X	X	X
Structural design of container	X	X	X	X	
Closure materials				X	X
Label materials				X	X
Adhesives, inks, coatings, laminates		X			X
Graphic design and labeling				X	
Note: Key environmental concerns are intended as an assessment of an attribute's *likely* significance.					

Figure 6.1

- ▶ Emissions released to the atmosphere (for example, GHGs, particulates, acid gases, and odors).
- ▶ Effluents released into water bodies (for example, suspended solids, toxins, oxygen-depleting chemicals).
- ▶ Solid waste (landfilled material and litter, for example).
- ▶ Habitat degradation (from non-sustainable timber harvesting, mining, and changes in water quantity and quality).
- ▶ Land erosion (from non-sustainable timber harvesting and/or mining practices).
- ▶ Noise and vibration (from harvesting raw materials, manufacture, distribution, collection, separation, and disposal).

Figure 6.1 on page 52 identifies different packaging considerations and their environmental significance.

Fiberboard Impacts

Figure 6.2 on page 54 describes the ecological impacts associated with the life cycle of various paper-based packaging. The figure shows the amount of trees used, the amount of energy consumed, and air emissions, wastewater volumes, and solid waste generated from different types of paper packaging. The worst offender is corrugated, bleached paperboard; coated paperboard made from 100-percent post-consumer content shows the most favorable impacts. If the type and amount (by weight) of the packaging consumption of an enterprise is known, the ecological impacts of the packaging can be easily estimated.

Plastic and Glass Impacts

Refillable bottles made from glass use less material and create less solid waste than their one-way cousins. The amount of resource saved is a function of the number of trips a refillable unit makes during its lifetime. One estimate shows refillable glass bottles using 93 percent less energy than one-way bottles.[2] Savings in water use, reduced contamination of air and water, and reduced raw material usage are additional benefits.

Eco-Friendly Packaging Principles

Eco-friendly packaging reduces ecological impacts by incorporating appropriate design principles throughout the life cycle of a package: acquiring the raw materials; manufacturing; filling, loading, and handling; distributing; using and reusing; recycling; and final disposal.

The Sustainable Packaging Coalition is a consortium of enterprises that have been organized by the GreenBlue Institute to encourage the development of packaging that is functional and cost-effective, while promoting environmental and human health. Essential criteria of the Coalition's definition of sustainable packaging are as follows:

- ▶ "Is beneficial, safe & healthy for individuals and communities throughout its life cycle.
- ▶ "Meets market criteria for performance and cost.

Estimated Lifecycle Environmental Impacts Associated With One Ton of Select Paper Packaging Products[3]

Paper Packaging Product	Post-consumer content (%)	Wood Use		Total Energy (million BTUs)	Air Emissions				Wastewater (gals)	Solid Waste (lbs)
		Tons	Trees		GHGs (lbs CO$_2$ equiv.)	Particulates (lbs)	HAPs (lbs)	VOCs (lbs)		
Corrugated unbleached	0	3	21	28	5,549	9	4	7	10,893	1,933
Corrugated unbleached	50	2	11	23	4,509	7	2	4	6,447	1,235
Corrugated semi-bleached	0	3	22	30	5,653	10	4	7	12,557	2,008
Corrugated bleached	0	4	29	43	5,812	14	3	7	21,470	2,359
Paperboard: solid, bleached sulfate	0	4	26	40	5,627	13	2	6	20,123	2,235
Paperboard: coated, unbleached Kraft	0	3	20	28	5,089	8	3	5	11,078	1,892
Paperboard: uncoated, bleached Kraft	0	4	29	43	5,796	14	4	7	21,415	2,281
Paperboard: uncoated, unbleached Kraft	0	3	23	30	5,204	9	3	6	11,522	1,913
Paperboard: 50% uncoated, unbleached Kraft; 50% recycled	50	2	11	24	4,286	7	2	3	6,750	1,225
Paperboard: coated, recycled	100	0	0	17	3,244	6	<1	<1	1,930	580

Figure 6.2

- ▶ "Is sourced, manufactured, transported, and recycled using renewable energy.
- ▶ "Maximizes the use of renewable or recycled source materials.
- ▶ "Is manufactured using clean production technologies and best practices.
- ▶ "Is made from materials healthy in all probable end-of-life scenarios.
- ▶ "Is physically designed to optimize materials and energy.
- ▶ "Is effectively recovered and utilized in biological and/or industrial closed loop cycles."[4]

Strategies for Eco-Friendly Packaging

Ecological packaging is most effective when it is integrated into the process for designing products. It is during the early product planning stages that environmental considerations can be addressed along with other product objectives. Such an integrated approach to design may be helpful in identifying solutions, such as the sale of concentrated product (laundry detergent, for example), that requires less product to be used (and packaged), or containers that can be refilled by the purchaser at the point of sale.

Four basic principles are the foundation of an eco-friendly packaging management plan:

- ▶ Using less packaging.
- ▶ Reusing packaging.
- ▶ Recycling packaging.
- ▶ Buying ecologically preferable packaging.

Use Less Packaging

Minimizing packaging is not necessarily an effective approach to packaging design because other packaging objectives, such as product protection, may be compromised. The following approaches can be considered as techniques for reducing the overall amount of resources used in packaging.

General

- ▷ Consider primary, secondary, and tertiary packaging as part of an integrated packaging system. Don't ecodesign one component at the expense of another.
- ▷ Work with an experienced professional in the design of the packaging system.
- ▷ Don't over-engineer single-use packages.
- ▷ Determine the reuse or alternative use of packaging (for example, a cardboard box can be designed as a "garage" for a toy truck).
- ▷ Evaluate whether a change in the design of the product could reduce packaging needs without sacrificing the function of the product.

▶ Offer at least one product line in reusable containers, when possible.

▶ During the packaging design stage, test different configurations to optimize packaging.
The American Society for Testing and Materials and International Safe Transit Association have promulgated standards for evaluating packaging performance.

▶ Maintain a feedback system to provide data on packaging performance. For example, all products returned due to damage during transport should be analyzed for cause.

▶ Communicate to customers that the organization is minimizing packaging to protect resources.

Primary Packaging

▶ Use the minimal amount of resources while achieving all other packaging objectives.
Downgauge—use the least thick material whenever possible.
Minimal may mean no packaging at all.

▶ Don't use packaging weight to convey value or larger product size.

▶ Design and develop (or use, if not a packaging producer) reusable packaging, where practical.

▶ Package larger quantities of product. (The purchase of a greater volume of product must be acceptable to the consumer, retailers, and distributors.)

▶ Design packages to minimize production waste (for example, a number of cardboard backings can be cut from a single sheet with minimal trimming left over).

▶ Eliminate plastic film "windows" that allow the prospective buyer to see inside the package. Instead, use a cutout or a photograph of the product.

▶ Design packaging to complement in-store merchandising and point-of-sale promotion.

Secondary Packaging

▶ Minimize the size of secondary packaging. Use only the size of box/bag necessary with sufficient protection for the shipped product—thereby eliminating excessive padding (such as bubble wrap and other void fillers).

▶ Optimize box geometry (provide the greatest shipping volume per material used).

▶ Substitute less resource-intensive packaging where feasible, (such as flexible packaging instead of cartons for soft goods).

▶ Have an inventory of various sizes and types of packaging that reduces the possibility of using oversized packaging when less would suffice.

▶ Use scored (variable depth) cartons that can be folded to an optimal size, thereby reducing the need for void filling.

▶ Create a set of packing guidelines to assist order fillers in selecting the appropriate packages, fill materials, adhesives, and labels for secondary and tertiary packages.

- ☒ Use a "strong enough" approach to design: Test packaging to assess ability to withstand expected stresses; don't over-design the packaging to remove all doubt of the product arriving unblemished.
- ☒ Use single-walled boxboard when possible. When extra protection is needed, use double-walled corrugated board rather than triple-walled.
- ☒ Apply structural solutions, such as corrugated flutes or honeycombed boxboard.
- ☒ Avoid unnecessary packaging layers.
- ☒ Minimize the size of labels on smaller packages.

Tertiary Packaging
- ☒ Design tertiary packaging for efficiency to optimize case stacking and packing in transit vehicles.
- ☒ Use a larger box instead of multiple, smaller packages.
- ☒ Design secondary packaging with pallet dimensions in mind. Eliminate overhang and cushion (fill voids) to prevent excessive underhang that also can damage products.
- ☒ Evaluate the need for pallets. (Can alternative support packaging, such as slip-sheets or corrugated trays, be used for lighter materials?)
- ☒ Purchase recycled pallets or pallets manufactured from previously used wood.
- ☒ Recycle pallets. Evaluate the choice between plastic and wooden pallets.
- ☒ Require repeat customers to return pallets or to reuse them.
- ☒ Use the least thickness shrink-wrap that still achieves product protection.
- ☒ Recycle low-density polyethylene (LDPE) stretch film.

Void Filling and Cushioning

Void filling fills the space between the product and the shipping carton. Cushioning material surrounds the product and is used to absorb shock and vibration. The four main blocking and filling materials are:
1. Paper pad.
2. Air pad.
3. Foam-in-place.
4. Loose fill.

Honeycomb, bubble wrap, and foam are other materials whose principal application is protection from shock and vibration, but that is sometimes used as blocking and filling. Evaluate the use of:

- ☒ Inflatable air pads, instead of packing peanuts, for secondary packaging.
- ☒ Packing peanuts manufactured from eco-friendly sources, such as cornstarch-based peanuts or peanuts made from recycled papers.
- ☒ Perforated wrap or foam that is sized to match the product being protected, instead of bubble wrap or foam.
- ☒ Crumpled Kraft papers or multi-layer paper for cushioning or void filling.

Encourage customers to reuse packing peanuts, bubble wrap, and other packing materials.

Closing Boxes
- ▣ Use the minimum thickness, width, and length of closing tape necessary.
- ▣ Consider using recyclable tape, such as Kraft paper tape. (It should be noted that there is some debate in the industry as to whether paper or plastic tape is better from a recyclability perspective.[5])
- ▣ Use automatic case sealers, which apply consistent and appropriate lengths of closing tapes, using less tape than the typical packer.
- ▣ Give preference to packaging materials that require less adhesive for closing: mailing bags, self-closing boxes, and end-loading boxes.

Strapping Pallets
- ▣ Plastic stretch film is the typical medium for securing packages to pallets. If used, the stretch film should be recycled.
- ▣ Stretchable tapes and rubber bands are suitable for light, uniform loads. However, they are not moisture-resistant.
- ▣ Plastic and steel strapping are extremely strong, but are difficult to apply and dangerous to remove.

Use Recycled and Renewable Materials in Packaging

Recycled materials usually are more eco-friendly than using virgin materials because less energy and processing is required to manufacture the packaging.

General
- ▣ Maximize post-consumer waste provided that other technical performance requirements are met.
- ▣ Incorporate post-industrial (cut-off) waste as a substitute for virgin material.

Paper and Board

Corrugated boxes typically contain 25- to 35-percent recycled material; however, some manufacturers are producing cartons from 100-percent recycled material.

The common way of measuring corrugated material strength is the Mullen Test, which measures box bursting strength. The Edge Crush Test (ECT) is an alternative measuring system that evaluates stacking strength. A box that meets the ECT standard is produced from less paperboard than its Mullen equivalent.[7]

- ▣ As an alternative to corrugated boxes, use a bookfold, which is a flat corrugated sheet with scored flaps that wrap tightly around the product(s) being packaged.[6] Bookfolds use less corrugated board than corrugated boxes and eliminate the need for void filling.
- ▣ Use the strongest and most ecologically benign materials.
- ▣ Consider using the Edge Crush Test instead of the Mullen Test to evaluate box strength. (See the sidebar.)
- ▣ Evaluate corrugated board (in small, such as E-flute, or micro-flute form) options.

▷ Consider the use of end-loaded boxes, which use less corrugated material and less adhesive for closing.[8]

▷ End-loaded boxes and telescoping design style trays are effective designs for shallow cartons.

▷ Maximize post-consumer waste in cartonboard.

▷ Food products may be able to use laminated recycled board or a plastic liner that would permit recycled board to be used, provided they meet FDA regulations.

Plastics

Plastic containers are a strong lightweight alternative to glass.

▷ Consider co-extruded bags and containers, which can incorporate post-consumer waste.

▷ Return plastic shrink-wrap to the manufacturer and purchase recycled shrink-wrap.

Glass

▷ If using glass, consider recycled glass.

▷ Evaluate the suitability of lightweighting glass containers.

▷ Consider alternatives to glass, such as flexible packaging.

▷ Retain flexibility in specifying glass color (to purchase the most currently available glass) by using plastic shrink sleeves or applying organic coatings to the glass.

Design Packaging for Reuse

Reusable shipping packages work best in closed distribution loop systems where there is a constant flow of product. The key considerations for designing packaging for reuse in delivering product are to:

▶ Integrate primary, secondary, and tertiary packaging.
▶ Design for durability.
▶ Design for weight control.
▶ Design for ease of handling.
▶ Design for cleanliness and ease of maintenance.

Figure 6.3 on page 60 presents an often-cited comparison of different shipping materials. The table indicates that although reusable containers are more expensive initially, their economic costs over their usable lifetime are very appealing. (It's important to note that the table presents historic data, with presumably historic prices, and no incorporation of return transportation, handling costs, or environmental burdens.)

Specific design considerations include:

▷ Develop protocols for return, to ensure the effectiveness of any take-back programs.

▷ Coordinate distribution of product with collection of packaging for reuse.

- ◧ Consider a tracking system to determine the locations of reusable drums, pallets, and other packaging.
- ◧ Assess suitability of integrating secondary and tertiary packaging into a point-of-purchase display of primary packages.
- ◧ Consider reinforcing existing designs, and use more durable packaging materials to enable packages to be reused. Reinforcing also could be accomplished with ribs, internal separators, edge strengthening, lamination, and so forth.
- ◧ Ensure that the overall design specifications are consistent with reuse of the package throughout its intended lifetime: finish, label removal and reapplication, and durability must all be matched.
- ◧ Make all components as lightweight as feasible.
- ◧ Make the package easily collapsible for storage and transport.
- ◧ Ensure packages can be opened and reclosed easily without compromising the integrity of the package for reuse.
- ◧ Invest in recyclable steel drums that are greater than 1 mm thick and suitable for reuse. Evaluate the suitability of thicker plastics as a lighter weight alternative to steel drums.
- ◧ Design the packaging for ease of cleaning (minimize dirt-catching crevices and surfaces in pallets; use liners in drums) and repair (use interchangeable modular components, such as wood slats on pallets).
- ◧ Store perishable packaging appropriately (for example, cardboard should be stored in a low humidity environment).
- ◧ If encouraging end users' reuse, provide information on how the package could be reused.

Comparison of Two Shipping Containers by Material[9]				
Container Attribute	Corrugated One-Way	Corrugated Reusable	Fiberboard Reusable	Plastic Reusable
Weight (lbs.)	1.5	2.2	5	5.5
Durability	Poor	Fair	Fair to good	Excellent
Initial cost	$0.53	$1.06	$6.05	$11.03
Estimated life	1 trip	5 trips	50 trips	250 trips
Procurement cost/trip	$0.53	$0.21	$0.12	$0.044
Other costs	•Setup •Disposal	•Setup •Breakdown •Return •Re-setup	•Return	•Return

Figure 6.3

Design Packaging Systems for Recycling and Disposal

The recycling packaging is determined by the collection, sorting, and recycling processes, as well as the use to which the recycled materials will be put. The key considerations for designing packaging for recycling and disposal are to:

- ▶ Minimize the handling of mixed recyclables.
- ▶ Minimize contamination of the base product (such as cardboard, glass, or plastic) that will be recycled.
- ▶ Make any contamination (that is, labels, sleeves, adhesives, and fasteners) easy to remove.

General

- ▷ Develop a system for accepting recycled packaging materials from customers.
- ▷ Minimize labels.
- ▷ Minimize ink surfaces and use readily soluble inks.
- ▷ Eliminate or reduce volumes of adhesives.
- ▷ Use water-based adhesives.
- ▷ Avoid use of plastics, chlorine, and heavy metals in order to reduce emissions of potentially harmful emissions if the disposed waste is incinerated.

Paper and Paperboard

- ▷ Avoid coatings, such as UV varnishes, wax, plastic, and foil laminates, that may be problematic for paper mill reprocessing.
Consider use of water/acrylic-based emulsions and starch-based coatings.
If coatings are needed, consider inorganic vapor-deposition coatings.
- ▷ Strive for an all-cardboard design that doesn't use EPS/plastic inserts.
- ▷ Avoid pressure-sensitive and cold-seal adhesives.
- ▷ Use "blobs" of adhesive on paper packaging, rather than thin strips that are more difficult to remove when papermaking.

Plastics

Plastic recycling requires the plastic to be sorted by color and by the type of plastic. Collected plastics are sorted by type of plastic, chopped/flaked, and washed to remove labels and adhesives. The cleaned, separated polymers are then further processed into granulate for new plastics. To facilitate recycling of plastic:

- ▷ Use single, readily recycled polymer types instead of multiple polymers that need to be separated.
- ▷ Avoid color in the plastic (clear and white plastics are the easiest to recycle) or color mixing in the same package.
- ▷ Minimize inks, adhesives, and coatings.
- ▷ Assess feasibility of molding label information into the package (similar to stamping the plastic identifier code).
- ▷ Assess whether a different manufacturing process (for example, blow-molded rather than injection-molded) would have a more favorable recycling capability.
- ▷ Use fasteners, such as press-studs and staples, which are easier to remove than tape or adhesives for secondary and tertiary packaging.
- ▷ Identify on the container the polymers used in the plastic packaging components.

Avoid Toxins

Toxic materials associated with packaging include materials that are incorporated intentionally or inadvertently:

- ▶ Heavy metals (lead, cadmium, hexavalent chrome, mercury) may be incorporated into some inks. They also can be introduced in minute quantities from recycled plastics, glass, and paperboard.[10]
- ▶ Solvents used in inks.
- ▶ Adhesives and coatings.
- ▶ Toxicants contained in plastics.
- ▶ Chlorine used in paper bleaching. (See Chapter 26.)

Eco-friendly packaging contain no hazardous materials:

- ▣ Use only unbleached paperboard or paperboard produced using totally chlorine-free (TCF) or elemental chlorine-free (ECF) processes.
- ▣ Select inks that have no heavy metals and don't require organic solvents. (See Chapter 15, regarding other environmental considerations when choosing inks.)
- ▣ Use water-based adhesives and hot-melts instead of solvent-based adhesives.
- ▣ Study *Material Safety Data Sheets* to identify toxic and/or hazardous characteristics of material.
- ▣ Avoid plastics containing toxins.

Receiving

Work with suppliers so that they are applying sound packaging principles to the products that are being delivered to the organization.

- ▣ Specify the use of eco-friendly packaging in procuring goods. (See Chapter 7.)
- ▣ Establish packaging guidelines for use by suppliers.
- ▣ Evaluate the packages arriving. If packaging can be improved, then address the matter with the vendor.
- ▣ Open packages carefully to protect their reusability.
- ▣ Segregate packaging upon receipt to protect their reusability and recyclability.
- ▣ Store packaging—whether for reuse or recycling—to use as little space as possible.
- ▣ Determine whether incoming packaging can be reused for outgoing product packaging, by another organization, or whether component material can be recovered.
- ▣ Ensure that packages and returned packaging is moved smoothly and without damage during the packing, fulfillment, shipping, return, and storage processes.
- ▣ Use rubber-tipped tines on forklifts to protect pallets and cartons from damage.
- ▣ Return packing materials to vendors or provide to materials reusers/recyclers.

Chapter 7

Green Purchasing

Green purchasing is an ecologically based procurement strategy that blends environmental considerations with traditional purchasing considerations. Green procurement is not the only criterion in purchasing, although some organizations may elect to make green characteristics a priority, if not the most important criterion.

Purchasing decisions are more and more influenced by the ecological performance of products and services and the enterprises that produce and sell them. (See Chapter 27.) When prospective purchasers are concerned about ecological impact, they may address only a single aspect of the ecological impact of a product or service, or they may be concerned about the ecological footprint throughout the lifetime of a product.

Effective green procurement results in the purchase of products that are energy-efficient, water-efficient, void of toxins, as well as the other impact areas outlined in Figure 5.4. These impact areas extend beyond the operational stage of product use to all stages of its life (as described in Figure 5.2).

The synthesis of these elements results in an organization that migrates from a (typically) least-cost purchasing policy to a holistic procurement policy that evaluates the purchase of products and services from a life cycle perspective, as well as in terms of compatibility with complementary organizational goals and strategies.

The steps for initiating a green purchasing program follow the process outlined in Chapter 4:

- ▶ Designating the person responsible for the Purchasing Plan.
- ▶ Conducting a review of current purchasing policies.
- ▶ Establishing goals, strategies, and actions.
- ▶ Implementing an Action Plan.
- ▶ Refining the Plan.

Designating the Person Responsible

Design of the green purchasing program should be assigned to a single individual. However, the responsible person's effectiveness in developing a successful program depends on involving stakeholders both in and out of the organization. It also is necessary to allocate sufficient resources to the project.

Evaluating Current Purchasing

Current procurement practices represent the baseline from which goals and strategies can be developed and evaluated. The procurement inventory should specify:

- ▶ Products and services purchased by the organization, including their specifications, and life cycle environmental characteristics, if known.
- ▶ Current suppliers of those products and services.
- ▶ Characterization of relations with suppliers, including how they are selected, cost-effectiveness, on-time delivery, payment terms, guarantees/warranties, and ease of conducting business with them.
- ▶ Frequency of purchase and cost.
- ▶ Identification of alternative products and services, and suppliers that meet the essential specifications and their environmental characteristics.

The Commission for Environmental Cooperation (whose three members are Canada, Mexico, and the United States), which houses the North American Green Purchasing Initiative, has drafted a detailed self-assessment survey, *Eco-S.A.T.*, that can be used to evaluate procurement practices for their ecological responsibility.[1]

Product and Service Evaluation

Organizations that purchase a limited amount of products or services may be able to evaluate the ecological impacts of their purchased products relatively easily.

Enterprises that purchase hundreds of products may elect to conduct a two-phase process: screening for high ecological impacts in the first phase (then creating green purchasing policies for those), followed by establishing green purchasing policies for remaining products in the second.

Supplier Evaluation

Evaluating the ecological responsibility of suppliers entails the consideration of the same topics that have been identified in the self-assessment described in Chapter 4. The following are criteria used by GRIP, which can be used to assess a supplier's eco-efficiency:

- ▶ "Environmental policy and environmental reporting.
- ▶ "Internal control and formal eco-management systems.
- ▶ "The relationship of foreign supplier/manufacturing firm to their authorities.
- ▶ "Raw materials and raw material extraction.
- ▶ "Energy.
- ▶ "Designs for recycling and repossession schemes.
- ▶ "Transport system."[2]

However, asking suppliers to describe their environmental practices may be a delicate matter if they are concerned about "grading" that may be done or if they consider such information proprietary. It's important to assure suppliers that any acquired information will be held in confidence, and to indicate that it's the objective to work together to ensure that acquired products and services are ecologically responsible.

Green Purchasing Planning

Green purchasing goals are ideally developed in conjunction with organization-wide goals, as they represent one of the implementation strategies for reducing the ecological impact of an enterprise.

Goals are best expressed as a measurable objective for the enterprise. (See Chapter 4.) A purchasing goal, such as the following, exemplifies a well-stated goal: *By January 31, 2010 the enterprise will purchase green office supplies with an ecological impact that is 20% less than the impact of the same types of supplies typically purchased at the time of the 2009 baseline assessment.*

The following are examples of strategies that may be considered to accomplish green procurement goals:

- ▣ Partner with suppliers in product development.
- ▣ Support suppliers in becoming more conversant in green procurement.
- ▣ Assist suppliers in evaluating their ecological performance.
- ▣ Develop ecologically responsible product specifications.

Implementing Green Purchasing Programs

Procurement specification is one of the most successful ways of implementing green purchasing. Alameda County, California, has prepared *A Resource Guide for Environmentally Preferable Products* that illustrates an effective specification-based procurement program. The Resources lists resources for developing specifications for various products and services.

If the procurement of an organization is complex, it may warrant a pilot program in which a single or limited set of products and services are "greened." Pilot programs can help identify the need for training, evaluate suppliers, and determine internal obstacles that require attention.

The GRIP Centre recommends that in addition to price appropriateness, availability, and ability to achieve the consumer's requirement of a given product, the following criteria should be applied to reveal the eco-efficiency of a product and the ability to meet enterprise requirements (all criteria do not apply to all products):

- ▣ "Raw materials are renewable, recyclable and designed for reuse.
- ▣ "Manufacturing process.
- ▣ "Content of environmentally hazardous substances.
- ▣ "Content of substances causing poor indoor climate.
- ▣ "Noise.
- ▣ "Energy consumption.

- ▶ "Water consumption.
- ▶ "Service life.
- ▶ "Useful qualities.
- ▶ "Disruption of production.
- ▶ "Repair possibilities and service.
- ▶ "Flexibility.
- ▶ "Multi-purpose fitness.
- ▶ "Upgradability.
- ▶ "Content of re-used parts.
- ▶ "Follow-up of warranty.
- ▶ "Recycling system for the product.
- ▶ "Recycling system for packaging.
- ▶ "Toxic waste.
- ▶ "Genetic engineering."[3]

Note that the characteristics being measured relate directly to the ecodesign guidelines described in Chapter 5.

Evaluating and Refining Procurement Programs

The success of the green purchasing program should be monitored through an assessment program that quantifies the ecological benefits and the cost savings, and compares those against any cost of the green procurement. (See also Chapter 30 on reporting and communicating environmental benefits.)

The program review may entail an assessment of the effectiveness of individual strategies and a determination of whether it's appropriate to revise strategies that are falling short of the expected results.

As part of the monitoring program, the enterprise should maintain contact with suppliers to address any issues that they may have with respect to providing green products and services.

Chapter 8

Facilities

This chapter addresses how to green the property, buildings, and landscape that are occupied by an enterprise.

Locating the Enterprise

Eco-friendly properties are characterized by easy access to an efficient transportation system, are served by utilities with stable supplies and capacity, and are close to enterprises that could potentially use waste materials (such as waste heat and water) generated by the organization.

Location and Transportation

The following considerations affect eco-friendly transportation choices:

- ► Manufacturers and distributors should consider locating their facilities in areas that are close to the locations where the raw materials and components of the enterprise are harvested and produced.
- ► Manufacturers should consider the location of their markets and optimize their choice of location so that the transportation network is able to efficiently distribute products to customers.
- ► Service-oriented enterprises should be located to facilitate employees' travel to customers.
- ► Within the optimal geographic region, consider locating in communities that offer affordable housing, education, healthcare, recreation, culture, and other amenities that appeal to employees.
- ► Look for a property served by public transportation and/or that can be accessed easily and safely by walking or bicycling.

See Chapter 21 for a discussion of eco-friendly practices related to the transportation of people and goods.

Location and Utilities

Organizations require supplies of water and energy, and the ability to cost-effectively manage solid wastes, wastewater, and storm water. The following are some utilities considerations for enterprises whose objective is to site their facility in a green location.

Water
- Evaluate (public and private) supply sources for the ability to meet enterprise demand (as represented by the calculated water budget; see Chapter 22) and expected community demand.
- Contact agencies responsible for surface and groundwater quality, and identify issues that are relevant to the enterprise.

Energy
- Profile electricity suppliers (see Chapter 9) in order to determine fuels that would be consumed in providing electricity and the greenhouse gas emissions associated with the generation of electricity for the enterprise.
- Determine sources of petroleum and natural gas supplied to the region.
- Identify price trends and supply vulnerabilities of energy sources.
- Evaluate the on-site potential of solar and wind energies to supply enterprise requirements.
- For enterprises with significant electric demand, mechanical energy needs, or heat requirements, identify opportunities for on-site combined heat and power and/or shared systems with other major producers/users of electricity and heat.

Solid Wastes
- Identify waste collectors that serve the area. Determine what types of wastes are collected and where collected wastes are transported for ultimate disposal.
- Based on the projected waste profile of the organization, determine the ability of local enterprises to accept and use wastes generated by the organization.

Wastewater
- Determine whether public wastewater treatment can accommodate expected wastewater generated by the enterprise or if on-site treatment will be necessary.
- If the organization generates substantial volumes of wastewater, determine whether local enterprises can accept and use the quantity and quality of wastewater generated.

Storm Water
- Determine disposition of storm water. Characterize receiving waters for drainage.
- Identify whether community collection combines wastewater and storm water that can result in insufficient treatment during major storm events.

Location: Existing Development, New Development, or Redevelopment

As enterprises grow and contract, change their business model, or alter their product/service mix, they may find it necessary to change the location of their business. There's a discrete set of basic options available; however, within those options there may be a variety of opportunities related to specific properties. The basic options are:
- Renovate existing space.
- Expand into adjacent space, with or without renovation.

◘ Move to new space, with or without renovation.

◘ Build anew.

In considering which of the options to select, it is important to understand the attributes of green facilities.

Green Site Development

The following considerations can guide green development for enterprises. These considerations can guide how an evaluator would gauge the eco-friendliness of an existing site, or serve as guidelines for specifying the attributes of a new development or renovation.

Site Development

▣ When evaluating site options, consider previously developed properties, which represent an inventory of embodied energy and often are served by existing infrastructure.

Consider the redevelopment of brownfield sites rather than developing previously undisturbed properties (greenfields).

▣ Create a development plan that is suited to the geological, hydrological, and ecological conditions of the site.

▣ Ensure adjacent and nearby surface waters are protected by sufficient development buffers.

▣ Minimize site disturbance by reducing development footprint:

▷ Optimize building footprint with a building envelope and orientation suited to bioclimatic conditions.

▷ Minimize impervious areas.

▷ Group utilities.

▣ Determine how property can connect with surrounding and nearby properties, sites, and amenities (such as connection to transit stations and stops, bicycle paths, open space, and so forth).

▣ Ensure minimal amount of desirable vegetation is removed or disturbed, while eradicating any invasive plant species.

▣ Ensure wildlife corridors and movement are not compromised.

▣ Respect the integrity of on-site, adjacent, or nearby historical and cultural resources.

▣ Examine site for evidence of toxins and remediate contaminated areas.

Developing With Microclimate in Mind

▣ Plan activity areas to benefit from site microclimatic features: solar radiation, thermal gradients and humidity created by site topography, and wind patterns that cool in the summer are blocked in the winter.

▣ Evaluate thermal properties (color and specific heat capacity) of site materials (ground, vegetation, water bodies, asphalt, gravel, building materials) and use to moderate site climate and thereby reduce energy needed to heat and cool occupied buildings.

☒ Examine regional architectural styles and materials that typically reflect building designs that are adapted to perform well in the climate of the location. (See Figure 8.1 on page 72 for specific considerations for different climatic zones.)

Developing With Energy Production in Mind

☒ Evaluate solar radiation and technical potential for use. (Keep in mind that technological advances will likely increase the efficiency of collection and reduce the cost.) Ensure that solar access is considered in site design decisions.

☒ Evaluate wind conditions and technical potential for capture (again remembering that technological advances, including advances in microturbines, may affect future cost-effectiveness). Ensure future use of wind is protected by site development decisions.

☒ Evaluate the potential for nearby vegetation or buildings to block solar access. Similarly, ensure on-site development and vegetation doesn't compromise solar and wind potential on adjacent and nearby properties.

☒ Identify the potential for on-site and nearby energy requirements to be provided all or in part by combined heat and power or renewable energy systems.

Developing With Storm Water Management in Mind

☒ Manage storm water to minimize flooding and uncontrolled surficial drainage.

☒ Evaluate potential for capture, collection, storage, and use of rainwater.

☒ Evaluate bioretention as a way to collect, store, filter, and manage the release of storm water.

Green Building

Construction of new buildings and renovation of old buildings are opportunities for enterprises to green the space in which they conduct their operations.

The U.S. Green Building Council (USGBC) is a nonprofit organization that has been a leader in green building and development since its inception in 1993. The USGBC's Leadership in Energy and Environmental Design (LEED) Green Building Rating System is a widely accepted benchmark for the design, construction, and operation of high-performance green buildings.

Heating and Cooling

Green buildings are designed to minimize the energy needed to achieve occupant comfort and appropriate operating conditions for temperature and humidity-sensitive equipment (such as computers and servers). Eco-effective structures also maximize the use of renewable resources to provide needed energy.

Space Conditioning for Occupant Comfort

Bioclimatic design relates the physical comfort of an individual to the temperature and relative humidity of their environment. Generally, humans are comfortable when they experience temperatures between 70 and 80 degrees Fahrenheit, and relative humidity between 20 and 78 percent (with reducing comfort as humidity increases beyond 50 percent).[1]

Perceptions of comfort can be altered. For example, shade and wind help moderate warm temperatures. Conversely, blocking wind and receiving solar radiation increases the comfort level in temperatures below the 70-degree comfort threshold. Uncomfortably dry conditions can be corrected by adding moisture (such as fountains), and high humidity can be counteracted by wind that helps evaporate moisture from the skin's surface.

Factors Affecting Space Conditioning Needs

Enterprises are housed in many different building types (including businesses operating from residences). Different building types and numerous other variables affect the space conditioning performance of a building, including:

- ▶ Climate.
- ▶ Orientation of the building to the sun and prevailing winds, and the effect that the surrounding topography, buildings and structures, and vegetation have in shaping local climatic conditions (the microclimate).
- ▶ Building size in terms of footprint and the volume of the structure.
- ▶ Materials (wood, brick, concrete, steel, and glass) that define the "envelope" of the building.
- ▶ Construction techniques that affect the infiltration of outside air into the building and conditioned air out of the building.
- ▶ Window and skylight placement, style, construction, and maintenance that affect solar gain (sunlight into the enclosed space) and natural ventilation.
- ▶ The arrangement of interior walls and spaces, equipment, and furniture that affects interior air movement.

These factors affect the heating and cooling loads of a building. Because each structure is unique, it's not possible to identify appropriate energy efficiency improvements for a particular building. However, the EPA's *Target Finder* tool helps architects and building owners assess the estimated energy use and establish energy performance targets of a building design.

Bioclimatic Structure Design

Figure 8.1 describes general design principles that promote natural heating and cooling in the four regional climate zones. Olgyay's *Design with Climate* is an excellent resource for applying microclimatic conditions to improve the energy performance of buildings, covering such topics as thermal massing; window selection, sizing, and placement; and overhang design.

Green Building Materials

Green building materials are durable, safe products that are manufactured with little life cycle impact. A growing selection of green building materials fulfills even the most demanding performance requirements. The guidelines starting on page 73 are intended to provide a sense of green materials that can be considered (the Resources provide greater detail on specific design practices and materials).

General Design Consideration for the Four Climatic Zones[2]

	Cool	Temperate	Hot-Arid	Hot-Humid
Objectives	Increase heat production. Increase radiation absorption. Decrease radiation loss. Reduce conduction loss. Reduce evaporation loss	Balance heat production, radiation, and convection on seasonal basis	Reduce heat gain. Promote radiation loss. Reduce conduction gain. Promote evaporation	Reduce heat gain. Reduce radiation fain. Promote evaporation loss
Site selection	SSE slopes for sun gain. Middle of slopes to avoid wind and cold air pools	East of south slopes. Upper part of slopes	SE-E slopes. Lower slopes	High, windward elevation S and N, preferable over E and W. Offset from prevailing wind
Public spaces	Wind-sheltered. Open. Periodic shading	Open with grouped shade trees	Nearby, shaded areas. Avoid paved surfaces. Water features	Minimum walking distance. Shaded areas
Vegetation	Evergreen windbreaks NE through SW at distance. Deciduous near building	Evergreen windbreaks on NW. Allow S-SW summer breezes. Deciduous on E and W	Desirable for radiation absorption, evaporative and shade-giving	High branches allow airflow. Minimize perimeter plantings. Invite air across cool surfaces
Form	Compact 1:1.1-1.3, elongated along E-W axis	Volume effect not important 1:1.6, elongated along E-W axis	Compact 1:1.3, elongated along E-W axis	1:1.7-3.0, elongated along E-W axis
Orientation	12° east of south	17° east of south	South to 35° east of south	5° east of south
Color	Medium colors for sun-exposed surfaces. Recessed surfaces dark, if shaded from summer sun	Medium colors for sun-exposed surfaces. Recessed surfaces dark, if shaded from summer sun	Whites and light colors. Dark colors under eaves to prevent reflection. Recessed surfaces dark, if shaded from summer sun. Light colored roofs	Reflective light pastels
Windows	Small, except on east and south. Shade windows in summer. Cross-ventilation desirable	South windows. Shade protect E, S, W windows in summer. Limit west windows. Orient for cross-ventilation	Openings on S, N and to lesser extent, on E sides. Small windows, shielded from direct radiation. External shading	Walls become windows, with screens, jalousies. Shade protected
Materials	High heat capacity mass to balance heat variations. West wall materials with 6-hour time lag	West wall materials with 6-hour time lag	High heat capacity walls: E, 0-hour time lag; S, N and W, 10-hour; roof; 12-hour	Light heat capacity

Figure 8.1

General

▣ Evaluate the potential for reuse of materials being dismantled. Recycle construction waste.

▣ Use engineering techniques to minimize material use (for example, the use of engineered trusses and I-beams, rather than solid woods).

▣ Use durable materials.

▣ Use materials that provide dual uses, such as structural insulated panels.

▣ Use insulation with recycled content.

▣ Design to minimize the need for cutting materials, which results in waste.

▣ Where practical, select materials with minimal embodied energy (energy needed to manufacture) and minimal maintenance requirements.

Concrete

▣ Consider use of concrete that incorporates non-toxic recycled fly ash or slag instead of Portland cement.

▣ Use recycled concrete for sub-base and aggregates.

▣ Use earth forms to eliminate need for formwork.
Alternatively, specify reusable formwork.
Consider permanent formwork (such as fiber-cement blocks) that adds insulating value.

▣ Use low-VOC (Volatile Organic Compounds) curing compounds.

▣ Use biodegradable form-release agents instead of petroleum-based products.

Parking, Drives

▣ Use recycled asphalt, gravel, eco-pavers, crushed shells, or other eco-friendly alternatives to asphalt paving.

Stonework and Masonry

▣ Consider use of salvage brick, stone, or cement block.

▣ Specify locally available materials to reduce transportation costs.

▣ Consider adobe, straw bale, pressed-soil cement, and other low-impact masonry technologies.

Metals

▣ Avoid using metals, especially aluminum, which requires significant quantities of energy to manufacture.

▣ Use recycled metals.

▣ Use physical finishing processes (blasting, grinding, buffing, polishing) instead of metal coatings.

▣ Where metal coatings are needed, use powder-coated fabrications to eliminate the need for solvents.

Woods

▣ Use recycled wood.

▣ Avoid the use of endangered wood species, as listed by the Convention on International Trade in Endangered Species. (See the Resources.)

- Use rot-resistant woods instead of treated woods, such as those treated with copper chromium arsenate.
- Seal treated wood.
- Consider the use of plywood alternatives, such as oriented strand board, agri-fiberboards, and fiberboards manufactured with post-consumer waste.
- Use formaldehyde-free plywood alternatives, such as particleboard and medium density fiberboard (MDF).
- Use woods certified or certifiable by the Forest Stewardship Council.

Drywall
- Use gypsum board containing at least 20-percent recycled gypsum.
- Use low-VOC joint compound.
- Use dry-mix joint compound to reduce transportation energy impacts.

Floor Covering
- Consider bamboo as an alternative to traditional hardwood flooring.
- Use installation techniques that avoid adhesives (such as floating floors or nailed).
- Use water-based, low-VOC adhesives if adhesives are used.
- Consider cork, linoleum-resilient, or rubber flooring.
- If vinyl is necessary, specify tile, rather than greater outgasing sheet vinyl.
- Use carpets manufactured with recycled content.
- Consider carpet tile, which is more easily replaced than broadloom in the event of damage.
- Specify "green label" or "green label plus" certifications from the Carpet and Rug Institute's Indoor Air Quality Testing Program.
- Consider wool or less durable natural alternatives (sea grass, jute, cotton, sisal) to synthetic carpets.
- Specify carpet colors achieved through solution-dying, rather than piece-dying.

Paints
- Use water-based rather than oil-based paints.
- Specify low- or no-VOC paints and sealants.
- Use high-performance acrylic paint rather than alkyd paints for applications requiring high resistance to weathering.
- Use recycled-content paints, and recycle or donate unused or excess paint.

Daylighting
Daylighting is the use of windows, glass-paneled doors, clerestories, and sky-lights to bring sunlight into interior spaces. The use of natural light reduces the need for artificial lighting and thereby saves electricity. Also note that:

- North-facing windows provide even, natural light with little glare and no direct radiation.
- East- and west-facing windows provide natural light in the morning and afternoon; however, there can be glare and shadowing unless

the sunrays are intercepted. East- and west-facing windows typically offer little solar heating gain during the winter months, and unwanted gain during the summer.

▶ South-facing windows allow the greatest amount of sunlight (and solar heating gain) into the structure. There is the potential for glare and it's critical to address shadowing and unwanted summer solar gain.

(Chapter 11 is devoted to lighting from an energy perspective.)

Greenscaping

The exterior environment is a place where workers and visitors can connect with nature. The eco-friendliness of the space is a reflection of design, planting, and construction choices that accomplish greenscaping objectives by:

▶ Blocking summer sun/allowing winter sun.
▶ Channeling cooling summer breezes into the structure and outdoor public spaces.
▶ Channeling winter winds away from the structure, walkways, and public spaces.
▶ Managing drainage and storm water.
▶ Connecting the site to nearby properties and amenities.
▶ Attracting desirable wildlife.
▶ Creating an edible landscape.
▶ Establishing inviting public spaces.
▶ Designing an appealing environment with visual interest.

These design principles can be augmented with the following considerations:

▶ Retain as many native plant species as possible.
▶ Eliminate invasive species. If unsure of a plant's character, contact the local extension service or consult the invasive species database.
▶ Heal damaged sites.
▶ Specify plantings that require little maintenance once established.
▶ Build the health of the soil with compost and non-petroleum based fertilizer soil amendments.
▶ Restore the property injured by contaminants.
▶ Shade and direct air flow to cool air conditioning units and compressors.
▶ Create space with living materials. For example, use hedges instead of fences.
▶ Use safe alternatives to persistent toxic chemicals for the control of pests.

(See also Chapter 22 regarding water-efficient landscaping. Many of the recommendations in that chapter contribute to a healthy site.)

Cleaning

Green cleaning in this chapter refers to maintaining the cleanliness of the facility. Cleaning chemicals often contain hazardous ingredients. Though some of the risks associated with the use or exposure to these cleaning substances have yet to be ascertained, it is prudent to avoid chemicals that pose a potential health threat.

The following considerations can help the organization reduce potential problems from exposure to cleaning chemicals:

▣ Minimize use of substances containing:
  ▷ Corrosives and irritating ingredients.
  ▷ Ozone-depleting chemicals.
  ▷ Ingredients of concern listed by authorities such as the National Toxicology Program, the U.S. Environmental Protection Agency, the International Agency for Research on Cancer, and the State of California.
  ▷ Regulated hazardous materials, such as products classified as hazardous waste or that trigger OSHA hazard communications.

▣ Use searchable databases, such as the Web-based Cleaner Solutions database, to identify potential substitutions for toxic cleaning products.

▣ Avoid products containing EDTA (ethylene diamine tetraacetic acid or ethylene dinitrilotetraacetic acid), NTA (nitrilotriacetic acid), chlorine, or sodium hypochlorite.[3]

▣ Use no- or low-phosphate cleaners (less than 0.5 percent by weight).[4]

▣ Use no- or low-VOC cleaners (less than 10 percent by weight for use-concentrations).[5]

▣ Use readily biodegradable cleaners, such as solvents produced from citrus, seed, vegetable, and pine oils, whose effectiveness should not be compromised by use with cold water.

▣ Use low flammability cleaning substances (flash points greater than 200 degrees Fahrenheit).

▣ Use neutral pH cleaning products.

▣ Use products that are non-toxic to aquatic species.

▣ Limit use of disinfectants to high-touch areas, bathroom fixture handles, and door knobs.

Chapter 9

Energy Supply and Use

U.S. Energy Consumption

Energy is the lifeblood of commerce. Historically, as the U.S. population and national economy have grown, so has energy consumption. Figure 9.1 illustrates energy consumption over the past 30 years for the four principal consumption sectors.[1]

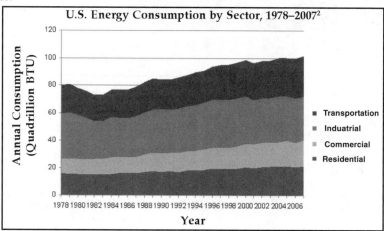

Figure 9.1

The U.S. Energy Information Agency forecasts that by 2030, U.S. energy demand will increase by approximately 18 percent, while global energy demand will increase by 50 percent, attributable mostly to the growth in demand from developing countries, such as China and India.[3] Commerce, as shown in Figure 9.2, accounted for one half of the total energy consumed in the United States in 2007.[4]

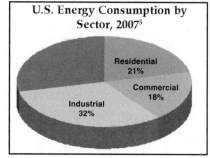

Figure 9.2

U.S. Energy Sources

Figure 9.3 illustrates the sources of energy that have powered the U.S. economy over the past 30 years. Inspection shows increases in contributions from all sources. Although not apparent at the scale of the figure, the most rapidly growing fuel source in recent years has been wind, whose contribution has increased tenfold over the past decade.

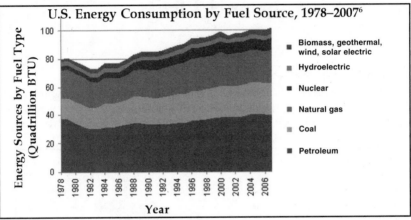

Figure 9.3

Conventional Energy Sources

Petroleum and Natural Gas

As illustrated in Figure 9.4 the United States is the greatest petroleum consumer of all nations. However, consumption is increasing, particularly in developing nations, such as China and India.

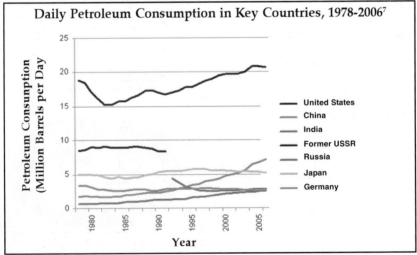

Figure 9.4

Slightly more than two-thirds of the petroleum consumed in the United Stated is used in transportation, with industrial uses consuming nearly 25 percent, and small amounts used for space heating and firing electric generating plants.[8] U.S. petroleum production peaked in the 1970s, necessitating a rise in imports from foreign sources, as illustrated in Figure 9.5.

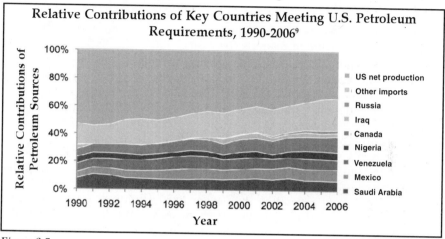

Figure 9.5

M.K. Hubbert, who predicted the U.S. peak production timetable, also has calculated that world petroleum and natural gas production will peak in the 2010s. This means escalation of oil prices (with volatility due to supply disruptions that result from political and events and storms). It also underscores the need to shift away from petroleum-based fuels.

Nuclear

Nuclear energy has been a quiet contributor to our nation's energy supplies, and is viewed by many industry analysts as a key bridge fuel to a more sustainable energy future. For many others nuclear power is deemed to have substantial drawbacks, including the generation of persistent radioactive waste materials (for which there is no commercially viable sequestration technology), the cost and time required to plan and construct nuclear power stations, and the risk of nuclear materials falling into the hands of terrorists.

Coal

The United States is rich in coal deposits, with nearly all of the mined coal used in electricity production. However, emissions from coal plants are a significant environmental and public health concern.

Public resistance to coal-generating facilities is increasing due to concerns about greenhouse gas emissions, worker safety in underground mines, and ecological impacts from surface (mountaintop removal) mining. Since 2006 some 60 coal-fired facilities in the United States have been cancelled, blocked, or delayed.[10]

CO_2 Emissions for Conventional Electricity-Generating Facilities

The following data reflect 1999 average CO_2 emissions for different types of generating plants:[11]

- ▶ Electric Generating Stations (Coal-fired)   2.095 lbs/kWh
- ▶ Electric Generating Stations (Petroleum-fired)   1.969 lbs/kWh
- ▶ Electric Generating Stations (Natural Gas-fired)   1.321 lbs/kWh
- ▶ Other (MSW, Tires and other fuels)   1.378 lbs/kWh
- ▶ Electric Generating Stations (Nuclear)   0 lbs/kWh

An organization can calculate the amount of carbon dioxide released as a consequence of generating the electricity used by the enterprise. A weighted average of emission rates can be determined from the EPA's interactive *Power Profiler* software, which describes the relative amounts of electricity contributed by different types of generating plants. For example, electricity in Minneapolis is supplied by Northern States Power Company. *Power Profiler* indicates that 73.5 percent of its electricity is produced from coal plants, 4 percent from gas-fired plants, 0.6 percent from petroleum-fired plants, 14.6 percent from nuclear, and the remainder from hydroelectric plants and other renewables. For every MWh generated, this mix of generating stations emits 3.71 lbs of nitrogen oxide, 5.65 lbs of sulfur dioxide, and 1,810 lbs of carbon dioxide. Generating station-specific data (for nitrogen oxides (NOx), sulfur dioxide (SO_2), carbon dioxide (CO_2), mercury (Hg), methane (CH_4) and nitrous oxide (N_2O)) are available for individual generating plants through the EPA's *eGRID* files.

Renewable Energy Sources

Renewable energy spans a variety of sources: hydroelectricity, biomass, geothermal, wind, solar electric and solar thermal, and ocean power.

Biomass

Biomass energy refers to the combustion of crop residues, forest residues, mill residues, and dedicated energy crops, as well as methane emitted from landfills, wastewater treatment facilities, and farm animals. Biomass can fuel industrial processes, generate electricity, and be converted into biofuels. Biofuels are liquid fuels that can replace or augment petroleum. (See Chapter 10 for a discussion of the advantages and disadvantages of this resource.)

Cogeneration, also referred to as Combined Heat and Power (CHP), is the simultaneous production of electricity and useful heat, which can be implemented at a number of scales. Smaller-scale cogeneration is appropriate to a business or group of buildings with a substantial electricity and heat demand, such as a hospital or school, while industrial users may have cogeneration plants that generate 25 megawatts (MW) or more of electricity.

Geothermal

Geothermal energy is derived from the naturally occurring heat in the earth. Most of the geothermal potential is located in the western third of the continental United States. Where high heat approaches the surface of the earth, temperatures are sufficient to create steam, which in turn can be used to generate electricity. The Geysers, 100 miles north of San Francisco, with 2050 MW of capacity, is the largest electricity-producing geothermal facility in the United States (and world).[12] In Boise, Idaho, geothermal energy is supplied to multiple buildings within a district heating system. On a smaller scale, heat pumps can take advantage of the energy content of the earth—"collecting" energy through a network of pipes in contact with the earth or groundwater and compressing that energy for space heating—and the same system can be used to cool buildings, using the relatively cool earth and groundwater.

Wind

Wind machines take the power of the wind to create mechanical or electrical energy. Wind turbines use wind energy to generate electricity. There are a variety of sizes of wind machines and the industry is a hotbed of innovation, resulting in wind machines that can be sited in previously challenging locations. The largest wind turbines have capacities of 5–6 MW, with rotor diameters of several hundred feet. Turbines used in wind farms range in size from several hundred kilowatts (kW) to 2–3 MW, and can be installed for as little as $1000/kW.[13] Average costs for wind turbines installed in 2007 were calculated as $1710/kW, a 9-percent increase over the previous year.[14] Small wind turbines are classified as having a capacity of 100 kW or less, and have an installed cost ranging between $3,000/kW and $5,000/kW.[15]

Solar

Solar energy can be used for daylighting, industrial processes, water heating, space heating and cooling, and to generate electricity. Solar energy can be captured at a variety of scales, from large-scale solar electricity-generating facilities to discrete projects scaled to provide a portion or all of the electrical, space heating, or water heating needs of individual enterprises.

Daylighting

Daylighting relies on building elements, such as windows, solar tubes, skylights, clerestories, solaria, and sawtooth roofs, to allow direct and indirect sunlight to illuminate the interior of a building. This use of natural light reduces the need for electric energy for lighting. (Chapter 8 addresses some of the design principles for using daylighting.)

Passive solar space heating

Passive solar heating refers to the capture of heat energy for warming interior spaces. In the northern hemisphere, this is usually accomplished with south-facing windows, which let in solar radiation that warms the air and the surfaces it strikes. The floors, walls, and furniture absorb the heat energy and release the heat back into the interior space.

Solar water heating

Solar water heating involves the use of a collection and storage system to heat water. Flat plate solar collectors are the most common collector system; they usually are thin rectangular boxes with a transparent cover that are placed on a south-facing roof.

Larger volumes of heated water can be generated by larger-scale systems (more collectors, greater storage volumes) and/or by more sophisticated collector systems. The most common systems for process heating are evacuated-tube collectors and parabolic-trough collectors.

Solar water heating costs depend on a number of variables. Installation costs may be as low as $1,700 to more than $15,000, depending upon the type of system.[16] Swimming pool water heating requires less equipment and costs $3,000–$4,000 for a residential-scale pool.[17]

Solar electric

Electric-generating power plants use the parabolic-trough collector technology, dish/engine technology, or power towers. The parabolic-trough system uses a field of collectors to boil water in a conventional steam generator to generate electricity. The dish/engine system uses a dish to concentrate sunlight onto a receiver that absorbs and transfers the heat to fluid within an engine. A power tower uses a field of concentrating mirrors to direct sunlight to a receiver at the top of a tower. The energy is then transferred to molten salts that flow through the receiver and can then be used to power a conventional steam generator to generate electricity.

Photovoltaics, also called PV or solar cells, convert sunlight directly into electricity. Solar cells are manufactured from relatively expensive semiconducting materials and typically are assembled into modules containing 40 cells, which in turn are mounted in arrays that hold about 10 modules. These arrays can be mounted directly on a flat surface, such as a rooftop, or mounted on a tracking device that follows the sun. A PV system may be as small as 10 arrays for a low-load business, or several hundred interconnected arrays for an industrial application.

Solar power from photovoltaics and concentrating solar systems contribute 1,284 MW to the nation's energy portfolio.[18] Costs for installed systems range from $10/watt to $12/watt for systems smaller than 1 kW, and from $7/watt to $10/watt for medium-sized systems (5 kW).[19] In certain expensive electricity markets (examples include Kauai, $0.398/kWh; Boston, $0.202/kWh; New York, $0.195/kWh; New Haven, $0.183/kWh; San Diego, $0.163; Long Island, $0.16/kWh), the price of solar generation compares favorably with current electricity prices.[20] Technological improvements are resulting in cost reductions, which are expected to continue with the growth of the solar electric market.

Hydropower

Hydroelectric power typically captures the energy of flowing rivers and streams. There are a variety of types of hydropower: run-of-the-river, which allows the river to run freely; storage dams, which allow collected water to be retained for conversion into electricity at designated (seasonal, daily, and hourly) times; and irrigation dams, which capture energy from the slower flows associated with irrigation projects. Not all hydroelectric potential has been realized.

Ocean power and tidal power are forms of hydropower. Tidal power is based on tidal flows: The potential energy in the tidal flow can be converted into electric energy using a barrage (a dam that spans an estuary) or with a turbine that spins in the current in a location that doesn't pose a hazard to marine traffic. An ocean power concept is a system that captures the flow of deep and shallow waters that have a heat differential.

Energy Use in the Commercial Sector

The commercial sector consumes energy for space conditioning, lighting, powering office equipment, water heating, refrigeration, and cooking. There is considerable variability in overall usage patterns depending upon general factors, such as the type of business and climatic conditions, as well as enterprise-specific characteristics, including the size of business; the size, orientation, and configuration of its building; the hours of operation; the equipment; and the desired occupant comfort. Figure 9.6 illustrates average energy usage for common types of businesses in the five U.S. climate regions (Figure 9.7). The table underscores the effect of space conditioning on commercial energy use.

Average Energy Intensity for Select Organization Types in U.S. Climate Zones[21]						
		Climate Zone				
		1	2	3	4	5
Organization Type	Heating degree days (HDD)	7,000+	5,500–7,000	4,000–5,499	< 4,000	< 4,000
	Cooling degree days (CDD)	< 2,000	< 2,000	< 2,000	< 2,000	2,000+
		Average Annual Energy Intensity (kBTU/sq. ft.)				
Education		77	88	69	66	56
Food service		155	169	213	232	195
Health care (inpatient)		270	269	204	227	202
Health care (outpatient)		118	84	80	74	100
Lodging		133	92	96	115	102
Office		93	95	80	72	68
Public assembly		66	77	66	72	54
Religious, worship		53	61	35	38	34
Restaurant		250	250	226	134	161
Retail		77	87	64	68	56
Warehouse (non-refrigerated)		59	64	51	36	33
Warehouse (refrigerated)		65	65	65	96	55

Figure 9.6

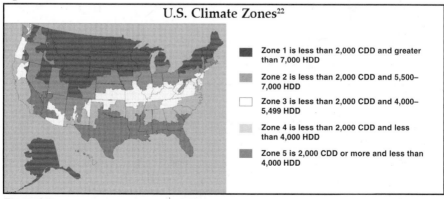

Figure 9.7

Figure 9.8 shows that most of the natural gas consumed in the commercial sector is used for space heating, water heating, and cooking. The remaining end commercial uses are powered primarily by electricity. The variability in commercial user activities and types of equipment and appliances affects the energy intensities of end uses that the electricity is applied toward, as shown in Figure 9.9.

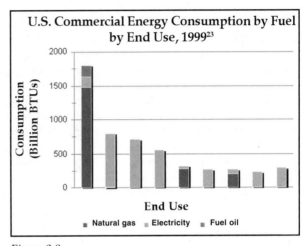

Figure 9.8

The U.S. Environmental Protection Agency promotes energy efficiency through various initiatives, such as the Commercial ENERGY STAR program. ENERGY STAR recognizes commercial buildings whose performance exceeds 75 percent of similar buildings (based on size, geography, hours of operation, number of employees, and other variables that influence energy consumption). An organization can evaluate its energy consumption relative to comparable enterprises by applying the EPA's *Portfolio Manager* software.

Distribution of Energy Use by Purpose for Various Organization Types in All-Electric Buildings[24]									
End use	Grocery	Health	Lodging	Misc.	Office	Restaurant	Retail	School	Warehouse
Lights	23	18	16	13	24	13	26	17	12
Refrigeration	38	3	4	20	1	16	10	2	32
Cooking	5	4	8	3	2	21	3	4	4
Water heating	2	8	14	4	4	11	4	8	2
Ventilation	4	10	5	7	11	5	6	6	7
Cooling	11	25	22	19	24	18	27	19	16
Heating	13	26	26	29	24	11	19	40	22
Other	3	6	5	5	10	5	5	4	5
	99	100	100	100	100	100	100	100	100

Figure 9.9

Energy Use in the Industrial Sector

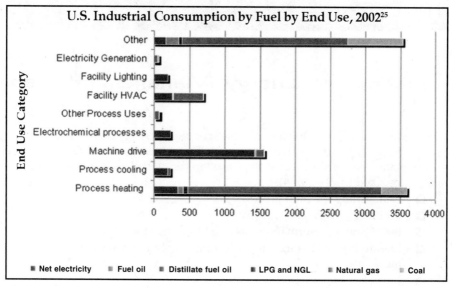

Figure 9.10

In the manufacturing sector, process heating and machine drive uses consume the largest quantities of energy. With energy costs being a significant expenditure for industry, energy consumption reduction is an important activity. In fact, a 2008 study of manufacturers indicated that 65 percent of survey respondents intended to invest in energy efficiency improvements during the next year.[26]

Chapter 10

Creating the Energy Management Plan

This and subsequent chapters address operational energy performance. Transportation energy is examined in Chapter 21. The process for creating an effective energy plan mirrors the principal steps used in the overall greening of the corporation (described in Chapter 4):

- ▶ Establishing the plan process.
- ▶ Profiling energy performance.
- ▶ Establishing performance goals and framing strategies.
- ▶ Identifying, evaluating, and selecting energy improvement measures.
- ▶ Implementing selected measures.
- ▶ Monitoring results/calibrating the plan.

The plan is iterative. Once the organization completes the process, it restarts the effort, establishing new performance goals whose achievement results in even greater energy efficiency. Thus, the organization is continuously improving its energy performance.

Establishing a Plan Process

As described in Chapter 4, a change initiative, such as implementing an Energy Management Plan, is likely to be successful when the appropriate people are involved at the right times, and the effort has the unequivocal support of leadership.

The process needs to include a plan for involving stakeholders inside and outside the organization (see Figure 4.1 in Chapter 4) and an individual needs to be assigned overall responsibility for plan management. With the responsibility comes the explicit authority and the resources (people, time, and budget) needed to complete the project.

Risk assessment is an incomplete component of the planning process. The organization faces several noteworthy risks related to energy:

- ▶ Regional differences in energy costs.
- ▶ Price escalation and increased cost of conducting business.
- ▶ Supply vulnerability.

Data on energy costs are available from the U.S. Energy Information Agency (*tonto.eia.doe.gov/state/SEP_MorePrices.cfm*).

Profiling Energy Performance

The energy performance profile is critical to understanding the energy consumption and energy management possibilities of the organization. The profile steps are:

- ▶ Establishing a boundary for the analysis.
- ▶ Determining energy consumption by fuel type and end use.
- ▶ Normalizing the consumption data.
- ▶ Evaluating the consumption data relative to similar enterprises.
- ▶ Characterizing indirect effects of energy consumption.

Establishing a Boundary for the Energy Analysis

Establishing an analytical boundary is the first step in creating an energy performance profile. There are three tiers of analyses.

The simplest analysis (Tier 1) addresses only the operational energy that is consumed directly by the organization.

A more detailed analysis (Tier 2) looks at the energy consumed directly by the organization and the indirect energy expended in the inputs (materials, supplies, equipment) to the operations of the enterprise.

The most comprehensive analysis (Tier 3) profiles energy use at all levels "upstream" and "downstream" of the enterprise: a life cycle assessment of direct and indirect operations. It examines not only the energy consumed directly by the enterprise and the energy associated with the materials provided by its suppliers, but also the indirect energy consumed by the suppliers.

Tier 1 analyses are appropriate for small enterprises, and can be used as starting points for larger organizations with complex energy consumption profiles. Tier 2 analyses are suitable starting points for manufacturers, and organizations with significant materials inputs from vendors with which they have influence in determining product specifications. Organizations that have accomplished energy goals established as a result of Tier 1 analyses also are candidates for Tier 2. Tier 3 analyses are suitable for organizations that are moving from eco-efficiency to eco-effectiveness.

Determining Energy Consumption by Energy Type and End Use

Energy Consumption by Energy Type

An *Energy Consumption Calculator* is included in the Appendix and illustrates the basic reporting form of a Tier 1 profile. It is suited to an enterprise that does not produce any of the energy that it consumes.

The annual consumption data are best derived from average monthly information for a period of two to four years. (The Appendix contains a *Fuel Consumption Profile Worksheet* template.) Averaging data facilitates the identification of seasonal and yearly variations due to changes in production, hours of operation, or weather.

If the enterprise produces energy, a more detailed calculator is better suited. (See the *Energy Consumption Worksheet* for producers in the Appendix.)

Energy demand is a crucial energy issue because it is a reflection of how much generating capacity a utility must have available to meet its customers' demands. There are hourly, daily, and seasonal fluctuations to energy demand. Demand over a 24-hour period typically shows greatest consumption rates during opening, when lights, equipment, and HVAC systems are being turned on. Weekly demand is greatest during weekdays, less on Saturday, when only some enterprises are open, and least on Sunday, when most enterprises are closed. Seasonal demands reflect the burden of space conditioning: Warm months require generating electrical capacity for air conditioning, whereas winter months create a demand for natural gas for heating.

In order to meet energy demand, electric utilities deploy an integrated system of electric-generating facilities. Baseload power plants are large generating facilities that operate 24 hours a day. When the baseload plants are unable to meet the overall demand, the utility purchases energy from outside suppliers or operates smaller peaking plant(s). Peaking power plants (such as natural gas–fired power stations or storage hydroelectric stations) are expensive because of the high capital costs invested in facilities that have a limited time of use. The utility passes this cost on through demand charges to commercial and industrial customers.

Peak electrical demand charges typically are based on the *average* demand for electricity over a fixed or rolling period that lasts 15–60 minutes.[1] If the facility incurs electrical demand charges (or is contemplating the generation of electricity), then the peak demand (represented as kW) should be tracked to determine daily and monthly peaks.

Energy Consumption by End Use

Chapter 9 describes how energy is used for different end uses in different types of commercial and industrial enterprises. Determining why energy is being used is one of the important aspects of an energy profile.

Industrial and commercial consumers may have electrical, gas, steam, or hot water sub-meters to monitor energy consumed by major sources, such as process equipment, computer servers, or fans. End use energy consumption also can be calculated by multiplying the average power draw of the use by the hours of operation. In a simple example, 30 75-watt light bulbs operating 12 hours a day consume

$$30 \times 75 \times 12 = 4{,}500 \text{ watt hours daily} = 4.5 \text{ kilowatt-hours (kWh)}.$$

Energy usage rates of smaller (120 volt) equipment and appliances can be determined by using a portable electric meter, such as the Kill A Watt™ meter. A simple template for tabulating end use data that would be suitable for various types of commercial buildings, *Energy Consumption by End Use*, is included in the Appendix.

Normalizing Energy Consumption Data

One of the reasons for assembling energy data from several years is to average out variations. Typical variations occur as a result of changes in hours of operations, changeout of equipment, alterations to production rates, enterprise growth resulting in more units being produced and/or more staff, facility expansion or renovations, or changes in weather patterns.

The internal events should be relatively straightforward to identify and compare with the usage data. Weather data (especially heating degree days and cooling degree days) usually can be acquired from Web sources, such as tabulated information from *www.degreedays.net* or graphic information from *www.degreedays.net*.

Based on known variables that influence the energy consumption of the organization, make adjustments in the aggregated consumption data.

Evaluating the Consumption Data Relative to Similar Enterprises

Figure 10.1 demonstrates how to calculate the overall energy intensity of the facility. The energy intensity of the enterprise can be compared to similar enterprises listed in Figure 9.6 (page 83), or usage data may be available from regional and local utilities, state energy offices, trade associations, or energy conservation specialists.

Energy Intensity Calculator Template[2]		
Factor		Unit
Normalized consumption		kBTU/year
Facility size		square feet
Energy intensity		kBTU/square foot/year

Instructions: 1.   Enter *normalized consumption* from the *Energy Consumption Calculator* (in the Appendix).
              2.   Enter *facility size* in square feet.
              3. Multiply *normalized consumption* by *facility size* to arrive at an overall intensity.		

Figure 10.1

Commercial enterprises can evaluate their energy consumption by end use category to similar organizations by comparing their data to the national data presented in Figures 9.8 and 9.9 (in Chapter 9). This comparison will provide a sense of whether the energy usage patterns of the enterprise are comparable to similar organizations. More applicable information may be available from regional and local utilities, state energy offices, trade associations, or energy conservation specialists. These groups, along with process engineers, are sources for consumption data for industrial users as well.

The enterprise may wish to consider energy intensity from perspectives other than "energy intensity per square foot," such as energy intensity per unit of production (kBTU/widget/year) and energy intensity per sales (kBTU/gross sales $/year).

Characterizing Indirect Effects of Energy Consumption

The indirect effect of greatest concern with the consumption of energy relates to the emission of greenhouse gases and other pollutants.

The U.S. EPA maintains *Power Profiler* (*www.epa.gov/cleanenergy/energy-and-you/how-clean.html*), a zip code–based lookup system to identify the types of fuels used by utilities to generate electricity. This aggregated information is derived from the *eGRID* database (*www.epa.gov/cleanenergy/energy-resources/egrid/index.html*), which contains generating station specific data for nitrogen oxides (NO_x), sulfur dioxide (SO_2), carbon dioxide (CO_2), mercury (Hg), methane (CH_4), and nitrous oxide (N_2O). Emissions from the combustion of other fossil fuels can be derived from Table A-30 of Annex 2 in the EPA's *Inventory of U.S. Greenhouse Gas Emissions and Sinks: 1990–2004*.

Indirect effects extend beyond air emissions and include, but are not limited to, health and safety impacts, thermal releases, land use, habitat, forestry and agriculture, and solid waste generation.

Establishing Performance Goals and Framing Strategies

Energy performance goals can be developed either from the top down or the bottom up. Top-down means that a goal is stated—say, the 10-percent reduction in energy for lighting within one year—and the strategies and specific actions to accomplish the goal then are assembled. A bottom-up goal can be established after the strategies and actions have been identified, evaluated, and selected.

There are five basic strategies for energy management. Two of the basic principles of energy efficiency are obvious:

1. Avoid using energy in the first place.
2. Reduce the amount of energy used when energy is needed to perform a function.

However, there are three additional strategic principles that build energy effectiveness:

3. Match the quality of the energy provided to the quality of the energy needed.
4. Capture and use energy that otherwise would be wasted.
5. Use renewable forms of energy instead of energy derived from fossil fuels.

Avoiding Energy Use

The first principle of energy efficiency is not to use it when it is not needed. It is the reminder to "turn off the lights when you leave the room." But multiplied in dozens of ways.

Reduce the Amount of Energy Used

The tenet of energy reduction is to use no more energy than necessary to achieve the desired end. Using a compact fluorescent light bulb instead of an incandescent bulb is a way of providing sufficient light while using less energy.

Capturing Wasted Energy

Another principle of energy effectiveness requires that we don't waste energy by allowing it to escape with usefulness remaining. Cogeneration (described in a sidebar in Chapter 9) is an example of recovering waste heat for energy efficiency. Cogeneration plants can operate at efficiencies upward of 80 percent, whereas conventional power plants convert only about a third of the fuel into useful energy.[3]

Matching Energy Quality

Energy quality can be thought of in terms of four useful forms:

1. Low-temperature heat.
2. High-temperature heat.
3. Mechanical power.
4. Electricity.

The amount of potential energy needed to produce low temperature heat, such as air warmed for space heating, is relatively low. As more heat is added to create high-temperature heat the capability increases, so that cooking, water heating, and other uses can be accomplished. A greater ordering of the energy creates mechanical energy that can be used to turn wheels, operate pumps, and power motors and turbines. The highest quality energy—electricity—can be used to power appliances, computers, and other equipment. The higher the quality of the energy, the more complex and more costly it is to produce. In the world of eco-effectiveness, matching the quality of energy input means that electricity is saved for powering systems that can operate only with electrical power.

Using Renewable Energy

The last principle is, wherever practical, to use energy from renewable sources instead of energy derived from fossil fuels or other harmful energy sources. Renewable energy sources may be generated on-site or off-site. The facilities may be owned entirely by the organization, owned in partnership with other parties, or leased. They may be operated and maintained by the enterprise or a third party may be responsible for operating the system.

For some organizations the best arrangement is simply to purchase renewable energy (green power) from utilities or other generators.

Identifying, Evaluating, and Selecting Energy-Improvement Measures

The identification process should be comprehensive in listing all potential measures. The subsequent process of evaluating measures filter out those improvement measures that are not feasible or practical. The selection process serves to organize the measures in a way that makes sense for the enterprise.

Identifying Energy-Efficiency Measures

There are several ways to identify energy efficiency measures that potentially could be applied:

- ▶ A checklist evaluation.
- ▶ An audit conducted by a staff person.
- ▶ An audit conducted by an outside professional.

Checklists for different improvements are presented for different end uses in subsequent chapters in this guide. These checklists are guidelines intended to suggest types of measures and are not a substitute for a site energy evaluation.

Smaller organizations with limited energy consumption and a modest understanding of energy topics would do well to work with an outside specialist (an auditor working with the utility, an energy service company, or independent contractor). The U.S. Department of Energy maintains a directory of specialists as part of their ENERGY STAR program. (Access the directory at *www.energystar.gov/index.cfm?c=spp_res.pt_spps.*)

For large and/or complex systems, facility engineers, system specialists, process engineers, and others with pertinent expertise should be involved in evaluating the systems of a facility and existing energy performance of the equipment against their designed performance level and/or against best practices. The variance represents the potential for energy savings and serves as the basis for identifying measures. On these larger assignments an audit team may wish to distribute responsibilities among members: One individual or sub-team addresses lighting; another, kitchen; and so forth.

Evaluating Energy-Efficiency Measures

The evaluation of the energy measures is intended to create an objective statement of the costs and benefits of implementing the energy efficiency measures that have been identified.

The types of considerations that should be addressed when profiling the measures include the following:

- Lifetime of measure.
- Projected savings in energy use (percent or amount of savings over a defined time period).
- Projected savings in energy demand (especially for enterprises with demand charges or considering the installation of solar, wind, or other production system).
- Projected associated savings (such as a longer life resulting in less maintenance costs; reduction in water purchase costs).
- Design or research costs (for example, redesign of a compressed air system, whether done by staff or outside specialists, if any).
- Capital costs of the measure (purchase cost).
- Installation cost of the measure (whether done by staff or outside specialists; including a determination of production downtime).
- Maintenance costs of the measure (whether done by staff or outside specialists).
- Decommissioning costs of the measure.
- Training requirements and costs.
- Additional equipment required.

This information can be assembled into the *Energy Efficiency Measure Evaluation Worksheet* in the Appendix.

One of the key considerations is the capital cost of the measure, which is affected by several variables, including the availability of rebates, and federal and state tax credits (including income tax and depreciation), deductions, and exemptions.

There are programs to help organizations finance energy efficiency improvements, including grants and loan programs. Consult *DSIRE* (*www.dsireusa.org*), a comprehensive database of federal, state, and local financial incentives for energy efficiency improvements to determine incentives that alter the effective capital cost of a potential measure.

There are several ways to describe the cost-effectiveness of potential measures: simple payback, cash flow analysis, internal rate of return, and net present value. Chapter 4 describes how to perform the calculations.

Selecting Energy-Efficiency Measures for Implementation

In addition to cost-effectiveness, other factors may influence the selection and sequencing of energy efficiency measures, such as:

- ▶ Initial cost: balanced against available resources.
- ▶ Sequencing measures: shorter paybacks generate savings faster to help pay for subsequent measures.
- ▶ Visibility: easily seen measures raise awareness, demonstrate commitment.
- ▶ Capacity building: measures requiring teams to implement can increase information sharing, collaboration, and innovation.

The *Energy Efficiency Measure Evaluation Worksheet* is a tool for organizing decision-making information on the individual energy efficiency improvement measures, and the *Energy Efficiency Measures Summary Worksheet* can be used to aggregate comparative data for measures being considered. Use of a *Summary Worksheet* facilitates the comparison and selection of measures.

Implementing Selected Measures

Selected energy efficiency measures should be assembled into an action plan. The plan should specify the individual responsible, the start and finish dates for installing the measures, resources allocated (time, people, equipment, supplies), and funding allocated and the source of that funding. See the Action Plan Format (Figure 4.11).

Simple measures (for example, replacement of a dozen incandescent lamps) for most organizations don't require a high degree of action planning, whereas complex measures (such as the upgrade of a compressed air system) are likely to require a series of steps and warrant their own action plan.

Monitoring Results and Calibrating the Plan

The person responsible for the plan should monitor progress toward achieving the goals. On an approximately monthly basis the individual should monitor:

- ▶ The status of Action Plan elements.
- ▶ Actual and any remaining costs against budgeted costs.
- ▶ Expected energy savings against actual savings.
- ▶ Factors that affect key assumptions, such as the cost of energy.

If a review of these elements suggests pressing issues, then the plan should be modified. For example, the individual responsible for upgrading the compressed air system may require additional training, and supplemental funds should be allocated.

Every few months a more comprehensive review of the goals, strategies, and individual actions should be accomplished. This detailed review should indicate where fine-tuning needs to occur.

As discussed in Chapters 4 and 30, it is important that the results of the effort are communicated to stakeholders.

Chapter 11

Lighting

Lighting Characteristics

Three characteristics determine how we perceive light:

1. The amount of light present.
2. The quality of the light.
3. The color characteristics of the light.

Light output is measured in lumens. (Light is not measured in watts, which is a measurement of the amount of power that energizes a light source; however, *watt* is a commonly used term that incorrectly describes the light output desired from an incandescent bulb. In replacing a lamp, ensure that the lumen value of the new lamp is comparable to that of the replaced lamp.)

Illumination provided by a light source is measured in footcandles and is inversely proportional to the distance between the light source and the illuminated object. Different activities require different lighting levels, as shown in Figure 11.1.

Lumens and footcandles aren't easily convertible data. The best method for determining illumination is to use a light meter. Light meters cost approximately $125 and are available from lighting supply houses. A cost-saving alternative is to use a gray card and a photographic light meter. (See the Resources.)

Light quality is described in terms of whether it is "bright" or "dull" or whether glare is present. Glare is created when direct or reflected light provides illumination that is greater than the luminance to which the eyes are adapted.

Lighting Level Recommendations[1]		
Activity/Functional area		Light level (average maintained footcandles)
Office	Private, without task lighting	50
	Open, with task lighting	30
	Computer work	30
	Conference	30–40
	Corridors	5–10
	Storage room	5–15
	Restrooms	10–20
Restaurant	Eating area	10–20
	Kitchen	50–100
Retail	Low-volume	30
	High-volume	100
Small warehouse	Storage	30
	Loading and unloading	10
Light industry	Work bench	50–100
Building entrances		5
Parking lots		0.8–3.6
Roadways		0.3–1.6

Figure 11.1

Color characteristics of a light source determine how accurately the color of an illuminated object is rendered, and are described using the Correlated Color Temperature (CCT) and the Color Rendering Index (CRI).

CCT measurements, use the Kelvin (K) scale, fall in the following ranges:[2]

- ▶ 2,650–3,200K: warm white
- ▶ 3,200–4,000K: neutral
- ▶ Above 4,000K: cool, "daylight"

Warm colors appear more natural, whereas cooler are often preferred for task lighting.

CRI is a scale from 0 to 100 with the rating of a light source indicating how "realistically" it renders an illuminated object. Good color rendering is distinguished by a CRI rating greater than 80.[3]

Light Sources

Lamp Characteristics[4]								
			Use			Color Temperature (K)	Lifetime (1,000s of hours)	Efficacy (lumens/ watt)
Lighting Type	Lamp	Description	Interior	Exterior	CRI			
Fluorescent	Straight tube	Short start-up. Good for ambient lighting over large areas. Dedicated fixtures with electronic ballasts. Principal sizes: T-8, T-12.	X	X	50–90	2,700–6,500	7–24	50–100
	Compact (CFL)	Short start-up. Popular choice over incandescent bulbs.	X	X	65–88	2,700–6,500	6–15	35–60
	Circline	Short start-up. Circular lamp.	X				12	40–50
Incandescent	Standard "A" bulb	Instant start-up. Least costly to buy. Excellent color. High energy use. Short life.	X	X	98–100	2,700–2,800	.75–2.5	10–18
	Halogen	Tungsten gas filling. Excellent color. Higher initial cost, more energy-efficient than standard "A."	X	X	98–100	2,900–3,200	2–4	15–20
High-intensity discharge	Mercury vapor	Long start-up, long life.		X	50	3,200–7,000	16–24	25–60
	Metal halide	Long start-up. Provides white light, good for high-ceilinged areas. Best color of HID.	X	X	70	3,700	5–20	50–90
	High-pressure sodium	Long start-up, long life. Poor (yellowish) color. High efficacy.		X	25	2,100	16–24	50–140
	Low-pressure sodium	Long start-up, long life. Ghastly (very yellow) color. High efficacy.		X	-44		12–18	60–150
Light emitting diode (LED)	Cool white	Developing technology. Very expensive.	X	X		3,500+	30–50	47–64
	Warm white	Efficacy lower than CFL. Exit signs.			80	2,600–3,500		25–44

Figure 11.2

There are a variety of light sources. Natural light sources include daylighting (described in Chapter 8) and solar lighting. Artificial light sources use electricity to power lamps (commonly called light bulbs).

There are different types of lamps appropriate to different lighting needs. Such factors as length of time to start the lamp and its color quality, lifetime, cost to purchase, and cost to operate must be balanced to determine the most energy-efficient illumination solution for a given lighting situation.

The characteristics of different types of lamps are shown in Figure 11.2. From an energy perspective the most important consideration is efficacy of a lamp, which describes the efficiency in transforming electrical power (watts) into light (lumens). The key for most enterprises is to use fluorescent and compact fluorescent fixtures and/or lamps, which typically use one quarter to a third of the energy to produce the same amount of light as incandescent lamps.

Figure 11.3 demonstrates the energy and cost savings one could expect with replacing a 100-watt incandescent bulb with a 23-watt CFL, which has a light output comparable to the incandescent being replaced. In this example, we're assuming that the fixture is on eight hours a day and six days a week and that the cost of electricity is 9.71¢ per kilowatt hour (the May 2008 national average). Based on these estimates the replacement would pay for itself in a little more than one third of a year, and result in annual electricity savings of nearly $19.

Light output deteriorates over time, as shown in Figure 11.4. Contrary to what "common sense" would suggest, it is usually more effective to replace lamps as their light output diminishes below an acceptable level, rather than waiting for the lamp to burn out. Replacing groups of older lamps takes less time on a per lamp basis than replacing individual lamps. (This is especially the case for fixtures installed in difficult-to-access locations, such as high ceilings and bays in interior locations, and high bays, tall light poles, and high on outside walls in exterior settings.)

Lamp Replacement Savings Example[5]		
	Base lamp	Replacement option
	Incandescent	CFL
Energy consumed (watts)	100	23
Rated lamp life (hours)	1,500	8,000
Cost per lamp ($)	$0.50	$6.50
Usage (hours per day)	8	8
Usage (days per week)	6	6
Life of lamp (years)	0.70	3.73
Energy use per year (kWh)	250	58
Electricity cost ($ per kWh)	$0.097	$0.097
Electricity cost per year ($)	$24.30	$5.59
Electricity savings per year	NA	$18.71
Payback time for option (years)	NA	0.35
Total life cycle costs	$80.35	$24.37
Total life cycle savings		$55.98

Note: For enterprises whose electricity tariff (rate) includes a demand charge, extra cost savings could accrue if the light is on when the peak electrical demand of the enterprise occurs. The monthly reduction = (Original Lamp Demand – Replacement Lamp Demand) × demand charge. In the above example, assuming a demand charge of $8.00/kW, the monthly reduction in demand charges = $(100 - 23)/1000 \times (8.00) = \$0.616$.

Figure 11.3

Lumen Maintenance Curve for Different Light Sources Over 10,000 Hours of Operation[6]

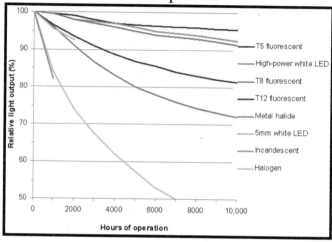

Figure 11.4

Incandescent Lamps

There are three types of incandescent bulbs: the familiar standard "A" bulb; tungsten halogen lamps; and two types of reflector lamps: Parabolic Aluminized Reflector (PAR) lamps and Ellipsoidal Reflector (ER) lamps.

Incandescent lights are widely used because of their low purchase cost, and ease of acquisition and control. However, incandescents convert only 10 percent of the energy they consume into light; the remainder is lost as heat energy. This makes incandescents the least energy-efficient of all lamps, which led to the federal Energy Independence and Security Act of 2007, establishing efficiency standards for incandescents, effectively phasing out bulbs in the 40–150 watt range by January 2014.

Figure 11.5 on page 98 describes the power savings, light output, and typical savings from various replacement options for incandescent lamps. Many of the options offer substantial savings with excellent returns on investment.

Fluorescent Lamps

Fluorescents are widely used in commercial settings, especially to provide general office illumination. There are a variety of fluorescent lamp configurations: tubular, u-shaped, circline, and compact (CFLs). Color problems associated with older fluorescents have been corrected by using phosphor coatings that provide more natural color rendering.

Increases in energy efficiency have been achieved by using an argon-krypton mixture as opposed to argon gas; using smaller lamp sizes (the "T" designation refers to the tubular bulb and the number following describes the lamp diameter in 1/8ths of an inch (thus, a T12 fluorescent is 1.5 inches in diameter); and by using more efficient ballasts that also reduce hum and flicker common to older fixtures.

Older magnetic core ballasts are candidates for replacement with energy-efficient alternatives:

- High-efficiency electromagnetic ballasts.
- Heater cutout ballasts, which turn off the heater function once the lamps illuminate.
- Electronic ballasts, whose solid-state circuitry require less energy and provides increased control, while operating more quietly and with less flicker.

Figure 11.6 describes the power savings, light output, and typical savings from various replacement options for four common types of fluorescent fixtures.

Replacement Options for Incandescent Lamps[7]				
Existing lamp	Replacement	Input power savings (watts)	Relative light output (%)	Annual value of energy savings ($)
Incandescent bulbs and fixtures				
60W incandescent	52W energy-saving	8	85	$4
	13W CFL	44	92	$21
	18W CFL	42	124	$20
75W incandescent	18W CFL	57	100	$28
150W incandescent	135W energy-saving	15	91	$7
	90W halogen	60	61	$29
500W	450W mercury vapor, self-ballasted	50	84	$24
	175W metal halide (fixture)	290	121	$140
1000W	750W mercury vapor, self-ballasted	250	59	$121
	250W hi-pressure sodium (fixture)	695	119	$336
Recessed, baffled incandescent downlight				
75W R30	18W CFL	57	96	$28
150W R40	120W energy-saving	30	100	$15
75W ER30		75	100	$36
150W R4075 W ER30	90W halogen	60	100	$29
300W R	120W ER40	180	100	$87
75W PAR	65W energy-saving PAR	10	100	$5
	45W halogen PAR	30	100	$15
150W PAR	120W energy-saving PAR	30	100	$15
	90W halogen PAR	60	100	$29
	60W HIR	90	100	$44

Figure 11.5

Fluorescent Replacement Options[8]				
Existing system	Replacement	Input power savings (watts)	Relative light output (%)	Annual value of energy savings ($)
FIXTURE Four-lamp 2′ x 4′ fluorescent fixture with flat prismatic lens **LAMPS** 4 40 W T12 **BALLAST** 2 magnetic high-efficiency	*Relamp only*			
	4 32W T12	30	88	$15
	4 34W T12	22	88	$11
	Reballast only			
	2 electronic ballasts	22-34	98-101	$11-16
	2 cathode cutout ballasts	22	86	$11
	Relamp and reballast			
	4 32W T8, 2 electronic ballasts	45-49	97-101	$22-24
	4 34W T12, 2 electronic ballasts	38-51	79-91	$18-25
	4 34W T12, 2 cathode cutout ballasts	41	79	$20
	4 32W T8, 2 magnetic ballasts	28	95	$14
	4 40W T10, 2 electronic ballasts	16-17	110	$8
	System replacement			
	3 40W T12, 1 electronic ballast	50-53	72-76	$24-26
	3 34W T12, 1 electronic ballast	65-73	61-67	$31-35
	3 40W T10, 1 electronic ballast	53	84	$26
	3 32W T8, 1 electronic ballast	63-76	65-73	$30-37
FIXTURE Three-lamp 2′ x 4′ parabolic fixture **LAMPS** 3 40W T12 **BALLAST** 1.5 magnetic high-efficiency(in tandem: 3 ballasts operate 6 lamps)	*Relamp only*			
	3 32W T8	27	92	$13
	3 34W T12	23	85	$11
	Reballast only			
	1 electronic ballast	20-26	93-106	$10-13
	1.5 cathode cutout ballasts (in tandem)	15	92	$7
	Relamp and reballast			
	3 32W T8, 1 electronic ballast	33-46	88-99	$16-22
	3 34W T12, 1 electronic ballast	35-41	88-92	$17-20
	3 34W T12, 2 cathode cutout ballasts	30	78	$15
	3 40W T10, 1 electronic ballast	23	114	$11
	3 32W T12, 1 magnetic high-eff ballast	23	87	$11
FIXTURE Two U-lamp 2′ x 2′ troffer **LAMPS** 2 40W T12/U (6″ lamps) **BALLAST** 1 magnetic high-efficiency	*Relamp only*			
	2 34W T12/U	11	88	$5
	Reballast only			
	1 electronic ballast	11-17	88-99	$5-8
	Relamp and reballast			
	2 34W T12/U, 1 electronic ballast	19-25	79-91	$9-12
	2 31W T8/U, 1 magnetic ballast	12	97	$6
	2 31W T8/U, 1 electronic ballast	9-21	97-115	$4-10
	System replacement			
	T5 system, 1 electronic ballast	14	111	$7
FIXTURE Two lamp 8′ with 35° CW shielding **LAMPS** 2 75W F96 T12 **BALLAST** 1 magnetic high-efficiency	*Relamp only*			
	2 60W F96 T12	35	83	$17
	Reballast only			
	1 electronic ballast	24	100	$12
	Relamp and reballast			
	2 60W F96 T12, 1 electronic ballast	46	83	$22

Figure 11.6

High-Intensity Discharge Lamps

Mercury vapor, metal halide, and high-pressure sodium lamps offer high illumination over extended lifetimes. Low-pressure sodium lamps are more energy-efficient than these three lamps; however, their color rendition is poor. Of the primary three, mercury vapor is the least efficient, with an efficacy only moderately better than incandescents. Mercury vapor lamps can be replaced with either metal halide or high-pressure sodium lamps. Figure 11.7 describes the power savings, light output, and typical savings for typical replacement options for metal halide lamps.

Replacement Options for Mercury Vapor Lamps[9]				
Existing lamp	Replacement	Input power savings (watts)	Relative light output (%)	Annual value of energy savings ($)
Relamp and reballast				
175W	70W high-pressure sodium	105	79	$51
	100W high-pressure sodium	75	112	$36
	100W metal halide	71	106	$34
250W	150W high-pressure sodium	97	147	$47
	150W metal halide	100	104	$48
	175W metal halide	70	106	$34
400W	150W high-pressure sodium	266	82	$129
	250W high-pressure sodium	150	141	$73
	250W metal halide	159	97	$77
1000W	250W metal halide, energy-saving	70	100	$34
	250W high-pressure sodium	775	62	$375
	400W high-pressure sodium	610	79	$295
	950W metal halide, energy saving	50	200	$24

Figure 11.7

Light-Emitting Diodes

LEDs are a promising energy-efficient lighting technology that uses a driver (current regulator) to provide electricity to a semi-conducting material whose stimulation results in the production of light. Unlike incandescent and fluorescent lamps that release light in all directions (and therefore incorporate reflectors and diffusers into their fixtures), LEDs focus their light output to a specific direction. LED technology is evolving rapidly with new generations of technology coming to market every four to six months.[10] Between 2001 and 2007, average prices for white light LED devices dropped by 85 percent.[11]

LED light output can be "tuned" to a particular color, which make them an efficient way to produce monochromatic light used in traffic signals, exit signs, and holiday lights (unlike full spectrum sources that are filtered to produce the desired color). In addition to these applications, LEDs are often used in electric signage and lighting for refrigerated display cases. Other applications to which LEDs are well suited are task lighting, recessed downlights, retail display, office undershelf lights, street and exterior area lights, and outdoor step and path lights. Estimates of energy savings potentials are described in Figures 11.8 and 11.9 on page 102.

Comparison of Energy Intensities of Lighting Alternatives in Interior Applications[12]					
Application	Description	Lamp Energy Intensity (watts)			
		Incandescent	Fluorescent	Halogen	LED
Conventional retail display case	Incandescent	67			9
	Incandescent with reflector	72			13
	T12 – less than 4'		31		29
	T12 – U shaped		49		46
	CFL		16		11
	Halogen – quartz			226	69
	Halogen – reflector, low-voltage			48	8
Refrigerated display cases	Angled without doors, 38° F		458		244
	Vertical without doors, 38° F		642		342
	Vertical with doors, 38° F		348		224
	Vertical with doors, 0° F		348		224
Task lighting	Incandescent	83			15
	Incandescent with reflector	72			11
	T12 – less than 4'		31		25
	T12 – circline		33		16
	CFL		16		11
	Halogen – quartz			78	15
Office, undershelf lighting	T12, magnetic ballast		36		19
	T8, electronic ballast		29		20
Recessed downlight			72		14
			16		11
Exit sign		10-50 (32)	10-24 (17)		2-10 (6)
Holiday lights	100 lamp, C-9 Incandescent string	125-175 (159)			2.5
	Miniature and icicle lights	24-42 (36)			5.0
Note: Exit sign and holiday light values show minimum-maximum range, with average intensity displayed in parentheses.					

Figure 11.8

In addition to reducing energy consumption, LED benefits include uniform lighting; compact fixture size; dimmability without loss of usable life; adjustable color; a long operating life, which in turn reduces maintenance costs because of the comparatively infrequent relamping; and the ability to direct LED light to a specific area to be illuminated, thereby reducing off-site light pollution in exterior applications and less scattered light in display cases and task lighting applications.

Developing a Plan for Energy-Efficient Lighting

A familiar set of tasks defines an approach to designing an energy-efficient lighting plan.

Perform a Lighting System Audit

The National Lighting Bureau's *Performing a Lighting System Audit* provides detail on individual steps.

1. Create a map of the organization that illustrates existing sources of illumination:
   ▷ For natural light sources (map the windows, skylights, and glass doors), determine when the light is available, the variability of the lighting level, and whether any glare or shadows are created.
   ▷ For artificial light sources, identify the types of fixtures (include descriptions of diffusers or reflectors), types and ages of lamps, the height of the fixtures, the outputs (in lumens), and the quality of the light.
   ▷ Identify colors and textures that affect reflectivity.
   Solicit input from workers on glare, shadows, and their perception of the effectiveness of lighting.

2. Map working areas. Determine distances of work surfaces from principle light sources illuminating the area.

   Identify the schedule of use of those areas (in some cases the schedule will be variable and/or unpredictable).

3. Determine existing lighting levels, either by asking a lighting contractor to measure or by using a light meter.

   In some situations, this may vary over the course of the day due to the orientation of windows and skylights to the path of the sun.

Comparison of Energy Intensities of Lighting Alternatives in Exterior Applications[13]			
		Lamp Energy Intensity (watts)	
Application	Base lamp description	Base lamp	LED replacement
Outdoor lighting	Incandescent	150	26
	Halogen quartz	150	31
	Fluorescent	159	151
	Mercury vapor	254	108
	Metal halide	458	327
	High pressure sodium	283	276
Step, path lighting	Incandescent	119	46
	Halogen	158	64
	Halogen quartz	432	211
Vehicle and pedestrian signals	3-colored ball – 12" red	135	8
	3-colored ball – 12" yellow	132	20
	3-colored ball – 12" green	132	9
	Arrow – yellow	132	7
	Arrow – green	132	9
	Walking person - white	132	8
	Hand – orange	132	8
	Countdown – orange	132	9
Advertising signs	Neon	3 watts/ft^2	0.96 watts/ft^2

Figure 11.9

Identify Lighting Improvement Options

Evaluate background data collected as part of the lighting audit, and identify goals for making lighting improvements. These goals generally will fall under the following categories:

- ▶ Increasing or reducing ambient lighting.
- ▶ Providing task lighting.
- ▶ Reducing glare and eliminating shadows.
- ▶ Selecting more energy-efficient lamp types.
- ▶ Selecting controls that are more energy-efficient.

Evaluate Identified Lighting Improvement Options

Perform economic evaluations of identified options, calculating both the energy and demand charges, if any, saved, as well as any indirect benefits or costs, such as:

- ▶ Reduced maintenance costs (from less frequent relamping).
- ▶ Increased productivity and quality due to less visual fatigue (that may lead to personal fatigue and absenteeism) and error reduction.
- ▶ Enhanced sales attributable to more effective merchandising.
- ▶ Improved appearance and attractiveness of the working and/or shopping environments.
- ▶ Heightened safety for workers and visitors.
- ▶ Less light pollution.
- ▶ Improved morale.

See the *Energy Efficiency Measures Evaluation Worksheet* in the Appendix.

Select and Incorporate Lighting Improvement Options

Based on the energy, economic, and indirect benefit assessment in the previous step, determine which options will be implemented.

Create a schedule for implementation, which should include a lighting maintenance calendar. See the *Action Plan Worksheet* in the Appendix.

Install the improvements and monitor their effect on achieving the desired outcomes established as part of the lighting planning process.

Actions for Increasing Lighting Energy Efficiency

An organization can take a number of actions in order to save energy. The actions correspond to the overall strategies of avoidance, efficiency, and effectiveness. The following lists provide an overview of key actions.

Improve Lighting Environment

General

- ▷ Use daylighting instead of artificial light, noting that direct sunlight should be avoided or diffused.

Use window treatments, such as blinds, exterior screens or shades, or solar screens, to reduce unwanted direct light and solar heat gain.

▣ Use light ceiling and wall colors that reflect light. Dark colors absorb light. As much as one-third of the energy of a light system is determined by room dimensions, windows, colors, and surface treatments.[14]

Recommended reflectances[15] for room surfaces are as follows:

▷ Window blinds 40–50 percent
▷ Walls 50 percent
▷ Business machines 50 percent
▷ Floor 20–40 percent
▷ Furniture 25–45 percent
▷ Ceiling 70–80 percent

▣ Reduce glare by shielding sources of unwanted illumination. Use curtains, shades, or solar film over windows.

Reduce glare by using a greater number of lower light output lamps rather than fewer high-output lamps.

Reduce glare from fluorescent fixtures by using fixtures that have parabolic louvers that direct light or diffusers that spread light. Select fixtures for use in general commercial areas that offer a Visual Comfort Probability rating greater than 70 (80 for computer areas).[16]

Reduce reflected glare by painting reflective surfaces with matte and/or dark-colored finishes.

▣ Position workers so that daylighting comes from the side (opposite their writing hand) or from behind (provided that the light does not create glare on computer monitor surfaces).

> All fluorescent bulbs contain small quantities of mercury (approximately 4 mg compared to old-style thermometers' 500 mg). Mercury vapor, metal halide, and sodium lamps contain mercury as well.[20] Using CFLs results in a reduction of mercury compared to emissions from coal-fuel power plants that power incandescent bulbs.[21] Magnetic ballasts and some CFLs with magnetic ballasts contain small quantities of short-lived radioactive materials. These hazardous materials need to be disposed of properly. Waste Management's and Earth911's Websites contain databases of locations that handle the disposal of these materials.

Lighting Computer Work Stations

Balance the amount of light in the room and the light emanating from the computer monitor. Too much room lighting washes out the image on the screen. Too much light from the monitor causes eyestrain.

▣ Create even light conditions within the computer operator's line of sight. Avoid high contrast created by the interaction of light and dark surfaces.

▣ Place monitors perpendicular to windows.

▣ Use window treatments to reduce glare from windows.

▣ Encourage workers to adjust the screen brightness as lighting conditions change over the course of the day.

▣ Orient the monitor so that the line of sight between the operator and light sources is greater than 30 degrees.

▣ Keep the screen clean.

▣ If overhead lighting causes glare, tilt the monitor downward or install diffusers to the offending light source.

▣ If glare continues to be a problem, attach a glare filter to the monitor screen.

Exterior Lighting

The State of California has promulgated standards for energy-efficient exterior lighting. Lighting levels requirements are based on the type of application and the lighting zone:[17]

▣ Hardscapes for vehicular use 0.05–0.19 W/ft²

▣ Hardscapes for pedestrian activity 0.06–0.21 W/ft²

▣ Building entrances without canopies 0.35–1.00 W/ft²

Use Energy-Efficient Fixtures

▣ Reduce over-illuminated areas by downsizing the energy intensity of lamps so that the recommended lighting level for the activity is achieved (see Figure 11.1) while maintaining the desired light quality.

This may be as simple as removing individual lamps from fixtures.

▣ Consider task lighting (such as desk lamps; hanging fixtures for work benches) to provide increased illumination at the point of need, which may allow overall ambient light levels in the room to be reduced.

▣ Replace inefficient lamps, ballasts, and fixtures.

▣ Replace incandescent lamps with fluorescent or compact fluorescent lamps (CFLs) in locations where the light is on for at least 15 minutes at a time (five minutes in areas with high electricity costs [for example, $0.15 or more per kWh]). Turning the lamp on and off shortens its lifetime.

In recessed fixtures, use a reflector CFL rather than a spiral CFL.

In locations controlled by a dimmer or 3-way switched, special CFLs designed for that purpose are needed.

Consider dedicated CFL fixtures that don't allow incandescents to be used. Some CFL lamps may require harp adapters or socket extenders to fit in incandescent fixtures.

▣ Replace fluorescent bulbs and ballasts more than eight years old with T-series lamps with electronic ballasts.

▣ Convert T-12 bulb fixtures to more energy-efficient fixtures ($50–100/fixture with 10-percent efficiency improvement; payback determined by hours used and electricity costs).

▣ Replace incandescent exit signs with LED exit signs.

▣ Replace incandescent or mercury vapor security lighting with metal halide or color-corrected sodium lamps.[18]

▣ Replace lamps whose output has deteriorated (one rule of thumb is 80 percent of output), although the conditions dictate replacement.

▣ Consider group relamping, reballasting, and fixture replacement as a cost-effective alternative to individual replacement.

⊠   Incorporate thoughtful lighting design into all construction and renovation projects.

⊠   Consider selecting lamps that have been awarded the ENERGY STAR label.

⊠   Be mindful of light pollution from exterior lighting. (See Chapter 8.)

⊠   Consider solar exterior lighting, which may be an effective alternative to electric lamps. Solar systems are particularly cost-effective where solar radiation is plentiful and electricity costs are high. Systems may be self-contained or connected to a photovoltaic panel. Illumination levels range from soft to beamed; and may be used as walkway lights, pole mounted, or attached to the building.

Use Effective Controls

The principal forms of control are the on-off switch, dimmers, timers, door-activated controls, photocells (that detect lighting levels), occupancy detectors, hybrid systems (for example, a timed photocell), centralized programmable controls, and smart controls that incorporate lighting control into the control of multiple facility systems.

⊠   Turn off lights in unoccupied spaces.

Turn off fluorescents if they won't be needed for more than five minutes (where electricity costs more than $0.15/kWh: balance reduction in lamp lifetime against energy savings).

In some cases there may be several controlled settings (for example, off when vacant, high illumination during normal use, and low illumination for lunch or maintenance times).

⊠   Where there are variable lighting needs in discrete task-lit areas, use dimming controls or use three-way bulbs (available in CFLs) that can match illumination levels to the need.

⊠   Consider installing dimmer controls, which provide variable lighting and energy-savings. Automatic dimmers that sense available daylighting and turn off or dim electric illumination may be a particularly cost-effective control.

⊠   Install occupancy sensors and timed lights (that turn off after a pre-set length of time), which are effective controls in bathrooms or conference rooms that are unoccupied for long periods of the day. Costing $25–80, these sensors may provide savings of 20–75 percent.[19]

⊠   Use photoelectric sensor controls in exterior settings that turn the lighting on in low-light conditions or, less desirably, a timer that is reset monthly or as needed. Incandescent security lighting also can be controlled by photoelectric and motion sensors that turn the system on when movement is detected in low-light conditions.

Lighting for security purposes does not have to be bright in order to be effective.

Maintain Lighting Systems

⊠   Establish a schedule for measuring light levels, light output, and relamping.

⊠   Clean lamps, reflective surfaces, and diffusers periodically.

Chapter 12

Space Conditioning

Space Conditioning Requirements

Space conditioning refers to the control of the indoor environment by caring for temperature, humidity, and air quality needed for the comfort of occupants and to maintain the recommended operating conditions of the equipment.

Occupant comfort is one of three parameters that space conditioning systems are designed for. (See Chapter 8 for a discussion of comfort and how solar radiation, wind, and moisture affect temperature and humidity, which are the two key variables that determine human comfort.)

The second determinant of space conditioning needs is the operating environment that is required for the functioning of many types of equipment and activities. For example, paint booths require control of both temperature and humidity; copy machines require optimal temperature and humidity conditions or else paper jams occur and print quality is compromised; servers and copier workstations emit sufficient volumes of heat so that ventilation may be needed to prevent room overheating.

The third factor is indoor air quality (IAQ), which also may be thought of as maintaining occupant health. Air quality in enclosed spaces can be compromised because of mold, bacteria, allergens, and chemicals, such as radon, carbon monoxide, and toxins routinely emitted from various products. Volatile organic chemicals (VOCs) are emitted from products commonly found in office settings: printers, copiers, marking pens, and cleaning products, as well as many building materials and furniture products. In general commercial and industrial enterprises VOCs may be released from paints, solvents, adhesives, and chemicals used in industry-specific processes. It is crucial that worker and customer health is not compromised by exposure to potentially hazardous substances. Ventilation is the way that healthy indoor air quality is maintained. The American Society of Heating, Refrigerating and Air Conditioning Engineers (ASHRAE) recommends ventilation rates for non-residential uses, and these rates should be considered in conjunction with OSHA standards.[1]

Planning for Energy-Efficient Space Conditioning Improvements

The principal methods for reducing the energy consumed in space conditioning are:

- ▶ Controlling the volume of air moving between the interior and exterior environment.

- ◻ Ensuring that space heating, cooling, and ventilation systems are sized correctly and operated to maximize their efficiency.
- ◻ Using energy sources that minimize the need for fossil fuel combustion.

Planning space conditioning improvements requires a starting point: an energy audit that profiles the base case. The space conditioning energy audit is typically part of a larger facility audit and is offered by virtually all electric and natural gas utilities.

The following tasks define an approach to designing an effective energy-efficiency plan for space conditioning:

1. Create a map of the organization that illustrates the major architectural features (exterior and interior walls, windows, doors), compass directions, sources of solar gain and prevailing winds, and neighboring buildings and landscaping that affect the microclimate.
   - ▷ Show the occupied rooms and areas, and their occupancy schedules.
   - ▷ Show unoccupied and transitional rooms (such as restrooms, conference, hallways, entries, and storage).
   - ▷ Show major process equipment (for example, servers and machines), and heating (drying rooms and so forth) and cooling (refrigeration).
   - ▷ Show the HVAC system including locations of inlets, outlets, and controls.
   - ▷ Identify hazardous substances stored or used in the building, their locations, and profile their use.
2. Characterize building components that affect space conditioning efficiency.
   - ▷ Attic insulation.
   - ▷ Exterior wall (and interior walls separating heated and unheated spaces) insulation.
   - ▷ Floor insulation.
   - ▷ Doors and windows.
   - ▷ Infiltration and air change rates.
3. Identify recommended insulation and ventilation values for the climate zone and suited to the types of uses and activities in the organization.
4. Determine desired temperatures, levels of humidity, and ventilation in each of the spaces. Variations in occupancy and equipment use during the day may affect target conditions.
5. Evaluate collected data and identify options for improving the energy efficiency of the building.
6. Evaluate identified options in terms of ease of implementation and expected ecological and economic benefit.

As described in Chapter 8, multiple factors affect the heating and cooling loads of a building. Because each structure is unique, the appropriate energy efficiency improvements for a particular organization are difficult to predict. Thus, the Guide's checklists must be considered to be a menu of possible actions.

Implementing energy efficiency measures is greatly influenced by the legal control that an organization has over making facility improvements. Generally, an enterprise falls into one of three situations:

1. The organization owns the building.
2. The organization leases all of a building, and the rental/lease contract allows the organization to make improvements outright.
3. The organization leases a portion or all of a building, and/or the rental/lease contract prohibits the organization from making major improvements without prior approval from the building owner.

If the organization owns the building, it has total control over improvements and need only balance the implementation with competing enterprise projects and any applicable regulations.

If the lease the organization has authorizes improvements (double check to confirm the legality of making unilateral improvements), then it is important to evaluate the return on investment for individual improvements against the time remaining on the term of the lease. Owners also may be willing to pay for all or a portion of the improvements that increase the value of the property.

If improvements require prior authorization or there are other occupants of the building, then the owner (and possibly other tenants) becomes a partner in developing the energy efficiency plan. It may complicate the process, but should not be a deterrent to taking action.

Air Sealing for Energy-Efficiency

Air sealing refers to the steps taken to reduce the volume of indoor, conditioned air escaping to the outside, and outdoor air infiltrating to the interior. These convective energy losses are different than the conductive energy losses reduced by insulation.

Air penetrates through openings in the building envelope, such as around:

- ▶ Door frames.
- ▶ Window frames.
- ▶ Electrical, natural gas, propane, and fuel oil service entry locations.
- ▶ Cable, TV, and phone lines.
- ▶ Water faucets, irrigation lines, and plumbing vents.
- ▶ Exhaust vents and fans, and condensate lines exit locations.

Professionals determine the air tightness of a space with a blower door test, which involves mounting a special fan into an exterior door frame. The fan pulls air out of the space so that air from the outside infiltrates into the building through openings in the building envelope. Measuring the pressure differential between the interior and exterior gives a reading of the air tightness. The created vacuum also allows infiltration locations to be identified.

Alternatively, infiltration problems can be identified through the following process:

1. Wait for a windy day or a time when there is a marked difference between interior and exterior temperatures.
2. Close all exterior windows and doors. Open all interior doors. Shut fireplace dampers and doors. Turn on any exhaust fans.

3. Holding a smoke stick (or similar commercial products) or an incense stick, trace the indoor perimeter of windows, doors, light fixtures, and penetrations. (Tape the stick to poles to reach out-of-reach locations.)

    Large interior spaces (such as warehouse spaces) may require smoke candles, which generate greater volumes of smoke than smoke sticks.

4. Record locations where air infiltration is indicated by the smoke stream.

5. Open windows and doors to exhaust the smoke.

    There are several ways to seal the structure to correct air infiltration problems:

▶ Install door sweeps or weatherstripping around exterior doors and interior doors that access highly conditioned (such as computer rooms or refrigerated rooms), unconditioned (for example, storage), or lightly conditioned spaces. Inspect interior door trim and, if needed, seal openings.

Inspect the exterior door trim and, if needed, caulk between trim pieces and the building siding.

▶ Caulk and weatherstrip around windows.

▶ Caulk around sill plates (at the top of foundation walls) and where walls and ceilings intersect.

▶ Plug gaps around electric, plumbing, cable, TV, irrigation, exhaust vents, fans, condensate lines, and other penetrations of exterior walls.

> There are more than a dozen types of weatherstripping systems, each with advantages and disadvantages. The U.S. DOE has an excellent chart for selecting and applying weatherstripping materials.[2] A similar chart compares the characteristics of different caulking materials.[3] It's critical to ensure that metal collar plates and heat-resistant caulking materials are used in conjunction with fireplace and wood stove flues, HVAC, and equipment exhausts.

▶ Use insulation to fill voids around pipes where they penetrate a wall, floor, or ceiling, and between conditioned and unconditioned (and lightly conditioned) spaces, and then patch or caulk around to create an air seal.

▶ Install foam insulation gaskets in outlets and switches located in exterior (more important) and interior walls.

▶ Inspect the exterior surfaces for uncaulked holes and caulking that has shrunk or detached. Remove, clean surfaces, and recaulk.

▶ Remove window air conditioning units during winter months.

In sealing the structure it is important not to make the structure so tight that air pollutants concentrate in the building. See the discussion that follows about maintaining healthy indoor air quality.

Increasing Insulation

Heat flows from a hot body to a colder one. Insulation reduces the amount of heat that is lost by conduction, which occurs when one material is in contact with another material (this concept extends to a material being in contact with air). The denser the material (think metal or glass), the greater the conductivity. More porous materials, such as cellulose, fiberglass, and foam, resist the flow of heat and therefore are excellent insulating materials.

Insulating Values of Select Insulation and Building Materials[4]			
	Material	R/inch	R/thickness
Insulation	Fiberglass batt	3.14 – 4.30	
	Rock wool batt	3.14 – 4.00	
	Rock wool blown (attic)	3.10 – 4.00	
	Rock wool blown (wall)	3.10 – 4.00	
	Cellulose blown (attic)	3.13	
	Cellulose blown (wall)	3.70	
	Vermiculite	2.13	
	Urea terpolymer foam	4.48	
	Expanded polystyrene	4.00	
Foundation framing, sheathing, exterior finish	Concrete block 4″		0.80
	Concrete block 8″		1.11
	Brick common 4″		0.80
	Poured concrete	0.08	
	Lumber 2x4		4.38
	Lumber 2x6		6.88
	Plywood ½″		0.63
	Plywood ¾″		0.94
	Foam insulated sheathing ½″		2.00-3.50
	Siding, beveled, lapped		0.80
	Siding, aluminum, steel, vinyl		0.61
	Roofing, asphalt shingles		0.44
	Roofing, wood shingles		0.97
Interior construction and finish	Gypsum board ½″		0.45
	Gypsum board 5/8″		0.56
	Paneling 3/8″		0.47
	Flooring underlay, plywood	1.25	
	Flooring underlay, particle board	1.31	
	Flooring, hardwood	0.91	
	Tile, linoleum		0.05
	Carpet		2.08
Windows	Glass single pane		0.91
	Glass single pane w storm		2.00
	Glass, double pane w. ¼″ airspace		1.69
	Glass, double pane w. ½″ airspace		2.04
	Glass, double pane w. ½″ airspace and Low-E 0.20		3.13
	Glass, triple pane w. ¼″ airspace		2.56
	Glass, triple pane w. ½″ airspace		3.23
Doors	Wood, hollow core flush 1 ¾″		2.17
	Wood, solid core flush 1 ¾″		3.03
	Storm door wood, 50% glass)		1.25
	Insulating door, metal (2″ w. urethane)		15.00
Air	Film layer, interior ceiling		0.61
	Film layer, interior wall		0.68
	Film layer, exterior		0.17
	Enclosed airspace, ½″ – 4″		1.00

Figure 12.1

Determining Insulation Levels

Figure 12.1 on page 111 identifies the insulating values of select insulation and building materials. (See also the ecological properties of the insulating materials described in Figure 12.4.)

Building energy audits determine the amount of insulation materials between conditioned spaces and unconditioned spaces. Using base data from Figure 12.1, one can calculate the effective R-value (insulating value) of the wall, ceiling, or floor separating the conditioned from unconditioned spaces.

Recommended Insulation Levels for Buildings (R-values)[5]						
Location		Attic	Wood Frame Wall Cavity	Floor	Crawl Space Wall	Basement Wall Interior
Zone	City					
1	Denver	38	13	30	25	11
1	Minneapolis	49	13	30	25	11
2	Chicago	49	13	30	25	11
2	Boston	49	13	30	25	11
3	St. Louis	49	13	30	25	11
3	Philadelphia	38	13	25	25	11
4	San Francisco	38	13	13	13	11
4	Atlanta	38	13	25	25	11
5	Phoenix	38	13	13	13	11
5	Miami	38	13	13	13	–

Notes: 1. Floor insulation only over unconditioned spaces.
2. Calculations based on residential buildings, heated by natural gas, using climatic data and energy cost data for the referenced City. Recommended R-values reasoned to be appropriate for energy–efficient enterprise use.

Figure 12.2

Examples of recommended insulation values for residential structures in select cities are shown in Figure 12.2. The ORNL *R-Value Recommendations for Building* software is a user-friendly tool for determining the recommended insulation levels for cities and towns whose R-values are not shown in Figure 12.2.

If the existing amount of insulation is less than the level recommended for the climate zone, then additional insulation should be installed. Increasing insulation levels is easiest during remodeling; however, insulation also can be retrofitted if remodeling is not in the foreseeable future. Figure 12.3 displays an example of how insulation improvements would be calculated for a hypothetical structure in Minneapolis.

The Appendix contains an *Insulation Improvement Worksheet* for planning improvements.

Insulation Worksheet Example

Surface being analyzed	Attic	Wood Frame Wall Cavity	Floor	Crawl Space Wall	Basement Wall Interior
Goal R-values	49	13	30	25	11

Surfaces	Location	Description	Existing R-Value	Additional R-value needed	Insulation Improvement
Attic	Above all rooms	60' x 40'10" fiberglass batt	=10 x 3.5 = 35	14	5" blown cellulose
Walls	North	3.5" fiberglass	= 4 x 3.5 =13.5	0	None needed
	East	3.5" fiberglass	= 4 x 3.5 =13.5	0	None needed
	South	3.5" fiberglass	= 4 x 3.5 =13.5	0	None needed
	West	0	0	13	3 ☐" expanded foam
Floor	Below all rooms	6" fiberglass	= 6 x 3.5 = 21	9	3 ☐" batt
Basement	All walls	0	0	11	3" polystyrene board

Note: Goal R-values determined from Figure 12.2; existing R-values are calculated based on the R-values of insulating materials (from Figure 12.1) that correspond to the hypothetical description; additional R-values needed are the difference between the goal R-values and the existing R-values; insulation improvement identified based on suitability of insulating option for location and the R-value of the option.

Figure 12.3

Overview of Ecological Properties of Building Insulation Materials[6]

	Material	Ingredients	Comments
Fiber	Cellulose fiber	85% shredded, fluffed newsprint 15% borate-based fire retardant	Borate is environmentally safe. Higher R-value than fiberglass. Blown-in exposes installer to airborne particles.
	Cotton fiber	Shredded, recycled cotton Treated w borate-based fire retardant	Low chemical choice. Blown-in exposes installer to airborne particles.
	Fiberglass	Manufacturers using (up to 40%) recycled glass	Bagged fiberglass reduces exposure to air-borne glass. Blown or batted exposes installer to glass.
	Mineral wool	Manufactured from recycled slag and mined basalt	Sound absorbent; pest and fire resistant. Blown-in exposes installer to airborne particles. Rigid board foundation insulation.
	Sheep's wool	Sheared from sheep Treated for moth- and mildew-prevention	Available in batts, loose fill. Healthy choice.
Foam	Cementitious	Manufactured from magnesium oxide cement	Fireproof. Mold and pest resistant.
	Polyicynene Polyurethane	Manufactured from petroleum-based oils	Water is blowing agent for polyicynene; chemical agent for polyurethane. Different formulations result in open-cell and, the more efficient, closed cell product.
	Agriculture-based	Soybean, corn, or sugar cane replace a portion of the petroleum-based polyurethane ingredients	Soy-based can form rigid board or can be sprayed.

Figure 12.4

Ecological Effects of Insulation

Insulation materials are by their nature an eco-friendly investment. However, some of the properties of insulation materials have adverse effects. In addition to the energy used to manufacture insulation, there are concerns about insulation. Figure 12.4 on page 113 identifies some of these concerns.

Building Envelope Energy Efficiency

Chapter 8 describes a variety of site development and green building considerations that can improve the space conditioning performance of a building.

Door Energy Efficiency

Doors often have a low insulation value. The Appendix contains a *Door Energy-Efficiency Improvement Worksheet* for planning improvements to standard doors.

Where an establishment has high traffic, with repeated opening and closing of doors, there can be a significant loss of energy. Consider these options:

- ▶ Revolving doors.
- ▶ Entries with two sets of doors that form an enclosed vestibule.
- ▶ Limiting entry and exit during non-peak times to a limited number of doors.
- ▶ Provide for use of single doors (instead of loading dock doors) for smaller deliveries.
- ▶ Keep loading dock doors closed during conditioning periods. Close doors to conditioned part of organization, when loading dock doors are opened.

Window Energy Efficiency

In selecting windows replacements, look for:

- ▶ Low solar gain window, which are identified by a Solar Heat Gain Coefficiency (SHGC) rating.
- ▶ High insulation values, as identified by low U-values (less than 0.35 recommended for cold climates).
- ▶ Low air leakage rates (less than 0.3 cubic feet per minute).
- ▶ Certification of the window performance by the National Fenestration Rating Council.

In addition to adding storms or replacing single pane windows, there are other ways of improving window energy performance (the suitability of the concepts depends on the space conditioning needs and the construction and orientation of the building). One example is to block incoming radiation during over-heated times by installing and using window awnings, blinds, draperies, shades, insulating shades, window quilts, architectural overhangs, or shutters. These are especially effective on south and west-facing windows, but may also be prudent investments in east-facing locations.

The Appendix contains a *Window Energy-Efficiency Improvement Worksheet* for planning improvements.

Heating, Ventilating, and Air Conditioning (HVAC)

HVAC refers to the mechanical systems that condition interior air. There is considerable variability in the types of systems that an enterprise might use:

- ▶ Fuel-fed furnace or boiler unit (natural gas, propane, petroleum, coal, or wood fuels with either forced air, steam, or water heat distribution).
- ▶ Heat pump (air, ground, or water heat source; also with either forced air or water used to distribute heat and coolth).
- ▶ Baseboard electric heater.
- ▶ Radiant heating.
- ▶ District heating system (shared with other buildings).
- ▶ Cogeneration involving the generation of electricity and heat.
- ▶ Passive and active solar systems.
- ▶ Air conditioning, as central chiller-based unit serving an entire building (or multiple spaces, users) or individual through-wall or window units.
- ▶ Natural air conditioning.

The energy efficiency of existing HVAC systems and the level of improvement to efficiency that may be available depends on a number of factors, such as the:

- ▶ Volume of the enclosure being conditioned.
- ▶ Age, expected lifetimes, and efficiency of the existing HVAC components, including air handling and water distribution efficiency.
- ▶ Ability of existing components to satisfy heating, cooling, and ventilating demands.
- ▶ Physical and technological ease of making identified improvements.

An organization contemplating HVAC system upgrades and changeouts has to evaluate these factors against financial considerations: current and projected prices of energy, availability of rebates and incentives, capital costs, and opportunity costs.

The variability of these factors and considerations make it impossible to specify energy-efficiency HVAC system improvements applicable to all enterprises. Instead, the Guide uses checklists to identify energy-efficiency improvement options and asks the reader to determine the suitability of the action to their situation.

Energy efficiency starts with a consideration of the energy efficiency of the building envelope, which is covered in the previous section of this chapter.

Maintain the Efficiency of Operating HVAC Systems

Regular maintenance is crucial to sustaining the efficiency of an HVAC system. Consider the following maintenance actions:

- ▷ Inspect operating systems regularly (daily for large systems, weekly for medium, and at least monthly for small).
- ▷ Eliminate or reduce flow of heat and coolth to rooms and spaces that do not require conditioning.

- Ensure that unobstructed airflow is maintained around air intakes and outlets, diffusers, radiators, and convectors.
- Clean air diffusers and air intakes.
- Clean radiators and heat transfer fins on baseboard systems.
- Periodically measure temperatures at different times of the day and in different heating and cooling modes, and rebalance the distribution system, as necessary.
- Monitor occupant work-arounds (vents that have been closed, personal fans, personal heaters) and rebalance the distribution system.
- Replace air filters regularly, usually monthly during operating seasons.
- Inspect cleanliness of heat transfer coils in heat pumps, air conditioners, and chiller units.
- Check the integrity of system connections.
- Inspect ductwork to ensure tightness of seals and insulation coverage (dirt lines on the ductwork or insulation is an indicator).

In addition to reducing energy consumption, regular maintenance also has the benefit of prolonging the lifetime of the system.

A more formal system tune-up should be conducted by a professional prior to the start of a heating or cooling season. Larger systems or HVAC systems under heavy load should be examined again during the working season. The following actions should be incorporated into HVAC tune-ups:

- Check combustion efficiency.
- Check refrigerant charge.
- Inspect and straighten heat transfer and condenser coils.
- Inspect, clean, and lubricate fans.
- Inspect steam valves for leakage and replace broken steam traps.
- Inspect ductwork and heat transfer pipes.
- Ensure proper economizer operation.
- Check for proper heat exchanger operation.
- Bleed trapped air from water distribution systems once or twice a heating season.
- Check condensate drains to confirm that air conditioning units are conveying water out of the building.

Minimize Distribution Losses

Take the following measures to minimize distribution losses:

- Seal air leaks and install insulation around ductwork (especially important for ducts passing through unconditioned spaces).
- Periodically clean air ducts to remove dust, dirt, and contaminants. (This is work that should be done by a trained professional.)
- Install pipe insulation around (water) heat transfer pipes (especially important for ducts passing through unconditioned spaces).

Control the System

Controlling temperature is an effective means of reducing energy consumption. The following control options should be considered:

▣ Reduce the temperature setting during the heating season and increase the set point to 78 degrees Fahrenheit during the cooling season. (An effective way of making the modification is to change the set point a degree every day or every other day, allowing occupants to acclimate to the new temperature.) See Figure 12.5 for a representation of setback savings.

▣ Install a programmable thermostat that schedules temperature changes automatically. The programmable thermostat should provide for manual override capability.

Approximate Savings From Thermostat Setback[7]			
	Setback temperature		
Degree Days	60° F	55° F	50° F
1,000	13%	25%	38%
2,000	12%	24%	26%
3,000	11%	22%	33%
4,000	10%	20%	30%
5,000	9%	19%	28%
6,000	8%	16%	24%
7,000	7%	15%	22%
8,000	7%	13%	19%

Note: Assumes a 65° F base temperature and setback lasting 14 hours a night and all weekend.

Figure 12.5

Use a programmable thermostat specifically designed for heat pumps in order to avoid using the inefficient electric strip heating of the system.

▣ Ensure system fans are set to "auto" position, which allow fan operation only when there is a demand for heating or cooling, and not the "on" position, which operates 24 hours a day.

▣ Experiment and adjust programmed settings.

"Coasting" refers to early setback (for example, setting back the temperature to 50 degrees Fahrenheit at 4:30 p.m. when the workplace closes at 5 p.m.).

During shoulder seasons (spring and fall) there may be less temperature differential to overcome, and the setback period can be lengthened so that the workspace is not heated to the desired temperature much before workers begin to arrive.

▣ It may be cost-effective to use personal space heaters that provide localized comfort for workers who come in early, work late, or work on weekends. This is more cost-effective than operating a central heating system that conditions a space larger than the limited area needed by the one worker.

▣ Install locking enclosures around thermostats to prevent temperature wars.

▣ Energy management systems (EMS) are "smart" electronics that extend control beyond the capability of programmable thermostats.

EMS can turn on economizers that circulate outside air instead of air-conditioned air, when there is a cooling load in the building, and the exterior temperature is low.

EMS can react to differentials in interior-exterior temperature and humidity to optimize comfort by adjusting supply air temperature and chilled water and heated water temperatures.

More sophisticated EMS can manage electric loads (to reduce electric utility demand charges) and control lighting systems.

EMS suppliers estimate savings of 10–50 percent (typically 20 percent) for buildings with central heating and chiller systems.[8]

Upgrade or Replace Inefficient HVAC Systems

The question of whether or not to upgrade or replace HVAC systems is best addressed after other energy-efficiency improvements are made. The improvements that have the greatest effect on HVAC loads are:

- ▶ Relamping (replacing incandescents with more efficient bulbs, such as CFLs, eliminates their heat emissions and reduce the cooling loads).
- ▶ Air sealing and weatherization measures that reduce the need for space conditioning.
- ▶ Sealing and insulation of distribution ducts and pipes.

Conducting these three measures before evaluating the performance of the existing HVAC systems provides a better, revised baseline for determining how efficient the existing systems are in delivering space conditioning requirements. In turn, the revised baseline enables a more accurate calculation of the payback on improvement options.

Evaluating HVAC improvement options is a relatively complex determination that is specific to the unique characteristics of the enterprise. The following overview of concepts is intended to provide a base knowledge of some of the options that a professional HVAC engineer might propose:

- ▶ Upgrade properly sized boilers with improvements, such as efficient burners, baffle inserts, combustion control, warm weather (temperature reduction) controls, and economizers.

  Efficient burners can operate at higher temperatures while consuming less fuel.

- ▶ Replace an oversized, inefficient boiler with a system matched to the requirement of the building.

  Make certain that equipment is properly sized. Undersized HVAC operates longer and may struggle to provide the desired comfort levels and is more expensive to operate than a properly sized unit. Oversized equipment often results in rapid cycling and also is more expensive to purchase and operate.

- ▶ Replace water-cooled centrifugal chillers that use R-11 or R-12 refrigerants that were banned by the 1990 amendments to the Clean Air Act.

- ▶ Consider replacing large central systems that serve multiple zones with comparatively large variations in their timing or duration of use, with individual systems that can be sized and operated to meet the needs of the zone(s) that they serve.

- ▶ Variable-speed drives match the different loads of HVAC pumps and air handlers that are created by different combinations of heating and/or cooling demands from multiple zones.

▣ Evaluate heat recovery from evacuated air. "Tight" structures and individual spaces in buildings (such as laboratories or paint booths) that require ventilation for maintaining air quality can capture the heat from the air that otherwise is exhausted from the building. Air-to-air heat exchangers recover a portion of the waste heat for reuse.

Heat recovery also is useful where heat from equipment (such as servers and printers) needs to be evacuated from an interior space.

▣ Consider heat recovery from process waste heat.

▣ Consider cogeneration systems and district heating systems that expand use of captured to offsite users in addition to the enterprise's need.

▣ Consider supplemental and pre-heat energy sources, such as active solar, heat pump systems, and geothermal systems.

▣ Radiant heating panels can be installed in areas where high ceilings or large air infiltration make convective HVAC systems costly. Radiant heating are options for loading areas, shop areas, and entry vestibules.

▣ Replace older, inefficient window air conditioning units with more energy-efficient models. Use Energy Guide labels and ENERGY STAR certification as guidance. Seasonal Energy Efficiency Ratio (SEER) ratings greater than 13 are recommended.

Consider features, such as fan-only operating mode, timer, digital controls, filter check light, and automatic delay fan, which turns off the fan several minutes after the compressor cycles off.

▣ When expanding or remodeling, consider a holistic approach to design whose objective is to minimize the consumption of fossil fuels for space conditioning. Super-insulation, passive solar design, and other design elements can effectively reduce energy use to zero. (See Chapter 8.)

Reduce HVAC Cooling Requirements

A number of measures can help reduce the need for air conditioning:

▣ Install attic fans that evacuate overheated air (during the summer months) that otherwise will conduct to the occupied space below.

▣ Use natural ventilation, ceiling fans, and personal fans instead of air conditioning.

▣ Close or cover heating air registers that allow cooled air to escape into ductwork.

▣ Ensure a tight seal between window air conditioning units and the frame that they're installed in.

▣ Relax the dress code on brutally hot days.

Boost Cooling Efficiency

A couple of considerations for improving the performance of a central air conditioning system are:

▣ Install a central system instead of individual units, unless there is substantial variability in use.

▣ Install the condenser unit outside, in the shade, and in a location where there is adequate airflow.

Chapter 13

Water Heating

As shown in Figure 9.9 water heating is a major energy use in lodging, restaurants, and healthcare organizations. Smaller enterprises and larger users that only have a small water heating demand (such as offices) often have water heaters that are similar or smaller in size compared to those used in houses. Commercial kitchens, laundries, restaurants, and industries with significant need for heated water have substantially greater water heating plants that either stand independently or are part of a space heating system or a cogeneration plant.

Strategies for reducing energy consumption for water heating fall into several categories:

▶ Minimizing water heating both in terms of the volume of water that is heated and the temperature to which the water is heated.

▶ Ensuring that the water heating system is properly sized and operated in a manner to maximize its efficiency.

▶ Using energy sources that minimize the need for fossil fuel combustion.

Minimize Water Heating Requirements

Many of the measures that reduce water consumption (see Chapter 22) also reduce water heating consumption—the key variable from an energy efficiency perspective being, of course, whether the water being conserved is cold water or hot water. The following are energy-conserving measures organized by activity. (Many of these measures also result in water savings.)

Faucets and Showers

Consider the following energy-conserving measures:

▶ Faucets: Aerators and flow restrictors reduce flow volumes; automatically closing, motion-activated, and metered (timed) faucets prevent excessive run times.

▶ Showers: Aerators, flow restrictors, and water-efficient fixtures reduce flow volumes.

Dishwashing

Smaller commercial enterprises often have break rooms and kitchens that are equipped with many of the same types of appliances one sees in a residential kitchen. Many of the water-conserving actions described in Chapter 22 also help reduce energy consumption. The following energy-conserving measures should be considered:

▣ Use a dishwasher, which is likely to be more energy-efficient than hand washing.

▣ Scrape—don't rinse—dishes.

▣ Use air dry instead of the heated dry function (or open the dishwasher door after the final rinse cycles has run).

▣ Run only full loads.

▣ Replace older dishwashers that have poor energy use characteristics with higher energy performance units (as shown on the ENERGY GUIDE label) and ENERGY STAR models that offer booster heating. Dishwashers with booster heaters increase the water temperature to 140 degrees Fahrenheit, which allows the water heater of the enterprise to be maintained at a lower temperature setting.

▣ Size the dishwasher to meet anticipated loads and use. Compact-capacity models may be sufficient for the requirements of the enterprise.

▣ Operate the dishwasher during off-peak periods.

▣ Maintain proper pressure settings.

▣ Maintain and replace washer curtains used with conveyor dishwasher units.

▣ Adjust dishwashing temperature setting to comply with recommendations of the manufacturer.

For commercial (restaurant) applications, consider the appropriateness of these actions as well as the following:

▶ Purchase energy- and water-efficient units sized to the expected demand.

▶ Turn off internal water heaters during the night and extended periods of non-use.

▶ Rinse pressures generally should be below 25 psi.

▶ Run conveyor-type dishwashers in automatic mode instead of leaving the conveyor on.

Clothes Washing Machines

Some enterprises regularly wash towels, uniforms, linens, and other items used in the business, and some property managers and hotels/motels offer clothes washers for tenants' and guests' use. The following energy conserving measures can be applied to residential-scaled machines:

▣ Reduce the amount of washing that needs to be done.

▣ Wash only full loads.

▣ For heavily soiled loads, soak the wash first, instead of an extended heavy wash cycle.

▣ Use shorter wash cycles for clothes that are less soiled.

▣ Use the lowest practical water level setting.

▣ Wash in cold water, and rinse in cold water. Water temperature doesn't affect cleaning.

- Select ENERGY STAR machines that provide for cold wash, and lower volumes.
- If purchasing a new unit, consider a clothes washer with an energy factor rating of 2.5 or more. ENERGY STAR certificates and ENERGY GUIDE labels are good indicators for buyers. Front-load washers are more efficient than top-load.
- Use high- or extended-spin feature, if available.
- Size laundry machines to the need of the organzation.
- Don't overuse detergent, which requires additional rinsing.

Other

Also consider the following energy-conserving measures:

- Garbage disposals: Avoid use, if possible. Operate using cold water.
- Encourage energy-efficient water use: Ask workers, guests, and customers to be mindful of their hot water consumption. Ask workers not to use hot water when cold will do (such as when cleaning equipment).

Ensure Water Heating System Efficiency

Once the demand for water heating is minimized, the efficiency of the delivery system can be optimized (the following are focused on smaller water heaters):

- Lower water-heater temperature to the minimum necessary to meet the requirements of the organization (115–120 degrees Fahrenheit is probably adequate). ASHRAE recommends water temperatures of 105 degrees for hand washing, 110 degrees for showers, 160 degrees for laundry, and 180–195 degrees for dishwasher rinse.[1] Dishwashers and clothes washing machines incorporate booster systems that heat the temperature of incoming water in order to reach operating temperatures.
- Insulate the water heater to R-24 in order to minimize standby losses. (The outside of the water heater should not feel warm to the touch.)
- Insulate hot water distribution pipes to prevent heat loss. Cold water inlet should be insulated for a minimum of 3 feet if the pipe is ever warm to the touch.
- Install heat traps that reduce the convection of heated water from the tank into the distribution lines. (Manufacturers are incorporating this feature into new water heaters.)
- Install a timer that shuts down the water heater if there are unoccupied periods (for example, during nights and on weekends).
- Perform routine maintenance: Flush a quart of water from the tank every three months, and completely drain and flush the tank annually (more frequently for larger water heaters or if the water source contains fine particles or minerals that deposit at the bottom of the heater).
- Replace leaking water heaters. Size the water heater to match the demand of the enterprise for hot water.

When replacing, ensure that the location of the tank is the shortest practical distance to the point of use.

For low hot water consumption situations, consider the cost-effectiveness of tankless heaters that operate only when there is a demand for hot water. Balance high initial costs with zero standby costs over the lifetime of the unit.

▷ When purchasing a new water heater, consider both the capacity of the tank and the ability of the tank to provide sufficient hot water during peak demand periods.

Calculate the maximum demand for hot water during the highest demand period by totaling the requirements from equipment, appliances, and activities that occur during the peak hour. Match the first-hour rating (FHR) of the water heater to the calculated peak demand.

Opt for natural gas fired heaters that deliver heated water more efficiently and with less ecological impact than water heaters that run on electricity.

Minimize the Need for Fossil Fuels

Examine the cost-effectiveness of heat recovery systems, which capture heat from water that otherwise would be disposed of. Sources of waste heat suitable for capture in commercial and industrial settings include wastewater from laundries and dishwashers, steam condensate lines, refrigeration and freezer systems, and process uses.

Solar water heating can be a cost-effective alternative and always is an ecologically friendly alternative to burning of fossil fuels for water heating. There are several different alternatives for solar water heating. (See Chapter 9.)

The Resources for Chapter 9 list the U.S. Department of Energy's link for evaluating the cost-effectiveness of solar water systems suitable for smaller organizations. Additionally, the American Solar Energy Society and Solar Energy Industries Association Websites offer resources to learn more about suitable systems, and locate manufacturers and installers.

Chapter 14

Refrigeration

Refrigeration is a major user of energy in groceries, restaurants, and cold-warehousing. Smaller enterprises and larger users that only have a small refrigeration requirements (such as offices) often have refrigerators that are similar or smaller in size to those used in houses.

General Considerations

There are a variety of actions that can reduce the amount of energy used for refrigeration—ranging from behavioral modifications to ensuring proper maintenance, to sizing the refrigeration system to the needs of the organization, to replacing or retrofitting inefficient units.

Refrigeration units have become more efficient in the past decade. Figure 14.1 illustrates the savings potential in replacing inefficient with efficient refrigeration units.

The following actions can help the energy performance of most refrigeration units:

Energy Use for Standard Refrigeration and Estimated Energy Savings[1]			
Technology		Estimated annual energy use for typical unit (kwh)	Energy savings potential
Refrigerator	Solid, reach-in	2,100	54%
	Under-counter	1,460	15%
	Glass, reach-in	3,250	50%
Freezer	Solid, reach-in	4,320	35%
	Under-counter	1,460	14%
Freezer-cooler	Walk-in	1,180	67%

Figure 14.1

◨ Keep the doors shut except when access is needed.
◨ Maintain optimal temperature settings:[2]

Offices and for non-commercial refrigeration: 35 to 38°

Groceries—produce, flowers: 35° and above

Groceries—meats, seafood: 10 to 25°

Groceries—dairy, produce, drinks, meat walk-in coolers: 15 to 25°

Groceries—dairy walk-in coolers: 25 to 35°

Groceries—frozen foods: −25 to −15°

Groceries—ice cream, frozen bakery: −35 to −25°

Beverage display cases: 35°

▶ Load units to allow free internal air circulation.

▶ If running more than one partially loaded refrigerator or freezer, consolidate their contents and turn off the unneeded unit.

▶ Determine whether it is possible to switch off the door heater without encountering frost build-up.

▶ Ensure proper airflow to the fan and condenser unit by providing adequate clearance around the refrigerator (typically 1 inch along the sides; 4 inches at the back, open top; or consistent with manufacturer's specifications).

▶ Periodically clean the cooling coils (at least once annually).

▶ Periodically check the integrity of door seals. (If a "trapped" piece of copy paper can be easily pulled out from a closed door, then replace the door seal.)

▶ Periodically inspect and, as needed, recharge refrigerant levels.

▶ Reduce defrost cycling time to the minimum necessary to keep frost from forming on the coils. (This is particularly appropriate for units in low-humidity climate zones and low-humidity seasons.)

▶ Use low-heat lamps to reduce the amount of cooling needed to compensate for the heat output of the lamp.

Small Refrigerators

In addition to the general measures just described, consider these energy-saving actions for refrigerators used in break rooms and organization kitchens:

▶ Maintain temperatures between 38 and 42 degrees Fahrenheit, with the freezer 0–5 degrees Fahrenheit.

▶ Defrost when the ice exceeds one-quarter inch.

▶ Size the refrigerator to the expected need.

▶ Locate the refrigerator away from heat sources.

▶ When purchasing a refrigerator look for ENERGY STAR logos and evaluate performance based on the ENERGY GUIDE label. ENERGY STAR refrigerators larger than 7.75 cubic feet are 15 percent more efficient than the federal standard.

Side-by-side refrigerator-freezer configurations, automatic ice making, and automatic defrost features add to energy consumption.

For low-temperature applications, look for units with an Energy Efficiency Ratio of 5–6. For medium temperature, 7–9.[3]

Display Case Refrigeration

Display case refrigeration units are typically found in groceries and convenience stores. The following actions can enhance the energy performance of display case units:

▶ Balance the energy efficiency of different case styles (glass-door reach in, open multi-deck, coffin/open-tub freezers, open seafood/deli display) to the type of use and temperature requirements that are needed.

▶ Specify glass display doors to reduce open-door searching.

- Use strip curtains in open (non-coffin) cases.
- Use night curtains to contain coolth when the store isn't open.
- Use a humidistat rather than a timed control to turn on and off the anti-sweat heater in display cases.
- Reduce defrost cycling time to the minimum necessary to keep frost from forming on the coils—usually no more than 15 minutes at a time, 4 times a day.[4]
- Consider energy-efficient evaporator fan motor (payback: .5–3 years)
  Consider energy-efficient compressors (payback: .5–5 years)
  Consider high-efficiency fan blades (payback: 0.5–3 years)
  Consider floating head pressure systems that allow compressors to work less when outside temperatures are cool (payback: 0.3–3 years)
  Consider other high-efficiency enhancements, such as electronic ballasts, non-electric anti-sweat components, and mechanical subcooling.[5]

Walk-In Refrigeration

Walk-in units are used in florists, cold-warehouses, groceries, commercial kitchens, restaurants, liquor stores, and institutions such as schools and hospitals. Storage-only walk-in freezers use an estimated 15,555 kwh/year; walk-in coolers used in merchandising (i.e. convenience stores) use 42,306 kwh/year.[6] The following actions can improve the energy performance of walk-in refrigeration units:

- Maintain low temperature differential between walk-in units and the working area.
- Ensure proper insulation levels around the enclosure.
- Use split systems (with the condensing unit remote from the walk-in) so that exhaust heat isn't added to the area adjacent to the walk-in.
- Use strip curtains and/or automatic door closers.

Chapter 15

Office Equipment

Common office equipment includes desktop and notebook computers, monitors and input devices, printers, scanners, copy machines, fax machines, multi-function devices, telephones, mobile phones, pagers, calculators, and personal digital assistants (PDAs). There are also "legacy" electronics, such as electric typewriters, microfiche readers, and adding machines, as well as clocks, time clocks, radios, televisions, personal fans and heaters, and water coolers.

Larger commercial establishments may have more intensive energy consuming equipment, such as printing stations, central computers, and servers. Figure 15.1 describes the operational energy profiles of the most common types of office equipment.

The energy profiles of office equipment include not only the energy consumed while operational, but also the energy involved in the manufacture, assembly, distribution, and disposal of the machines. Because the equipment are so reliant on plastics and metals, they have a large footprint: Manufacturing energy is typically several times greater than the energy consumed in operation alone.

Sample Power Consumption Rates and Annual Energy Use for Select Office Equipment					
Equipment		Power Consumption Rate (watts)		Annual Energy Use (kWh)	
		Operating	Sleep	Power management*	24/7
Computer	Desktop	55	4	27.6	481.8
	Notebook	20	2	10.8	175.2
Monitor	15-inch	75	4	49.8	657
Laser printer		350	20	102	3,066
Fax machine		300	10	145.6	2,628
Copier	Small	300	20	92	2,628
	Large	1,400	40	888	12,264

*Assuming five-workday weeks, power-management mode for computer assumes operating 2 hours/workday, sleeping 7 hours/workday, off remainder; for monitor operating 3 hours/workday, sleeping 6, off remainder; for printer and small copiers assumes operating 1 hours/workday, sleeping 8 hours workday, off remainder; for large copier assumes operating 3 hours workday, sleeping 6, off remainder; for fax machine assumes on 1 hour/workday, sleep remainder.

Figure 15.1

There is increasing interest in "green technology" or "low carbon information technology" that reduces the ecological impacts of office equipment. In addition to saving energy used to operate office machines, green IT reduces the amount of cooling energy used to compensate for the waste heat emitted from equipment. Other benefits include reducing peak demand charges and enhancing data security.

There is considerable variation in the eco-friendliness of computers themselves: Greenpeace regularly evaluates 18 manufacturers on the basis of materials use, energy consumption, and recycling programs. Their *Guide to Greener Electronics* is a valuable resource. Chapters 25 (Resources) and 26 (Paper) of this guide address non-energy aspects of office equipment.

Note that even when in "off mode" computers draw a small amount of energy. Only disconnecting the equipment from the power source, either by unplugging the machine or turning off the power strip/surge protector, eliminates "phantom load."

Computers

In general notebook computers are more energy-efficient than desktops. They are smaller and offer energy-saving features to increase the time the machine can run on battery power. Power-management turns off the computer monitor and idles the hard drive after a preset period of non-use. Power-management settings also allow computers to turn themselves on at a preset time so that the machine is available for use as workers arrive at their desk.

Power management features have been increasingly incorporated into desktop computers, so that virtually all new computers are shipped with that feature installed and enabled. The result has been substantial gains in the energy performance of desktops.

The following can increase the energy efficiency of computers:

☒ Enable power-management system settings in individual computers. If an older system does not have the software installed, then purchase, install, and enable power management utility software.
There are a variety of free and low-cost software tools to activate sleep settings across the network of an organization.

> When installing or enabling power-management software, test legacy hardware and software to be certain they are compatible with sleep mode. It's also crucial that automatic software update capabilities continue to function.

☒ Use sleep mode rather than screen saver mode. Screen savers reduce the possibility of pixel burnout on a monitor and provide entertainment value; however, screen savers continue to draw energy from the computer.

☒ Shut down the computer when not being used. A rule of thumb is that the start-up surge in power uses less energy than a computer left on more than three minutes.

☒ When replacing computers, select ENERGY STAR–qualified machines. (See the link to ENERGY STAR profiles in the Resources.)

ENERGY STAR desktop computers draw less than 95 watts during idle state, less than 4 watts of power in sleep mode, and less than 2 watts when in off mode. Some desktop computers draw less than 45 watts while idle.

ENERGY STAR–qualified notebooks draw less than 22 watts during idle state, less than 1.7 watts of power in sleep mode, and less than 1 watt when in off mode.

ENERGY STAR–qualified workstations have maximum power draws calculated as

$$P \leq 0.35 \times (Pmax + (HD \times 5))$$

where Pmax is the maximum power drawn by the system and HD is the number of installed hard drives in the system.

▣ For telecommuters, road warriors, and other workers who use both notebook and desktop computers, consider using only a notebook. Alternatively, if a larger screen is desired at the office, the notebook can be connected to a larger display monitor (and input devices). This avoids the energy consumption associated with the manufacture of a second computer.

▣ Running applications increases memory usage and processing time. Reducing the installed features of applications to a minimum (by performing custom installs) increases efficiency.

Installing only those capabilities of an application that will be used reduces memory usage and improves processing time.

Monitors

The size and type of monitor have the greatest impact on the energy efficiency of desktop computers. (Liquid crystal display (LCD) screens use one third to half as much energy as older cathode ray tube (CRT). Other actions for reducing monitor energy use are:

▣ Enable power-saving features that put the monitor into sleep mode after being idle. The shorter the duration of time before the monitor defaults into sleep mode, the more energy will be saved.

Screen savers are not effective in saving energy.

▣ When replacing monitors, select ENERGY STAR–qualified machines. These monitors use less than 2 watts of power while in sleep mode, and less than 1 watt in off mode.

Copiers, Printers, Fax Machines, Scanners, and Multi-Function Devices

Copiers, printers, scanners, and multi-function devices also are large energy users. Similar to copiers, ENERGY STAR–qualified imaging equipment is 25 percent more efficient than machines that do not achieve the specification criteria. The following actions can improve the energy performance of these types of equipment:

- ☒ Enable power-saving features that put the device into sleep mode after being idle. The shorter the duration of time before the device defaults into sleep mode, the more energy will be saved.
- ☒ When replacing devices, select ENERGY STAR–qualified equipment whose capacity matches the expected printing output.
- ☒ Smaller offices and enterprises with low demands may wish to consider multifunction machines that require less (embodied and operational) energy than the total of the individual machines it replaces.
- ☒ Print copies in batches, so that the amount of time the printer is in high-powered mode is minimized.
- ☒ Create a network of shared printers that allow individual printers to be turned off or retired.

Data Centers

Data centers are industrial-scale computer and telecommunications facilities that house computers, data storage devices, data communications, backup power, and environmental controls (space cooling and fire suppression). These facilities range in scale from single rooms to one or more floors, to entire buildings. In 2006 data centers consumed 1.5 percent of all electricity in the United States, and this energy use is growing at a rate of 12 percent a year.[1]

The principal energy load of a data center is space conditioning—not the energy used to run the computer or telecommunications equipment. Temperature and humidity control are crucial to the proper functioning of computer equipment. Optimum temperatures are between 68 and 75 degrees Fahrenheit and optimum humidity between 40 and 55 percent.[2] The equipment generates heat that must be evacuated from the data center. If the humidity of the data center decreases below 40 percent, there is the potential for electrostatic discharge, which can compromise data integrity. If the humidity is too great, condensation can occur and there then is the potential for corrosion. (In reality hot surfaces of data equipment in the data center environment do not allow condensation to occur.[3])

The following concepts help guide the design and operation of an energy-efficient data center:

- ☒ Monitor the data center environment, particularly equipment air intake temperatures.
- ☒ Conduct system review using the Department of Energy's *DC Pro* software, which identifies energy efficiency improvement measure options.
- ☒ Evaluate individual components, racks, and the system as a whole.
- ☒ Turn off or consolidate under-capacity or non-operating servers.
- ☒ Replace older, energy-intensive servers with newer servers whose performance meet or exceed ENERGY STAR specifications (scheduled for release at the time this guide goes to print).
- ☒ Match power supplies to the load of equipment that is being supplied.
- ☒ Evaluate use of high-efficiency (80-plus percent) power supplies that offer better performance at lower server utilization rates.

▶ Design and operate the center to meet equipment operating environment requirements, specified by the manufacturer.

▶ Configure the data center so that cooling air inflows are deposited directly onto server racks in "cold aisles." The cooling air should be drawn into the fans of the equipment with warmed air evacuated into "warm aisles" where it is pulled out of the data center.

▶ Consider overhead (conditioning) system location, which provides for better temperature control at rack inlets, compared to underfloor configurations.

▶ Consider an economizer option that draws in outside air when temperature conditions are favorable.

▶ Ensure HVAC system is functioning as necessary, including provision for clean intake air.

▶ Consider temperature-controlled variable airflow server fans.

▶ Except in high-humidity climates (where pre-conditioning outdoor air may be necessary) consider eliminating upper humidity limit controls.[4]

Consider adiabatic humidifiers (ultrasonic or direct evaporative cooler).[5]

▶ Ensure incandescent lamps are changed out to reduce heat output into the data center.

▶ Evaluate the feasibility of heat recovery for use outside the data center environment.

On the Web

Organizations also can reduce the amount of energy associated with the use of the Internet and reduce the amount of fossil fuels consumed by their Website. Consider the following:

▶ Consider the energy impacts of Website design choices. Flash animations, music, and high-resolution graphics increase the amount of energy used to experience a site. High load time is an indicator of energy consumption.

▶ Consider being hosted by "green" Internet Service Providers (ISPs), whose equipment is powered by renewable energy resources or that purchase offsets to compensate for the electricity of the servers that is produced from fossil fuels.

Green ISPs are launching frequently. Use an Internet search to locate green ISPs, price their services, and be certain to perform due diligence to evaluate their reliability and service.

Chapter 16

Miscellaneous Equipment and Appliances

This chapter addresses the performance of miscellaneous energy-consuming appliances frequently found in organizations. Dishwashers and clothes washers are addressed in Chapter 13.

The ENERGY STAR program is designed to increase the efficiency of common appliances, whereas the ENERGY GUIDE program is designed to inform consumers about the energy consumption characteristics of small and medium appliances.

Ice Machines

Ice machines, commonly used in lodging and restaurants, use about 6 kWh per 100 lbs of ice produced in the larger capacity units (approximately 1,400 lbs/day) and 10 kWh per 100 lbs of ice produced in the smaller capacity machines (approximately 100 lbs/day).[1]

Larger ice machines typically have better insulated ice compartments and more efficient compressors with large evaporators. In purchasing ice makers, look at the life cycle operating costs: The machines have relatively short lives (seven to 10 years), so the cost of energy can be an important determinant when considering more expensive, energy-efficient models. Consider the following measures:

- Ensure the ice machine is sized to meet the expected demand for ice.
- Balance the convenience of smaller ice machines in multiple locations against larger, more efficient units.
- Purchase energy-efficient models, which can offer savings of 20 percent compared to standard icemakers.
- Evaluate the cost-effectiveness of both air-cooled and water-cooled models.
- Locate the machines in cool areas, where there is good air circulation around the machine.
- If possible, locate the heat generating compressor unit away from the ice storage unit.
- Maintain tight-fitting door seals.
- Post reminders to close the ice storage door after accessing ice and to take no more ice than necessary.

Vending Machines

The majority of vending machines (and there are more than a million of them installed in the United States) are used for selling food and bottled and canned beverages. Consumption typically ranges between 2,763 kWh/year and 3,165 kWh/year.[2] Higher compressor efficiencies, and low wattage and low heat output lighting are the distinguishing features of energy-efficient vending machines. The following energy-saving measures may be considered:

- Ask vendors to supply energy-efficient vending machines that use LED or T8 lamps, efficient compressors, and timers, and incorporate tight seals.
- Enterprise-owned vending machines can install after-market smart controls, such as VendingMiser®, which limit energy except when the unit senses people or the machine temperature needs to be lowered.
- Site machines in cool locations and provide sufficient airflow around the unit.

A thorough description of energy-efficient refrigeration technologies that apply to the different equipment described in this chapter is presented in *Energy Savings Potential for Commercial Refrigeration Equipment: Final Report.* (See the Resources.)

Water Coolers

Water coolers typically are gravity-fed devices that offer chilled or heated water. Consider the following to reduce their energy consumption:

- Place the unit on a timer so that cold and hot water temperatures are not maintained during nights and weekends when there is no demand.
- Replace older units with an energy-efficient unit that uses approximately 55 percent of the energy of an older water cooler.

Clothes Dryers

Clothes dryers are energy-intensive appliances that deserve attention to reduce their energy use. Consider the following measures:

- Evaluate gas-powered dryers, which are more energy-efficient than electric models.
- Clean lint traps after each load.
- Minimize bends in the dryer vent line. Clean dryer venting lines at least annually.
- Use the moisture sensor control instead of timed-dry settings.
- Dry loads in sequence to take advantage of the heat built up in the drum of the dryer.
- Consider heat recovery.

Cooking Equipment

Commercial kitchens offer special challenges because modifications to more energy-efficient cooking techniques and styles may not be gladly received. The heavy-energy-using equipment (broilers, hot top ranges, steamers, pasta cookers, conveyor ovens, and combination ovens) should be the focus of energy conserving attention. Estimates of energy-saving potential for energy-efficient cooking appliances versus standard equipment are illustrated in Figure 16.1.

Some of the areas that can be examined include:

Energy Savings With Efficient Cooking Equipment[3]	
Technology	Energy Savings Potential
Broiler	19%
Fryer	31%
Griddle	5%
Hot food holding cabinet	43%
Combination oven	39%
Steamer	73%
Toaster	87%

Figure 16.1

⊠ Encourage use of microwaves and gas stoves as alternatives to electric resistance cooking; encourage ovens instead of rotisseries; griddles instead of broilers; convection setting instead of bake.

⊠ Ensure the size of the cooking appliances isn't excessive for the demand.

⊠ Purchase energy-efficient models of fryers, broilers, soup kettles, and other appliances.

⊠ Use appliances with multiple compartments or systems that provide for using only the portion of the appliance or system needed. Reduce infrared warming lights, reduce cooking areas of broilers, and reduce use of steamer compartments.

⊠ Turn off exhaust vents when not needed and at night.

⊠ Consider demand control exhaust hoods, which use two-thirds the energy of a standard exhaust hood.[4]

⊠ Cook in large batches when practical.

⊠ Regularly inspect, repair, and maintain cooking appliances.

⊠ Periodically recalibrate thermostats and controls.

⊠ Dial in minimum settings needed to achieve the result required.

⊠ Adjust burners and pilot lights if the flame appears yellow.

⊠ Consider "connectionless" steamers as opposed to boiler-based steam systems.

⊠ Contain heat with lids.

⊠ Consider induction technology ranges.

⊠ Cut idle and standby times for fryers, steamers, conveyor ovens, combination ovens, griddles, pasta cookers, and other appliances.

Chapter 17

Steam and Process Heating

This chapter provides an overview of energy-conserving actions for reducing energy consumption related to steam and process heating. Specific improvements appropriate to a particular facility should be evaluated in the context of the industrial processes that the steam and process heat serves.

Steam used for space heating also is addressed in Chapter 12.

Steam

More than 45 percent of the fuel burned by industry is used to make steam. A typical facility can increase the performance of steam systems by making improvements to the steam generation and distribution components, and by recovering heat from the steam once it has been used in the industrial process.

Steam Generation

Consider the following actions to increase the efficiency of steam generation:

☒ Minimize excess air during combustion so that generated heat is transferred to the steam and not lost as heated air up the stack.

☒ Maintain clean boiler heat transfer surfaces.

☒ Use feedwater economizers and/or combustion air preheaters to recover heat from exhausted gases.

☒ Maintain high water quality to minimize boiler blowdown caused by total dissolved solids in the boiler water.

☒ Recover energy from boiler blowdown.

☒ Add or restore boiler refractory.

☒ Optimize de-aerator venting rate to eliminate excessive venting of steam.

☒ Consider high-pressure boilers with a turbine generator.

☒ Consider steam turbine drives for powering rotating equipment.

Steam Distribution

The following measures can be considered:

☒ Repair leaks to steam lines.

☒ Minimize vented steam.

☒ Ensure that insulation is installed and maintained on steam lines, fittings, and vessels to reduce heat losses.

☒ Maintain steam traps so live steam does not enter the condensate system.

▣   Ensure steam does not enter distribution lines to locations where it is not used.

▣   Use backpressure turbines instead of pressure-reducing valves.

Steam Recovery

The useful energy in steam can be recovered by considering the following:

▣   Insulate condensate return lines.

▣   Optimize condensate recovery to reduce the amount of makeup water needed and to increase the temperature of the feedwater base.

▣   Use high-pressure condensate to make low-pressure steam.

▣   Use steam jet ejectors or thermocompressors to reduce venting of low-pressure steam.

▣   Use vapor recompression to recover low-pressure waste steam.

▣   Use a vent condenser to recover flash steam energy.

The best practices listed here are described in greater detail in *Improving Steam System Performance: A Sourcebook for Industry.* (See the Bibliography.) DOE also provides a set of resources to assist in the identification of steam system performance options; these tools include profiling templates assessment tools for generation, distribution, and recovery operations, and insulation appraisal software.

Process Heating

Process heating refers to different systems that generate heat required for an industrial process. Process heating types include:

▶   Fuel-based process heating, which uses natural gas, biomass, or liquid fuels for direct or indirect heating in furnaces, kilns, and melters.

▶   Electric-based process heating uses electric currents or electromagnetic fields to heat materials, such as electric arc furnaces.

▶   Steam-based process heating.

Some industrial processes are hybrid, which use a combination of the process heating methods.

Process heating is a significant component of the energy use profiles in metals, stone, glass, ceramics, pulp and paper, plastics, rubber, chemicals, and agriculture and food processing industries. Businesses in these industries typically operate at scales outside the small to medium-sized enterprise that is the focus of this guide, although some may incorporate fuel-based process heating systems.

Energy-efficiency improvement opportunities are related to the functioning of the heat-generating system and the properties of the heated materials. Typical energy-conserving actions for fuel-based systems include:

▣   Optimizing control systems, such as air to fuel ratio controls.

▣   Using oxygen-enriched combustion air.

▣   Preheating combustion air.

▣   Improving heat transfer.

▣   Reducing heat losses.

▣   Recovering waste heat for secondary use.

▣   Avoiding the heating of low quantities of material.

Chapter 18

Industrial Equipment

Motors and Direct Drive Systems

Electric motors usually run at a constant speed. However, not all work that a motor powers requires a constant output. Adjustable speed drives can vary the energy output of the motor to match the load and increase efficiency ranging from 3 to 60 percent, depending on how the motor is used.

The following best practices reflect energy-efficient motor applications:

- ▶ Turn motors off when not in use.
- ▶ Ensure that the motor is properly sized to its intended function.
- ▶ Replace inefficient motors with energy-efficient motors, such as National Electrical Manufacturers Association NEMA Premium motors, which typically carry a 10- to 15-percent price premium.[1] Replacement is cost-effective in areas with high electricity costs, when motor maintenance and repair costs represent a significant percentage of the price of a new motor, and/or if utility rebates or incentives contribute to a favorable ROI.
- ▶ Use DOE's *MotorMaster+* and *MotorMaster+ International* software suites to conduct repair versus replacement analyses, calculate efficiency analyses, and identify and evaluate replacement options. The software also includes maintenance and reporting functions.
- ▶ Maintain the continued operation and efficiency of motors with a regular inspection, repair, and maintenance program.
- ▶ Maintain a proper operating environment for the motor by controlling dirt and corrosives, voltage irregularities, temperature extremes, and overload.
- ▶ Consider cogged belts and synchronous belts as alternatives to typical V-belts.
- ▶ Consider adjustable speed drive motors that control the rotational speed of the motor.

Variable frequency drives use external sensors to monitor conditions (for example, liquid levels, pressure, or flow) and automatically adjust rotational speeds over a wide range.

The best practices listed here are described in greater detail in Tip Sheets appended to the document *Improving Motor and Drive System Performance: A Sourcebook for Industry.* (See the Bibliography.)

Pumps

Pumps transfer liquid from one location to another by using mechanical energy to create pressure. A number of factors affect pump operations:

▶ Volume of liquid being transferred (for example, the flow rate required of process equipment receiving the liquid).

▶ Volume and flow consistency of pumped liquid (volume of liquid, required rate of flow, and timing).

▶ Characteristics of the piping system (capacity of pipes relative to volume of liquid being pumped; friction within the pipes, valves, and fittings).

▶ Distance and change of elevation in the pumping.

▶ Chemical properties of the liquid (viscosity, temperature, alkalinity).

▶ Return (closed loop) system or delivered system (open loop).

The following best practices contribute to energy-efficient pumping operations:

▣ Identify system requirements and determine the efficiency of current operations, using evaluation tools such as the *Pumping System Assessment Tool*.

▣ Match the pump size to the system needs determined by process flow. (Correct the imbalance if the system requirement and measured discharge rate and flow rate exceed 20 percent.)

▣ Trim or change pump impellers to match output to system requirements.

▣ Use adjustable speed drive pump, optimized multiple pumps, an auxiliary pump, or slower synchronous speed motor to meet flow rate variations (as opposed to throttling back valve(s) and operating a single pump).

▣ Routinely monitor pump performance by watching for indicators of energy inefficiencies: continuous pump operation to support batch processes; clogs in pumps and lines; throttle valve controlling (override used to reduce the flow rate of oversized pumps); noise in pumps and valves; high maintenance; and constant number of pumps supporting a process with changing demands.[2]

▣ Conduct routine maintenance to ensure proper packing, integrity of seals, condition, and lubrication of bearings, alignment of the motor and the pump, and overall condition including motor, pump, piping, valves, and fittings.

▣ Size piping to meet need: The larger the pipe diameter, the greater the friction and energy required to pump the liquid.

▣ Shut down unnecessary pumps.

▣ Replace standard efficiency drive motors with NEMA Premium™ motors.

▣ Consider off-peak timing of pumps to reduce demand charges (for example, replenishing stored water).

The best practices listed are described in greater detail in Tip Sheets appended to the document *Improving Pumping System Performance: A Sourcebook for Industry*. (See the Bibliography.)

Fans

Fans move air typically for space conditioning, ventilation, and process uses. (High pressure air is generated by compressors, which are addressed in the following section.) Fan systems typically are comprised of a fan, an electric motor, a drive system, ducts or piping, flow control devices, and, often, air conditioning components (filters, cooling coils, heat exchangers, and so forth).

Factors that affect pump operations include:

- Volume of air being moved.
- Consistency of pumped air (both volume of air and timing).
- Characteristics of the duct or piping system (capacity of pipes relative to volume of air being pumped; friction within the pipes, due to baffles, filters, cooling coils, heat exchangers, and other components that restrict or cause turbulent flow).
- Distance in ventilating, and the temperature and pressure differentials in inlet and outlet environments.
- Chemical properties of the air (temperature, particulate load, alkalinity).
- Return (closed loop) system or delivered system (open loop).

There are two different fan types. Axial fans resemble propellers with fan blades creating airflow along the same axis as the fans rotation. The second type of fan, a centrifugal fan, is more common in industrial applications. Centrifugal fans, which have a variety of blade designs, offer high efficiencies and adaptability to many different types of operating environments.

In order to improve the performance of a fan system it is crucial that the operator take a holistic approach—recognizing that improvements to one component of the system may compromise the overall performance of the fan. The following best practices contribute to energy-efficient fan operation:

- Conduct routine inspections and complete necessary maintenance to ensure proper functioning of fan motor; belt condition, tightness, and alignment; and bearing condition.

  Inspect ductwork and repair leaks. Clean ducts when inspection reveals deposits of friction-causing material.

  Clean contaminant build-up on fan blades. High air contaminant and high moisture content environments are particularly vulnerable to buildup. In those conditions, radial and radial-tip blades may be less susceptible to build-up.

- Change filters regularly.
- Evaluate the efficiency of the fan system using DOE's *Fan System Assessment Tool,* which calculates energy use and efficiency, and quantifies savings from potential system upgrades.
- Replace oversized fans, decrease their operating speed, install an adjustable speed drive or multiple-speed motor, or install an axial fan with controllable pitch blades.

- ◨ Evaluate control options for variable load fan conditions: fan speed controls, inlet vanes, and outlet dampers.
- ◨ If corrosive contaminants are degrading fan system components, consider components manufactured with resistant materials and coatings.
- ◨ Correct imbalances in the ductwork: Size ductwork correctly for calculated air volumes; ensure adequate distance between fan and split locations, between splits and inlets, and between splits and outlets.
- ◨ Evaluate more efficient options to flat belt drives, such as V-belts, cogged V-belts, synchronous belts, and direct drives.

   Belts should be selected to match the environmental conditions of their work environment.

Compressed Air Systems

Many businesses use compressed air for sand blasting, painting, and powering hand tools. The energy efficiency of many compressed air systems can be improved by 20–50 percent.

Factors that affect compressed air system operations include:

- ▶ Volume and demand for compressed air (both volume, duration and timing, and peak demand).
- ▶ Quality requirement of the delivered, compressed air (from low to high quality, they are: plant air used for powering air tools; instrument air for paint spraying and climate control; process air for food, pharmaceutical, and electronics applications; and breathing air).
- ▶ Characteristics of the piping system (capacity of pipes relative to volume of liquid being pumped; friction within the pipes, valves, and fittings).
- ▶ Distance between compressor and point(s) of use.
- ▶ Chemical properties of ambient air (contaminant types and amounts, moisture, and temperature).

A holistic approach to increasing the performance of a compressed air system can reduce energy consumption by 20–50 percent and result in less downtime.[3] The magnitude of the opportunity is reflected in typical system efficiencies being only 10 percent (that is, 10 percent of the input energy is delivered in the form of compressed air, most of the remaining energy is converted into heat).[4] The following best practices contribute to energy-efficient compressed air system operation:

- ◨ Conduct routine inspections and complete necessary repairs and maintenance to ensure proper operating conditions are sustained.

   Clean and lubricate prime driver and compressor unit; replace filters as needed. (See also the previous section on maintaining motors.)

   Inspect distribution lines and repair leaks.

   Clean and maintain separators, aftercoolers, and dryers.

   Ensure moisture traps are functioning properly.

Ensure point-of-use tool filters, regulators, and lubricators are functioning as designed.

☒ Ensure that compressed air systems requirements are well understood: locations, volumes, quality, and timing (load profile) requirements.

☒ Size the system to the calculated demand, considering the potential use of compressed air storage or multiple compressors to meet fluctuating demands.

☒ Evaluate the use of other ways to accomplish the tasks that compressed air is being used for, such as the use of vacuums for cleaning or the use of fans or mixers for oxygenation.

☒ Locate air receivers (compressed air storage tanks) close to high demand locations.

☒ Reduce delivery pressures to the lowest practical pressure for accomplishing the job effectively.

☒ Eliminate distribution of compressed air along lines to equipment no longer operating.

☒ Eliminate leaks in pipes, hoses, tubes, fittings, pressure regulators, open condensate traps, valves, and joints.

☒ Minimize pressure drop by selecting moisture separators, aftercoolers, dryers, and filters whose specifications are optimal for the operating conditions.

☒ Use controls suited to the complexity of the system being controlled.

☒ Ensure compressor unit and prime mover are suited to the application.

☒ Determine whether excess heat can be recovered and used for space heating, industrial drying, or another application using warmed air, or for water heating via heat exchangers.

Industry-Specific Energy Efficiency

The U.S. Department of Energy has prepared energy efficiency guides for the following industries (see the Resources):

▶ Breweries.

▶ Cement manufacturing.

▶ Corn refining.

▶ Food processing.

▶ Glass manufacturing.

▶ Motor vehicle manufacturing.

▶ Petroleum refining.

▶ Pharmaceutical manufacturing.

Chapter 19

Renewable Energy Resources

An energy-*efficient* organization ensures that it uses the least amount of energy throughout its operations. Efficiencies also may be achieved through technologies that convert energy input into multiple usable outputs, such as:

- ▶ Combined heat and power that produces electricity, space heating and cooling, and process energy.
- ▶ Microturbines (typically between 25 and 500 kW) that produce electricity and 50–80 degrees Celsius water.
- ▶ Fuel cells (see Chapter 20) that produce electricity and usable heat.

An energy-*effective* organization goes a step further by using ecologically friendly renewable resources to fuel its energy needs. Ecologically friendly energy resources and their typical end uses include:

- ▶ Solar energy for heating, pumping, or electricity generation.
- ▶ Wind energy for pumping or electricity generation.
- ▶ Biomass from sustainably managed, net (ecologically) positive sources that can be used for heating and electricity generation.
- ▶ Geothermal energy for heating and electricity generation.
- ▶ Hydropower for mechanical systems and electricity generation from rivers, and electricity generation from ocean (tidal, wave, thermal) systems.

There are two principal mechanisms for acquiring power from renewable energy sources to meet the requirements of an organization: become a producer, or become a buyer.

Produce Energy From Renewable Sources

The production of energy from renewable resources varies by resource type, the local availability of the resource, and feasibility and ballpark cost, as outlined in Figure 19.1 shown on page 144.

The National Renewable Energy Laboratory offers free, downloadable software, *HOMER,* that can be used to evaluate the suitability and economic feasibility of different renewable energy systems (as well as distributed power sources, such as generators, that run on fossil fuels).

The following process can be used to evaluate the feasibility of installing renewable energy systems into the facility of the organization:

1. Determine the minimal energy requirements (by end use) for the organization. The profile should reflect the expected energy use after all practical energy-efficiency improvement measures have been implemented. (These efficiency improvements should occur before investing in renewable energy systems.)

2. Based on resource maps, assess the general availability of individual resources for the location of the organization.[2]

3. For those resources that are determined from step 2 to be favorably available, evaluate specific feasibility for the location of the organization. Primary evaluation criteria include:

  ▷ Energy quality match between end use and energy source.

  ▷ Energy timing match between energy demand and resource availability (daily and seasonal).

  ▷ Expected scale of the individual systems. (The final system may be comprised of a single resource or multiple resources (a hybrid system) and with different hybrid options characterized by various configurations.)

  ▷ Estimate of generated energy that exceeds requirements (and, therefore, may be sold to an off-site user).

  ▷ Net capital and operating costs of the system, where the capital costs are calculated:

    Capital cost = Equipment cost – discount + installation cost – rebate
    See the Database of State Incentives for Renewables and Efficiency (DSIRE) for comprehensive information on federal and state tax incentives.
    And the operating costs are computed as:
    Operating cost = Fuel cost – Maintenance cost + energy sales
    The energy sales in this formula are a negotiated agreement between the producer and the purchaser. The federal government requires electric utilities to purchase excess generation from their customers, usually in the form of an offset against customer purchases. States are enacting different policies. (For example, in some states only investor-owned utilities are required to purchase excess generation and there are limits on the size of the generating facility that must be offset if requested by the producer [typically 2 MW]). See the Net metering requirements for different states in the DSIRE database (*www.dsireusa.org/*).

  ▷ Additional financial considerations include the value of depreciating the purchased energy system, added property value, and the increase in property taxes.

  ▷ Compatibility with regulations governing the installation and operation of the resource (consistency with zoning, building codes, and other permitting requirements).

Viability of Renewable Energy Resources for Commercial Use[1]		
Resource	Viability	Cost ($/kW)
Fuel cells	Technologies developing. Good for remote locations.	$5,500/kW
Combined heat and power	Microturbines (25–500kW) in early deployment stage. Commercial and industrial applications may be as large as 25 MW. Various fuels—including dual fuels—may be used. Electric/mechanical/heat outputs determine configuration and costs.	$700–1,200/kW
Solar	Solar viable for passive space conditioning: daylighting, summer pool heating just about everywhere. Electric generation can be scaled to serve single buildings, shared systems, or utility-scale centralized facilities. Feasibility increases at lower latitudes.*	WATER HEATING domestic $1,700–15,000 POOL HEATING $3,000–4,000 PHOTOVOLTAIC < 1 kW: $10,000–12,000/kW < 5 kW: $7,000–10,000/Kw
Wind	Wind viable on varying scales provided wind is available. Wind farms for utility scale applications. Single, towered units serve individual users, typically in non-urban settings with available land, and allowed under zoning. Microturbines being developed for unique applications, such as along building parapets and in rooftop settings.**	SMALL SYSTEM < 100 kW $3,000–5,000/kW LARGER SYSTEMS 2007 average: $1,700/kW
*Access solar resource maps at NREL's Renewable Resource Data Center (*www.nrel.gov/rredc*.) ** Access wind resource maps at NREL's Renewable Resource Data Center (*www.nrel.gov/rredc*).		

Figure 19.1

Cost considerations for renewable energy projects include:

- System planning and design costs.
- Resource availability.
- Prevailing and projected cost of energy.
- Market for "excess" energy that may be produced.
- Net metering availability.
- Permitting fees.
- Equipment cost, including sales tax.
- Installation cost.
- Rebates.
- Federal, state, and local tax credits and incentives.
- Depreciation allowance.
- Operations and maintenance.
- Insurance.
- Financing cost.
- Tax increase (property).
- Property value.

Buy Green Power

Purchasing green power is an energy-effective alternative for organizations that are unable or unwilling to produce energy from renewable sources. Green power programs, first introduced in the early 1990s, are available through more than 850 utilities in 47 states.[3] Green power sales have averaged a 43-percent growth rate since 2004.[4]

There are three types of green power: renewable energy purchased from utilities; renewable energy purchased from independent retailers; and renewable energy certificates (RECs).

Green power programs allow consumers to purchase some portion of their electricity from renewable sources. Some utilities and independent retailers are selling electricity that is completely generated from renewable resources.

Green power is usually more expensive than energy generated from conventional resources: The median premium for residential customers is 1.5¢/kWh; however, the premium is decreasing (a reflection of the declining cost of renewable energy).[5]

RECs (also known as green tags, renewable energy credits, and tradable renewable certificates) represent the "green" characteristics of renewable energy generation and are a tradable commodity sold separately from electricity. Green energy producers sell green power into the grid and are credited with one certificate for every 1 MWh of green electricity produced. RECs typically are certified in order to demonstrate that there is no double-counting (selling of the electricity *and* selling of the credit). Owners of purchased RECs can claim that they "purchased" renewable energy. The Center for Resource Solutions offers a certification program, Green-e, which awards certification to green energy producers that meet their standards.

The U.S. Department of Energy offers information on green power and the *DSIRE* database has searchable information on programs offered in individual states.

Chapter 20

Batteries and Fuel Cells

Batteries

Batteries are devices that convert chemical energy into electrical energy. There are two types of batteries: primary batteries and secondary (rechargeable) batteries.

Primary Batteries

Primary batteries commonly used in commerce include button cells; AA, AAA, and AAAA batteries; C and D batteries; 9-volt batteries; lantern batteries; and a variety of specialized batteries. The batteries usually cannot be recharged and so, once used, they typically are disposed of.

Alkaline batteries are manufactured from zinc and manganese dioxide; other primary battery types include lithium, silver oxide, zinc-air, zinc-carbon, and zinc-chloride. Batteries are shipped "charged" and, even without being used (remaining in the package or idle in the device in which they've been installed), they slowly lose their charge, a phenomenon known as self-discharge.

Secondary Batteries

Secondary batteries can be recharged by applying an electrical current that reverses the chemical processes that occur as the battery discharges. The lead acid car battery is the most familiar of the secondary batteries; however, other rechargeables include nickel-cadmium, nickel metal hydride, and lithium-ion.

In commerce secondary batteries are often found in rechargeable battery packs for tools, notebook computers, mobile phones, and other mobile electronics.

Saving Battery Energy

Energy-efficient battery use involves avoidance (it's more effective to use energy from conventional and renewable energy sources) and prolonging battery life. Consider the following:

- ☒ Use battery-powered devices only when necessary.
- ☒ Match the battery type to the application. The Battery University (*www.batteryuniversity.com*) has recommendations for battery types for a variety of commercial devices.
- ☒ Store batteries at low (but above-freezing) temperatures. Avoid high temperatures.

⊠ Buy only the number of batteries needed. For primary batteries this is especially important as, once discharged (and because of self-discharge they lose their charge even when not installed in a device), they are worthless energy sources.

⊠ Slow recharges are preferred over rapid recharging.

⊠ Recharge before the battery has lost it entire charge.

⊠ Unplug battery, computer, and mobile phone rechargers when not in use.

Optimizing Rechargeable Batteries[1]			
	Nickel-cadmium Nickel metal hydride	Lithium-ion	Lead-acid
Initial use	Distributed partially charged. Prime with 14–16 hour charge.	Avoid purchase for later use. Distributed partially charged. Charge when needed.	Distributed fully charged. Top off.
Charging frequency	Fully discharge every 1–3 months. Not necessary to fully deplete before charging. Overcycling harms NiMH.	Recharge more often; avoid frequent full discharges. Fully discharge once every 30 charges or once a month for batteries with fuel gauges.	Recharge more often; avoid frequent full discharges.
Charging level	Charge fully without interruption.	Full or partial charges acceptable.	Full or partial charges acceptable.
Chargers	Fast charge, with termination determined by other than temperature.	Charger should apply full charge. Avoid "1-hour" chargers.	Charge should fully saturate
Fastest full charge	1 hour	2–3 hours	8–14 hours
Long Storage	40% charge. Store in cool place.	40% charge. Store in cool place.	Always keep fully charged.

Figure 20.1

Figure 20.1 describes how to optimize the performance of rechargeable batteries.

Information on managing batteries at the end of their useful life is included in Chapter 25.

Fuel Cells

Fuel cells are devices that convert chemical energy into electrical energy, but, unlike closed system batteries, fuel cells require the addition of reactants, such as hydrogen, diesel, ethanol, or other alcohols. Fuel cells are able to generate more power (wattage) than batteries.

Phosphoric acid fuel cells are the most mature of the major fuel cell technologies. However, fuel cell research and development has gained momentum. Figure 20.2 presents an overview of the characteristics of four fuel cell systems.

Fuel Cell Characteristics[2]				
Descriptor	Phosphoric Acid (PAFC)	Molten Carbonate (MCFC)	Solid Oxide (SOFC)	Proton Exchange Membrane (PEMFC)
Size	120–200 kW	1kW–10 MW	250 kW–10 MW	3–250 kW
Fuel	Natural gas Landfill gas Digester gas Propane	Natural gas Landfill gas Hydrogen Fuel oil	Natural gas Hydrogen	Natural gas Hydrogen Propane Diesel
Efficiency	36–42%	45–60%	45–55%	25–40%
Features	~ 0 emissions Cogen (hot water)	~ 0 emissions Cogen (hot water, LP or HP steam)	~ 0 emissions Cogen (hot water, LP or HP steam)	~ 0 emissions Cogen (80° C water)
Installed cost	$5,500/kW			
Projected cost (uninstalled)	$1,500/kW	$1,200–1,500/kW	$1,000–1,500/kW	$1,000/kW

Figure 20.2

Fuel cells are relatively high priced on an installed kilowatt basis; however, they often are cost-effective in remote locations where they compete with the costly extension of grid-based power, or operating and maintaining fossil fuel–powered generators.

In addition to remote applications fuel cells are being developed for vehicles, aircraft, and boats; as components to micropower systems for buildings; and as storage medium for power derived from solar and wind systems.

Chapter 21

Transportation of People and Goods

Motorized vehicles—aircraft, ships, trains, trucks, vans, and automobiles—involved in the movement of people and goods consume fuel. Operational vehicles—for example, fork lifts and construction equipment—also use energy. Exhaust from all these sources, particularly those powered by diesel engines, is a major source of air pollution and greenhouse gas (GHG) emissions, and generates noise.

To evaluate options for reducing the transportation footprint of an enterprise, it's valuable to be familiar with transportation usage patterns, the efficiency of passenger and freight options, and the ecological impacts of options.

In 2006, transportation consumed 29 percent of the total energy used in the United States.[1] Nearly all of the energy was petroleum-based with the remainder from natural gas and electricity. Approximately two-thirds of the petroleum consumed in the United States is used by transportation.[2]

Figure 21.1 shows the relative distribution of vehicles in the U.S. Highway Fleet and their petroleum use. What stands out is that heavy trucks (tractor trailers) comprise less than one percent of the fleet but consumes nearly one-fifth of the petroleum.

Fuels used in transportation represented 28 percent of the total greenhouse gas (GHG) emissions.[4] Cars and light trucks accounted for nearly 95 percent of the vehicles on the road while emitting 60 percent of the GHGs of the sector; most of the emissions are attributable to diesel trucks.[5] Chapter 24 includes a discussion of GHG sources.

U.S. Vehicle Fleet and Petroleum Consumption by Vehicle Type, 2006[3]				
Vehicle type	Number of vehicles (millions)	% of total	Petroleum consumption (1000s of barrels per day)	% of total transportation sector petroleum use
Motorcycle	6.7	2.7	14	0.1
Passenger car	135.4	54.2	4,891	36.0
Light truck	105.8	42.3	3,957	29.1
Heavy truck	2.2	0.9	2,473	18.2
Bus			93	0.7
Other			2,163	15.9

Figure 21.1

Transportation in Commerce

Business is dependent upon the transportation system for:
- ▶ Commuting to work.
- ▶ Worker travel for business.

- Raw materials and finished products transport (freight).
- Finished product delivery.
- Customers traveling to businesses.

Commuting to Work

As illustrated in Figure 21.2, in 2006 three-quarters of U.S. workers commuted to work in single occupancy vehicles, 11 percent carpooled, 4 percent used public transportation, and 4 percent worked at home. The trip to and from work averaged 12.1 miles.

Worker Travel for Business

Workers traveled for their business for sales calls, meetings, and training. The median business trip is 123 miles round trip.[7] Eighty percent of long-distance business trips are by personal vehicle, and 16 percent by air.[8] Air is the mode of choice for longer distances.[9]

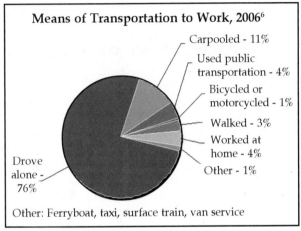

Means of Transportation to Work, 2006[6]

- Carpooled - 11%
- Used public transportation - 4%
- Bicycled or motorcycled - 1%
- Walked - 3%
- Worked at home - 4%
- Other - 1%
- Drove alone - 76%

Other: Ferryboat, taxi, surface train, van service

Figure 21.2

Means of Freight Transport by Weight, 2002[10]		
Freight Mode	2002 Ton-miles (billions)	Percentage of 2002 Ton-miles
Rail	1261.6	38.4%
Truck, for hire	959.6	29.2%
Truck, private	291.1	8.9%
Water, deep	282.6	8.6%
Water, shallow draft	211.5	6.4%
Parcel, USPS, courier	19.0	0.6%
Truck and rail	45.5	1.4%
Truck and water	32.4	1.0%
Rail and water	115.0	3.5%
Other multiple modes	13.8	0.4%
Air	5.8	0.2%
Unknown	44.2	1.3%
TOTAL	3282.1	100%

Figure 21.3

Distribution of Raw Materials and Finished Products (Freight)

The selection of freight mode is a function of how quickly the product must arrive at its destination, the volume and weight of the product, service availability, and cost. Figure 21.3 shows that two-thirds of the 2002 freight (excluding piped product) in the United States was moved by rail or by hired truck. Approximately 9 percent of the total freight was moved by businesses with their own fleet.

Delivery (and Returns) of Finished Products

Most finished products are delivered by businesses using their own vehicles or courier services, or are picked up by customers or their agents.

Customer Travel to Business

In 2001, approximately 21.1 percent of household trips were from home to businesses for shopping purposes, and 24.7 percent were for family or personal business (some of which might be considered to be customers traveling to business establishments, such as medical offices).[11]

Ecological Impact of Passenger and Freight Transportation

The ecological impacts of transportation options are derived from the transportation use data of the organization, such as vehicle miles traveled (VMT), passenger-miles, and ton-miles. Four indicators can be used to characterize ecological impact:

1. **Vehicle operational energy efficiency** is an expression of how efficiently a vehicle runs. It is a function of the size, weight, aerodynamic or hydrodynamic design, and engine type of the vehicle. It is reported in miles per gallon of fuel. The U.S. Environmental Protection Agency's expression of vehicle miles per gallon in city or highway traffic is a statement of operational energy efficiency.

2. **Vehicle energy intensity** is an expression of the efficiency of the vehicle in accomplishing its purpose. It is reported as BTUs per passenger-mile or BTUs per ton-mile.

3. **Vehicle life cycle energy cost** (see Chapter 5) is a summary of the energy inputs over the course of the entire lifetime of the vehicle. The life cycle energy cost sums the energy required to process raw materials, manufacture, deliver, operate, and decommission the vehicle. It is reported as an allocation of those total energy inputs on a per-mile basis over the expected lifetime of the vehicle.

4. **Vehicle emissions** are expressed as the amount of exhaust that is created as a function of the operation of a vehicle—and is expressed either as grams per passenger-mile, grams per freight-mile, or grams per vehicle-mile. Emission impacts also may express the amount of exhaust for different fuel types.

Passenger Vehicle Efficiency

Figure 21.4 illustrates that intercity buses and motorcycles are the most efficient vehicles, and light trucks are the least efficient from the perspective of operational energy intensity.

A caveat is that the values are based on vehicle load factors—defined as the average number of passengers transported by the vehicle—and not the capacity of the vehicle. For example, although an automobile normally can accommodate four to five passengers, the average occupancy is 1.1 persons. If one assumed a load factor of four people, the energy intensity of an automobile would equal 865 BTUs per passenger-mile.

Freight Mode Energy Efficiency

Data sources caution that it is difficult to compare the energy intensity of freight modes. Not only are there inherent difference due to locational variables (proximity to rail lines, navigable waterways, and so forth) there also are variability due to load size and weight, engines, and many other factors.

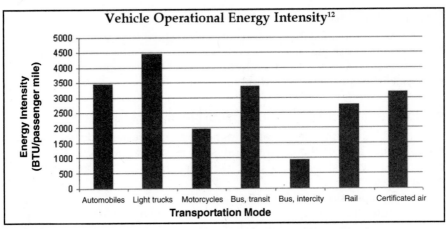

Fig 21.4

Generally, rail is the most energy-efficient freight mode, using 337 BTUs per ton-mile.[13] Barge and shallow draft vessels are the next most efficient, using 514 BTUs/ton-mile. The least energy-efficient freight mode is the heavy-duty truck, which consumes 3,357 BTUs/ton-mile.[14]

In some cases, multi-modal options (more than six percent of 2002 shipments by weight) are the most energy-efficient.

Vehicle Emissions

Figure 21.5 presents emissions data compiled from U.S. EPA modeling. Motorcycles have a favorable operational energy intensity, but their emissions profile is

Select Operational Emissions by Vehicle Type and Conventional Fuels[15]				
		Emissions (grams per vehicle-mile)		
Vehicle	Fuel	Hydrocarbons	Carbon Monoxide	Nitrogen Oxides
Motorcycles	Gasoline	2.29	14.59	1.25
	Reformulated gas****	2.03	12.56	1.25
Passenger cars*	Gasoline	1.04	10.28	0.73
	Reformulated gas****	0.85	9.29	0.72
	Diesel	0.36	1.21	0.85
Trucks and minivans**	Gasoline	1.31	13.52	1.02
	Reformulated gas****	1.09	12.03	1.01
	Diesel	0.63	1.06	1.09
Heavy duty trucks***	Gasoline	1.54	13.55	3.33
	Reformulated gas****	1.23	11.25	3.39
	Diesel	0.48	2.66	9.60
Notes: *Lighter than 6,000 pounds.				
**Pickups and minivans up to 8,500 pounds.				
***More than 8,500 pounds.				
****Assumed 100-percent reformulated gas, which contains oxygenating additives—either ethanol or MBTE.				

Figure 21.5

poor. It is important to note that diesel exhaust contains several components that are public health concerns: nitrogen oxides, fine particulate matter and toxics (including more than 40 chemicals "listed by California and the U.S. EPA as toxic air contaminants, probable human carcinogens, known human carcinogens, reproductive toxicants or endocrine disrupters"[16]).

Approximately 70 percent of the freight vehicle emissions are associated with the operational stage of the life cycle.[17] Figure 21.6 compares emissions data for three freight modes. Rail emissions are the least polluting freight transport mode, with 50–94 percent less emissions than heavy trucks. Air freight is the most polluting mode (with the exception of CO emissions).

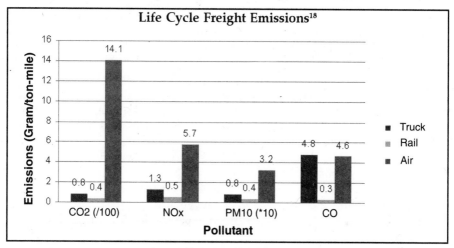

Figure 21.6

Marine freight calculations indicate the following for ocean vessels: 0.0003 kilograms of NOx emissions per ton-mile; 0.00003 kilograms of PM emissions per ton-mile; 0.00001 kilograms of HC emissions per ton-mile; and 0.00003 kilograms of CO emissions per ton-mile.[19] Calculations for inland traffic are generally somewhat lower. (Caution should be exercised in comparing these data to the data presented in Figure 21.6.)

Alternative Vehicle Power Plants and Fuels

Hybrid-Electric Vehicles (HEVs) have an internal combustion engine (ICE) as well as a battery system. The ICE produces most of the power required to operate the vehicle. The battery system powers the vehicle when idling, when cruising, or when extra power is needed. The ICE engages when the batteries need recharging. HEVs, although more expensive to purchase, use less fuel, emit fewer pollutants, and are quieter than ICE vehicles.

Battery-Electric Vehicles (BEVs) have no ICE. BEVs have a limited range because they require periodic recharge from an electric source. The battery plants are heavier than HEV battery systems. BEVs are quieter and use less fuel than HEVs (no fuel if their electricity is produced from renewable sources).

Fuel cell vehicles (FCVs) combine oxygen from the air with a hydrogen-rich fuel, such as gasoline, natural gas, propane, or pure hydrogen that has been separated from water, to produce electricity and water. (See also Chapter 20 on fuel cells used for non-transportation purposes.)

Biofuels (fuels from plant sources) are an alternative to petroleum-based fuels that are produced through two principle processes:

1. Ethanols (ethyl alcohols) are produced from the fermentation of:
    ▶ Crops that have high sugar content, such as sugar cane, sugar beets, or sweet sorghum.
    ▶ Starchy plants, such as corn or maize.
    ▶ Cellulosic sources, such as switchgrass and agricultural residue (plant stalks and leaves).
2. Biodiesel fuels are produced from vegetable oils, such as oil palm, soybean, algae, or recycled cooking oils.

The Argonne National Laboratory has created a downloadable model, *GREET 2.7*, which allows the user to manipulate data inputs to calculate energy use and emissions for select passenger vehicle types. The Laboratory is in the process of expanding the model to apply to other vehicles. *GREET* sums the life cycle from three components:

1. **Fuel cycle,** the energy and emissions associated with producing and transporting the fuel to the pump.
2. **Vehicle cycle,** the energy and emissions embedded in the manufacture and maintenance of the vehicle.
3. **Operational energy** consumed by the vehicle while operating.

Alternative Passenger Vehicle Energy Use and Emissions

Figure 21.7 illustrates total energy use and emissions data for 15 vehicle fuel configurations. The best performing vehicle type is a Fuel Cell Vehicle (FCV) powered by hydrogen produced from renewable energy. The two other vehicle types that derive their power from renewable energy (the hydrogen-powered Hybrid-Electric Vehicle [HEV] and the Hydrogen-powered internal combustion energy [ICE] vehicle) also have low emissions and comparatively low energy requirements. Flex-Fuel Vehicles (FFVs) fueled by cellulosic ethanol have low emissions but a relatively high-energy requirement. The Compressed Natural Gas (CNG) vehicle and diesel-fueled HEV have low energy requirements and favorable emissions. Grid-derived hydrogen-fueled vehicles have the worst performance characteristics, followed by grid-derived hydrogen fueled HEVs.

Transportation Management Planning

Planning for transportation efficiencies begins with a transportation audit that establishes a baseline and then uses that data as the basis for goal, strategy, and action plan development.

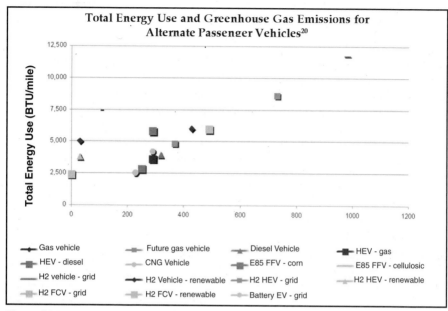

Figure 21.7

The Transportation Audit

The audit starts with a characterization of the fleet of the organization, including the number of vehicles, and fuel use. (Much of the data can be summarized from vehicle logs.)

Organizational travel patterns, transportation modes, energy efficiency, and emissions also should be assembled. (A *Transportation Audit Worksheet* for recording summarized transportation data is included in the Appendix.)

Developing Strategies for Transportation Efficiency

A review of the audit data enables setting of transportation goals. Goals should be established for VMT, reducing fossil fuel use, and reducing emissions.

Greening the transportation footprint of an organization involves four strategies:

1. Reducing the number of vehicle miles traveled.
2. Making eco-friendly mode choices.
3. Increasing the performance of vehicles.
4. Shifting to more benign vehicles (and fuels).

Potential measures for increasing transportation efficiencies are organized by category of travel.

Efficient Worker Travel

Commuting Efficiency

Consider the following for improving the energy efficiency of commuting:

- Encourage transit use by subsidizing transit passes.
- If the transit stop is outside easy walking distance, provide shuttle service.
- Encourage carpooling and vanpooling by assisting with ride matching, providing preferential parking, and/or paying for the purchase or maintenance of the vehicle. Many metropolitan areas offer ride-share matching services. (See the Resources for rideshare-matching databases.)
- Allow a compressed work week schedule, such as:
    - Four 10-hour days in a week.
    - Three 12-hour days (36-hour) week.
    - Nine nine-hour days over a two-week period (work 5, off 2, work 4, off 3).
- Have employees stagger their off days, which reduces traffic congestion and lessens parking needs.
- Allow flextime, which enables workers to alter their arrival and departure times in order to avoid peak traffic periods, match with transit schedules, or join vanpools/carpools.
- Encourage walking and bicycling to work.
- Provide secure storage for bikes, ideally on the ground floor near changing rooms and showers; or covered bike racks or outdoor bike lockers.
- Provide private changing rooms and showers, ideally. If not possible, arrange for shower facilities nearby, such as at a health club.
- Provide a tire pump, bike tools, extra tubes, and a patch kit for workers and clients.
- Reimburse bicycling workers for work-related trips at the same rate as workers who use their own vehicles.

Telecommuting

Telecommuting enables employees to work from home, and is successful when the worker normally spends a significant portion of his or her time at the computer or on the phone.

Along with saving energy, reducing emissions, and eliminating commute time, telecommuting has a number of additional benefits: improved productivity, less absenteeism, greater worker retention, and ease of attracting talent.

Policies and guidelines that address key issues make it easier to administer a successful telecommuting program include:

- Evaluating initial and ongoing suitability of telecommuting.
- Providing equipment, software, and supplies.
- Establishing expectations regarding when to work where, availability, and other factors.
- Supplying technical support.
- Ensuring adequacy of insurance.

- Monitoring legal issues, safety, and productivity.
- Training in remote-work efficiency.
- Maintaining security of confidential data.

Reduce the Need for Personal Trips

The following techniques can reduce the need for workers to leave the place of business to conduct personal errands that consume energy:

- Provide food storage, food preparation, and dining amenities. Most enterprises can offer a small kitchen with refrigerator, microwave, sink, utensils, and comfortable seating.

  Organizations can add limited cooking, dishwashing, and (preferably healthy choice) vending; or provide cafeteria services.
- Encourage workers to share rides to errand destinations and back.
- Establish a concierge service that performs routine errands, such as:
  - ▷ Automatic (electronic) deposit of paychecks.
  - ▷ Pickup and delivery of clothes washing and dry cleaning.
  - ▷ Post office.
  - ▷ Personal shopping.
  - ▷ Vehicle care, inspections, licensing, and registration.

This may be as simple as working with a single vendor who orchestrates all the "concierge" services or finding one or more vendors, such as one dry cleaner who will perform pickups and deliveries.

Meetings

There are three main alternatives for reducing the adverse impacts of off-site meetings.

Don't Meet/Don't Go/Limit Attendees

Assess whether the outcomes of a meeting can be efficiently accomplished in some other way, such as telephone or e-mail. If a physical gathering is necessary, invite only those who need to be present (others can join via conference call). Meeting minutes can be distributed to those who didn't attend.

Teleconference

Teleconferencing can be used for shareholder meetings, board meetings, management meetings, sales meetings, press conferences, promotional meetings, and training.

Follow best practices to ensure teleconferencing success:

- Start and end on schedule.
- Distribute an agenda that specifies discussion topics, who's in charge of leading each topic discussion, and duration and outcome of discussion (such as decision, approval, for information only, and so forth).
- Ensure support materials are distributed sufficiently ahead of time to enable participants to prepare.
- If needed, identify yourself before speaking.
- Speak slowly and distinctly.

▶ Avoid the speaker function of desk phones, as they compromise sound quality.

▶ Control the environment to minimize distractions and noise.

Examples of conference calling services include Adium, Digsby, Free Conference, and Genesys.

Some teleconferences require the participants to view or work from documents, presentations, and graphics in real time. Collaboration software may be useful in providing this capability.

Videoconference

Videoconferencing allows meeting participants in different locations to communicate with one another visually and audibly in real time. Videoconferencing has evolved dramatically since the technology first emerged. Even so, use of the technology may be challenging for some members of virtual teams. Cisco's report, *The Psychology of Effective Business Communications in Geographically Dispersed Teams*, offers advice on establishing videoconferencing capability.

Many of the best practices previously cited for teleconferencing also are suitable to videoconferencing.

The following vendors offer free demonstration trials of their videoconferencing technology:

▶ WebEx.

▶ Genesys.

▶ GoToMeeting

▶ MegaMeeting.

▶ LiveMeeting.

▶ Adobe Acrobat Connect Professional.

Use Efficient Travel Modes

The transportation audit outlines the travel demand of organization. If a vehicle is warranted, then its type, size, and features should match the requirements determined through an evaluation of requirements.

There are several alternatives an organization has for meeting its passenger travel needs with less of an ecological impact than a company-owned vehicle:

▶ Use efficient travel modes for individual trips: walk, bicycle, transit, intercity bus, or rail. (See Figure 21.4.)

▶ Use an *existing* passenger vehicle rather than purchasing a vehicle (which results in the consumption of energy and materials embedded in its manufacture): taxis, rental cars (especially a "green" vehicle), or worker-owned vehicle.

▶ Maintain an optimal fleet size. Not all trips need to be via organization-owned or organization-leased vehicles.

Reimburse workers for use of their own vehicles.

▶ Maintain a mix of vehicle types (sedan, van, truck) that accommodate the calculated needs for transporting workers and their accompanying materials.

▶ Size the vehicle according to need. Generally, the larger and heavier the vehicle, the more fuel it consumes.

◪ Select an energy-efficient vehicle, considering the engine type, size, and fuel. (See figures 21.4 and 21.7.)

Increase Passenger Vehicle Efficiency

The energy efficiency of a vehicle can be maximized through trip planning, proper maintenance, load reduction, and effective driving practices.

Plan Trips

Consider the following best practices in planning for energy-efficient travel:

◪ Schedule trips for when fewer vehicles are on the road, such as off-commute times.

◪ Combine trips. Sixty percent of the vehicle emissions occur during the first mile of cold operation.

◪ Avoid dirt and gravel roads.

◪ Always use the shortest, practical route. Check with *www.mapquest.com* or other resources. Alternatively, use on-board navigation systems.

◪ Check traffic reports on the Internet or radio before leaving on your trip. Accurate reports have been reported from the following Websites:

  ▷ *www.traffic.com*

  ▷ *www.accutraffic.com*

◪ Use electronic toll-paying technology.

Maintain Vehicles

Maintain vehicles for peak performance by incorporating appropriate suggestions:

◪ Keep vehicles properly tuned for top fuel efficiency: check spark plugs, oxygen sensors, hoses, and belts. (Fuel economy benefit of 4 percent.)

◪ Clean battery cable corrosion, which can cause the alternator to work harder.

◪ Check oil regularly. Change oil and oil filter as recommended by the car manufacturer, and use the grade of oil recommended by the manufacturer. (Fuel economy benefit of 1–2 percent.) Use heavier weight oils during overheated periods. Used oil can be recycled; *www.earth911.org* lists oil-recycling centers.

◪ Radial tires create less friction than standard tires. Low-rolling resistance tires are specifically designed to reduce friction without sacrificing traction.

◪ Use chains and snow tires sparingly.

◪ Under inflated tires generate more friction, wear faster, and waste fuel. For most tires, each drop of 1 psi leads to a 1.4 percent increase in its rolling resistance.[21] (Fuel economy benefit of 0.4 percent for every 1 psi of under inflation.)

◪ Check tires at least weekly—when they're cold—using an accurate air pressure gauge and adjust the pressure to match the optimal. (Optimal pressure is usually listed on a label inside the frame of the driver's door, or in the glove box or owner's manual. Do not use the manufacturer's recommendation printed on the tire; that's the "maximum permissible" pressure.)

- ▣ Inspect tires every month for tread wear and evidence that the vehicle is aligned and balanced properly.
- ▣ Garage vehicles or keep them protected from the elements to extend their lifetime.
- ▣ Use "gas-saving" devices cautiously. They may damage a car engine or increase exhaust emissions. For more information and a full list of tested products, check *www.epa.gov/otaq/consumer.htm*.

Reduce Loads, Increase Aerodynamics

Best practices for achieving energy savings through load reduction and favorable vehicle aerodynamics include the following:

- ▣ Remove non-essential weight from the vehicle. (An extra 100 lbs reduces fuel economy by 1–2 percent.)
- ▣ Place loads in the car, instead of in carriers or the roof rack, if possible. (A loaded roof rack can decrease fuel economy by 5 percent.)
- ▣ Remove a detachable roof rack or carrier if not being used.
- ▣ Remove snow and ice before driving.
- ▣ Inspect suspension and chassis to ensure proper alignment and operation of axles, springs, shock absorbers, and wheels.
- ▣ Keep windows closed at highway speeds. Open windows increase drag.
- ▣ Be mindful in the use of air conditioning (which can decrease energy efficiency by up to 12 percent[22]), heater fans, heated seats, and power windows, which place a load on the engine and reduce mileage.
- ▣ Washed and waxed vehicles offer less air resistance.
- ▣ Park in the garage or in the shade or use windshield shades. The vehicle requires less air conditioning to become comfortable.
- ▣ Open windows and vents to blow the hot air out faster before turning the air conditioner on full blast.
- ▣ Fan speed does not affect fuel economy. Initially, turn the fan on the highest setting to cool the vehicle down faster, then adjust for comfort.
- ▣ Select the "recycle inside air" feature. It recirculates the cooled inside air, rather than pulling in and cooling the hot outside air.

Fueling

Energy also can be saved through the following practices while fueling the vehicle:

- ▣ Reduce evaporation by using the correct gas cap for the vehicle.
- ▣ Keep the hose in the tank until after the all of the fuel has drained out of the nozzle and hose of the shutoff pump.
- ▣ Don't overfill the tank; fuel expands and can leak out.

Fuel-Efficient Driving Practices

Best practices for saving fuel while driving include the following:

- ▣ Don't race or idle the engine when starting. Drive off right away.

▷ Accelerate slowly and smoothly.

▷ Select lanes that offer the smoothest (least friction) ride. Avoid potholes, manholes, uneven or rough pavement, puddles, snow, and mud.

▷ Use engine gears wisely. Drive in the highest gear possible without causing the engine to labor.

▷ Stoplights are often timed to maintain traffic flow. Driving steadily at the speed limit can limit the need to accelerate then stop.

▷ Mind speed. Cars achieve about 21 percent better mileage at 55 mph than at 70 mph.

▷ Maintain even engine load, as indicated by a steady reading on the tachometer. Don't cycle between pressing and releasing the accelerator.

▷ Don't ride the brake pedal, which wastes fuel and reduces brake life.

▷ Don't ride the clutch pedal.

▷ Accelerate smoothly and avoid heavy braking, saving both fuel and wear and tear.

▷ Build up speed as you approach a hill instead of accelerating once on the slope.

▷ When appropriate, use cruise control, which saves up to 6 percent on the highway.

▷ Idling consumes 0.5–1 gallon of fuel per hour. If at a standstill for more than a minute, switch off the engine. Alternatively, idle in neutral.

▷ When safe and possible coast to stops.

▷ To help maintain traffic flow, communicate intentions: signal lane changes, motioning other motorists to proceed, and so forth.

Use Fuel-Efficient Vehicles

New technologies are enhancing the fuel economy of vehicles. In addition to the fuel-efficient vehicles described in Figure 21.7, the following are examples of advanced vehicle technologies:

▶ Continuously Variable Transmissions use belt-pulley systems instead of traditional gear sets to optimize the drive-ratio (4–8 percent improvement in fuel economy).

▶ Cylinder Deactivation shuts down half of the cylinders during light driving conditions (5–10 percent).

▶ Variable Valve Timing continually adjusts valve timing to optimize (4–8 percent).[23]

Various databases (listed in the Resources) facilitate the identification and selection of suitable vehicles.

Before replacing vehicle(s), examine the feasibility of converting an existing vehicle to a more benign fuel system.

Increase Freight Transport Efficiency

The goal of the green shipper is to understand and control the transportation footprint.

The principal strategies for achieving high freight transportation efficiencies are:

- ▶ Using ecologically friendly freight modes.
- ▶ Increasing vehicle load factors.
- ▶ Improving the technical efficiency of existing vehicles, or introducing new, more efficient replacement vehicles.
- ▶ Reducing the number and length of trips made.
- ▶ Shifting to non-oil-based fuels and lubricants.

Use Ecologically Friendly Freight Modes

Several variables come into play when selecting a freight mode: ability to accommodate weight and dimensions of freight, geographic coverage, speed of delivery, energy efficiency, cost, and ecological impact.

Rail and barge are the two most eco-friendly freight modes. However, trains only can serve areas along rail lines. Barge service is practically limited to the coasts, wide/deep rivers, and large water bodies.

Multi-modal services (for example, train and truck) can be an effective alternative for delivering freight over distances. Organizations with substantial freight movement requirements should conduct a review of their needs and options with multi-modal experts, third-party logistics providers, and freight forwarders to determine whether multi-modal options are suitable choices.

Reduce the Number and Length of Trips

Techniques for reducing the number and length of freight trips include the following:

- ▶ Restructure delivery territories using alternate carriers.
- ▶ Use computerized tracking and software technologies that allow for optimal routing of individual vehicles and the fleet.

Maintain High Load Factors

Trucks loads are constrained by two factors: weight and volume. The greater the weight of a truck, the more energy is used, the greater the emissions, the more wear and tear on roads, and the more noise. The greater the volume of a shipped product, the more space in the vehicle is required; the smaller the volume, the easier to use smaller, more efficient vehicles.

The two strategies for increasing load factors are reducing the volume and weight of the product to be shipped (see Chapter 5) and reduce the volume and weight of the crating and/or packaging used to protect the shipped product (see Chapter 6).

Eliminate deadheading, which refers to trucks having no load on a leg of their route. Load matching, which "finds" loads for trucks, can be accomplished through Internet-based load matching services, freight forwarding services, and load boards at truck stops.

Optimize Truck Routing

Freight and delivery fleets can optimize routing and loads by using routing and scheduling software that incorporate multiple variables. Affordable software for smaller organizations includes *Roadnet Anywhere*™ (from UPS) and Web-based *RouteSmith*ˢᴹ.

Work with other organizations and governmental transportation planners to address the potential for shared pickups and/or deliveries.

Use an Efficient Fleet of Vehicles

Enterprises that ship and/or deliver their own products can ensure energy- and resource-efficient trucks are used through their internal fleet management. Those that outsource product shipping and/or delivery to a freight/delivery enterprise can use procurement practices to specify that energy-efficient vehicles and driving practices are used by their selected supplier.

Increasingly manufacturers are developing truck technologies to make vehicles more energy efficient. These vehicles first incorporate aerodynamic design principals and weight reduction through materials engineering. This allows less powerful engines to be used.

Truck Aerodynamics

According to Kenworth, at truck speeds of 55–60 mph, half of the fuel is used to overcome air resistance: the remainder to move the load.[24] For every 2-percent reduction in trucks aerodynamic drag there is a 1-percent increase in fuel efficiency.[25] Principal improvements to truck aerodynamics include:

- ⊠ Cab extenders that reduce aerodynamic drag created by the gap between the tractor and trailer (~2-percent savings[26]).
- ⊠ Side skirts that reduce airflow under the trailer in crosswinds (4-percent savings).
- ⊠ Boat tails that tapering the rear of the trailer to minimize wake airflow.
- ⊠ Side mirror design with a minimal friction mirror shape and mounting support to reduce drag.[27]

Truck Ground Friction

Principal improvements for reducing truck friction include:

- ⊠ Reducing tractor and trailer weight.
- ⊠ Using radial tires, or "low rolling resistance tires" on light trucks and cargo vans. Optimize the width of the tire for the type of load being hauled. If the vehicle typically transports high-volume, low-weight loads, then smaller diameter tires can be used.
- ⊠ Using "single wide" or "wide base" tires instead of two standard wheels and tires on combination trucks. This substitution reduces lowers rolling resistance, drag, and weight by 800–1,000 pounds, providing a 4-percent to 6-percent improvement in fuel economy for a given load or increasing the cargo capacity of weight-limited trucks.[28]
- ⊠ Ensuring that tire pressures are optimized, either through frequent manual checks or through remote sensing.

Shift to Non-Oil-Based Fuels and Lubricants

Fossil fuels also can be saved through the following:

▶ B2 (and possibly B5) biodiesel fuel can be used in any diesel-fueled truck without modifying the engine.

▶ Low-viscosity lubricants, made from synthetic or mineral oil blends, are less resistant to flow than conventional petroleum-based lubricant. This reduces friction in engines, transmissions, and drive trains, providing at least a 3-percent increase in fuel economy.[29]

Use Efficient Practices

Reduce Idling

In order to maintain minimum engine temperature, battery charge, and the comfort of the cab or sleeping quarters, drivers often run truck engines when the vehicle isn't moving. Although starting ease is also cited as a reason for drivers to idle, there is no data supporting that starting is hard on the engine.[30] Idling can be improved through:

▶ Spend off hours in truck stops that offer vehicle electrification. Automatic shutdown and start-up systems governed by engine oil temperature, cab temperature or battery voltage can be installed.

▶ Use auxiliary power units (APUs), generator sets, or battery units to power heating and air conditioning, and other electricity-drawing appliances. APUs use approximately 0.2 gallon of fuel per hour, compared to 1 gallon/hour for an idling truck.[31]

▶ Use direct-fired bunk heaters and coolers.

Apply Best-Performance Practices

Operational energy energy also can be saved in the following ways:

▶ Provide fuel consumption display and monitoring devices so drivers receive real-time feedback on vehicle performance. Alternatively, monitor fuel economy manually through vehicle logs.

▶ Train drivers in fuel-efficient practices: maintaining optimal RPM for the engine; not speeding; using cruise control; convoying with minimum (safe) separation.

▶ Reward drivers for fuel-efficient performance.

Other

Additional energy-saving transportation-related actions include the following efforts:

▶ Evaluate the need to provide recharging capabilities for customers, workers, or the fleet.

▶ Support public transit improvements.

▶ Support bicycle infrastructure plans.

Chapter 22

Water

Enterprise Water Use

Most of the water consumed in the United States is used for irrigation and to cool electric generating stations. Industrial, commercial, and institutional water consumption amounts to approximately 15 percent of total U.S. water use.[1]

Figure 22.1 illustrates the variability in the overall water consumption of different categories of commercial enterprises. The variability is dependent on a number of factors: end uses, geography (temperature, rainfall), amenities, served population (number of employees, customers, students, visitors and/or patients), hours of operation, and other considerations.

Water Usage by Various Commercial Business Categories[2]					
Category	Gallons per Capita per Day	Gallons per Employee per Day	Category	Gallons per Capita per Day	Gallons per Employee per Day
Apparel and accessory stores	–	68	Laundromats	50**	–
Auto dealers and service stations	–	49	Movie theaters	5***	–
Auto repair, services, and parking	–	217	Nursing homes	–	197
Dentist offices	–	259	Restaurants	2-10****	–
Food stores		98	Retail Stores	400*****	–
Hotels	60*		Schools (day)	15-25******	–

*2-person room with private bath   ***Per patron   *****Per restroom
**Self-service, per customer   ****Per patron   ******Per pupil

Figure 22.1

Water use in restrooms, cleaning, laundry, production, irrigation, and heating and cooling is very different from business to business. Figure 22.2 shows how different commercial business types use water.

Even within a business category there can be wide variability depending on the characteristics of the different businesses. For example, a downtown hotel with minimal landscaping that caters to business conferences and meetings would use more water for kitchen uses and less for irrigation and domestic services than a suburban hotel on a landscaped property with large pools and water features.

Relative Water Use in Different Enterprises[3]					
	Heating and Cooling	Domestic	Landscaping	Laundry	Kitchen	Other
Hospitals	13%	40%	5%	10%	8%	Sterilizers: 10% X-ray machines: 6%
Hotels and motels	15%		10%	20%	25%	Guest rooms: 30% Swimming pools: <1%
Offices	28%	40%	22%		1%	9%
Schools	20%	45%	25%		10%	Swimming pools: <1%

Figure 22.2

The variability of usage patterns underscores the importance of using enterprise-specific data to create a baseline of water consumption, rather than relying on business category benchmarks. By extension, this also suggests that the opportunities for saving water are specific to the individual enterprise.

Production processes dominate water consumption in industry. Actual consumption may be proportional to production (for example, refineries), be linear (bottling plant), or experience decreased unit consumption (where economies of scale generate water use per widget produced).[4]

The remainder of this chapter describes how to develop a water management plan that is tailored to the opportunities of an individual enterprise; describes water management options to reduce water consumption for domestic, heating and cooling, cleaning, process, landscaping, and swimming pool uses; and the reuse of water.

Water Management Planning

Water management options range from behavioral changes, to modifying the way that equipment and fixtures are operated or maintained, to retrofitting or replacing equipment and fixtures. An effective water management planning process creates an Action Plan that fits the particular enterprise.

The level of detail of the water management plan should be tailored to the amount of water used and impacts by the enterprise, to a determination of the business risks, and lastly to the importance of water strategy in combination with other organizational goals and strategies.

Creating a successful water management plan follows the process outlined in Chapter 4:

- ▶ Designating the person responsible for the plan.
- ▶ Assessing water-related risks.
- ▶ Conducting a water audit.
- ▶ Determining goals, strategies, and actions.
- ▶ Implementing an Action Plan.
- ▶ Refining the Plan.

Water-Related Risks

Understanding water-related risks is important to assessing the significance of the water management efforts of the enterprise. Some risks with potential consequences to the enterprise are the following:

- Water supply cost increases that are a result of diminishing supplies from "upstream" users and/or growing demand from the suppliers' customer base.
- Changes in water availability due to variances in precipitation patterns (attributable to long-term climate change or shorter-term droughts) that reduce the supplies of water.
- Water supply disruption due to sabotage or infrastructure failure.
- Regulatory changes that mandate conservation, specify minimum performance (water efficiency) levels, or require reporting.
- Changes in water quality that result in supplies of water that are short of the purity needed by the enterprise.

The Water Audit

The water management plan starts with preparing an audit that is drawn from utility data, on-site meter data, facility and plumbing drawings, facility walkthroughs, and equipment specification data.

The water audit characterizes overall water use:

- Overall water consumption for two to three years on a monthly basis from metered data that are available from utility billing statements, the water supplier, or onsite sources. (A *Water Consumption Worksheet* is appended.)
- Process uses that include both onsite processing activities as well as a description of major water-consuming processes used in the manufacture of supplied components should be described.
- Water conservation and efficiency improvements implemented to date, including an assessment of their effectiveness.
- Water supply capacity, quality, and reliability for offsite or onsite (wells, rainwater collection) sources. This profile may include precipitation data.
- Facility description, including the location and specifications of fixtures and equipment used for domestic purposes, heating and cooling, and landscaping. Include the location of meters and submeters, and the fixtures/equipment that they measure.
- Wastewater treatment and sewer bills should be assembled and tabulated.
- The water balance, which is the sum of the water consumed by usage category, should be calculated based on metered or inferred data. Figure 22.3 presents a simplified water balance sample for a fictitious manufacturing facility. (A *Water Balance Worksheet* is appended.)
- The maintenance schedule, which should describe proactive and reactive labor and supplies used for maintaining process equipment and domestic fixtures.

▶ The total cost of water calculated as the sum of water purchased from utilities, energy costs of water pumping from wells owned or operated by the enterprise, wastewater charges, wastewater pre-treatment costs (including labor, chemical, energy, and residual disposal), energy for heating water, and onsite water treatment (such as water softening or ionization).

▶ The overall water consumption is usually expressed as cubic feet consumed, and the cost is expressed as dollars per 100 cubic feet ($/ccf), which incorporates indirect costs such as energy, chemical treatment, and labor. The water cost also can be expressed as dollars per units of produced output.

Normally the audit profiles the facility and processes of the enterprise. If water is an issue in the production of raw materials or components, or if a more detailed audit is desired, the analysis can be broadened. Assembling this secondary level of information is challenging and entails the cooperation of suppliers and vendors. Conversely, an organization that has limited water use may restrict the audit to the preparation of a water balance.

Strategies for Water Efficiency

Managing water resources relies on three general categories of action:
1. Reducing losses.
2. Reducing use.
3. Reusing water that is currently being discarded.

Water Balance Sample		
	Quantity in Gallons	% Consumption
Water purchased	14, 300,000	
Water pumped from onsite wells	810,000	
TOTAL WATER PURCHASED	*15,110,000*	
Cooling tower make-up and boiler makeup	5,953,000	39.4%
Process use	2,795,000	18.5%
Once-through cooling: air compressors and pumps	1,723,000	11.4%
Landscaping	484,000	3.2%
Kitchen	287,000	1.9%
Domestic: faucets, toilets, showers	2,327,000	15.4%
General washing, cleaning, and maintenance	468,000	3.1%
Leaks (detected)	393,000	2.6%
TOTAL WATER USED	*14,430,000*	*95.5%*
TOTAL WATER UNACCOUNTED FOR	*680,000*	*4.5%*

Figure 22.3

Examples of water efficiency actions are organized by end use. The descriptions of measures are intended to reflect general options and may not include all measures or be appropriate for all organizations.

Domestic Water Use Management Options

Some of the domestic water conservation measures are relatively inexpensive with immediate and substantial payback; others, such as replacing inefficient fixtures, will have a longer-term payback.

General

Several measures should be considered by all enterprises:

▣ Weekly inspections of fixtures should be conducted to ensure proper operation.
▣ Supply line pressure should be maintained between 40 and 60 psi or as low as practicable. A pressure-reducing valve can be installed to achieve appropriate pressure.
▣ Insulate hot water supply lines to reduce loss from users' running water waiting for the water temperature to rise.

Restrooms and Showers

Water consumption in restrooms and shower facilities is a function of user behavior and the efficiency of different types of fixtures:

Commodes (Toilets)

Commodes installed before the 1970s typically use 5–7 gallons per flush (gpf). Toilets installed after 1993 are required to meet the federal standard of 1.6 gpf (referred to as ultra low flush toilets [ULF]).

There are three common types of toilets:

▶ Gravity-fed tank toilets—like those typically found in homes—rely on siphon action from the tank to the bowl to evacuate waste into the sewer line.
▶ Flushometer (tankless) toilets release a measured amount of water from a pressurized supply pipe to force the waste into the sewer line.
▶ Pressurized tank toilets are the most efficient toilet fixture. These units use supply-line water pressure to compress air in a sealed tank within the toilet, thereby releasing greater flush water force.

The following are options to consider for saving water used in toilets:

▣ Test for leaks in all tank type toilets every six months by putting a dye-Figuret or several drops of food coloring in the tank. If after 10 minutes dye has leaked into the bowl, identify the leak source and repair.
▣ Replace deteriorated flapper valves, a common source of leaks and a relatively easy maintenance procedure.
▣ Optimize length of chain connecting the valve and flush lever so that it cannot become lodged under the flapper valve.
▣ Minimize the volume of water used in flushing, while remaining consistent with manufacturer specifications.
  ▷ Early closure devices can be installed in gravity-fed toilets, saving 0.5–2 gpf.
  ▷ Dual-flush adapters can be installed to allow the user to select the type of flush: low-volume flush for liquids and paper; higher-volume for solids and paper.
  ▷ In tank toilets adjust the ballcock position. (The black ball can be screwed in/out of the connecting rod.) Alternatively, the rod can be gently bent; however, manufacturers disdain the practice because the soft metal is easily broken.

- ▷ Install compatible water-displacement devices, such as water-filled bags or tank dams (plastic or metal sheets) that reduce the amount of water entering the tank, saving up to 1.0 gpf. Do not use bricks.
- ▷ In many cases the valve adjustment is not as effective as replacing the fixture with a more water-efficient model.
- ▷ In tankless toilets install an insert or valve-replacement device that reduces volumes by 1.0 gpf.
- ▷ Infrared motion detectors are sanitary options that eliminate double flushing, and are more easily used by individuals with disabilities.

☒ Replace inefficient toilets with water-efficient fixtures. First replace the highest use toilets. It's important that sewer pipes be of sufficient size to carry wastes flushed from ULF toilets. It may be necessary to regrade (increase the pitch of) sewer pipes with a diameter of 4 inches or larger.

- ▷ Replace 3.5 gpf toilets with ULF toilets. If payback is not economically attractive, install toilet dams and/or low-flow flapper valves.
- ▷ Install a water-efficient urinal or dual-flush toilet if only commodes are in place.
- ▷ Change out inefficient commodes with water-efficient fixtures that incorporate features such as ultra-low flush, dual flush, and infrared/motion-sensing flush activation.
- ▷ Composting toilets are a particularly efficient option, but rare in the United States because we are so uptight about poop. They require no water for evacuation of the waste, which can be recovered for fertilizer after it has decomposed. The units are sanitary and non-aromatic when properly used and maintained. Before purchasing a composting toilet ensure that local regulations allow their installation and use.

☒ Consider "if it's yellow, let it mellow; if it's brown, flush it down." (an option that isn't accepted by everybody).

Urinals

There are several types of urinals:

- ▶ Washdown or washout urinals are activated by the user or by infrared/motion sensors.
- ▶ Siphonic jet urinals use an elevated flush tank that periodically rinse the fixture without being user-activated. This makes them more sanitary than other units, but more water-intensive.
- ▶ Waterless urinals have no handles, sensors, or moving parts. Following use a liquid floats to the top of the urine (much the way that oil floats on water), preventing odors and gases from escaping into the restroom.

The federal Energy Policy Act of 1992 established maximum water usage of 1.0 gpf flush for urinals. Conserving water in urinals can be accomplished by the following actions:

☒ Install timers on siphonic jet urinals so no automated flushing occurs when the building is not occupied.

☒ Install infrared or ultrasonic sensors that control flushing.

Faucets

The federal Energy Policy Act of 1992 established maximum water usage of 2.5 gallons per minute (gpm) (at 80 pouns per square inch [psi] of water pressure) for lavatory faucets. There are several ways that existing faucets can be modified to reduce water usage. Not all faucets should be replaced/modified.

Options for increasing faucet efficiency include:

▷ Install an aerator, which adds air to the water stream, thereby reducing water flow. Aerators come in a variety of sizes: Aerators that allow 0.5–0.75 gpm are suitable for handwashing in restrooms.

▷ Install a flow restrictor into the faucet head, which reduces maximum flow to 0.5–1.5 gpm.

▷ Replace older fixtures with new faucets with lower flow volumes, or that control the length of time that water runs. (See the sidebar.)

▷ Encourage users not to open the faucet handle to its widest flow and to turn off the faucet when lathering and scrubbing.

> Metered valve faucets deliver water for a preset length of time (usually five to 20 seconds) before automatically shutting off. Self-closing faucets automatically shut off when the user releases the handle.
>
> Motion-activated faucets are activated while the user's hands are placed beneath the faucet head, usually turning off after a preset volume of water or length of time passes.

Showers

The federal Energy Policy Act of 1992 established maximum water usage of 2.5 gpm (at 80 psi of water pressure) for showerheads.

Options for saving water in showers include:

▷ Maintain the shower valves by checking frequently for leaks.

▷ Install an aerator.

▷ Install a flow restrictor.

▷ Replace older showerheads with water-efficient fixtures that reduce flows to 2.5 gpm or less.

> One drip per second translates into a loss of 36 gallons per day.

▷ Encourage users to use as little water as possible by encouraging shorter showers, turning off the water when soaping and scrubbing, and discouraging shaving in the shower.

Kitchen, Cafeterias, and Staff Rooms

Water conservation in kitchen facilities is a function of fixture efficiency and user practices.

Dishwashing

Washing dishes, cups, and glasses by hand is common to smaller enterprises. Automatic, residential-sized dishwashing machines typically are used with moderate volumes of dishes (usually no more than a couple of loads per day) or where staff allows unwashed dishes to accumulate. Restaurants, cafeterias, and institutional kitchens use commercial-scale dishwashing equipment with scrap stations, prewash stations, and high-capacity dishwashing machines.

Options for conserving water used in dishwashing include:

▶ If handwashing, use only the amount of water necessary.

▶ Use dishwashing machines (2–7 gpm), which are often more water-efficient than handwashing. Use water- and energy-efficient models (see Chapter 16) that are matched to the expected usage:

   ▷ Under counter units   60 people

   ▷ Door-type units   50–200 people

   ▷ Rack Conveyor   200 or more people

▶ Scrape plates—without rinsing—before handwashing or placing in dishwasher.

▶ Pre-soak utensils in basins rather than in running water.

▶ At prewashing stations reduce water flow to the minimum needed to dislodge food. Manual stations, which shut off when the operator lets go of the nozzle handle, are more efficient (1.8–2.5 gpm) than conventional spray units (4.5 gpm).

▶ Use automated prewashers (only requiring operator loading of the unit), which consume 3–6 gpm. These units can be retrofitted with low-flow, high-pressure spray heads or a flow-reduction valve in the supply line.

▶ Check prewashers frequently for leaks.

▶ Fit conveyor-type dishwashers with an automatic shutdown device that deactivates the rinse water when dishes are not passing through the system.

▶ Run dishwashers only when there is a full load.

▶ Recycle final rinse water to the next dishwasher load, the prewash load, or the garbage disposer.

Garbage Disposers

It's not necessary to dispose of food waste in the sewer system (and it's not recommended for onsite [septic system] disposal). Commercial disposers use approximately 4–10 gpm.

Options for conserving water used in garbage disposers include:

▶ Choose not to use a disposer.

▶ Donate extra food.

▶ Scrape food from pots, pans, and dishes before washing.

▶ Compost vegetable scraps, coffee filters and grounds, and other suitable waste.

▶ Run the disposer only as long as needed to evacuate waste into the sewer. For timed units, reduce the operating period to the minimum needed.

▶ Adjust the disposer to the manufacturer-specified minimum acceptable water flow rate. The volume can be adjusted manually or with flow regulators for commercial units.

▶ Use recycled dishwasher or prewasher water.

Ice-making machines

There are two types of stand-alone machines: ice cube makers and ice flake makers. Icemakers consume water in the ice-making process and some machines use water for cooling (air-cooled ice machines use less water, but more electricity).

There is a large variability in the amount of water individual machines need to produce ice: 20–90 gallons of water to produce 100 pounds of ice cubes; 15–20 gallons of water to produce 100 pounds of ice flakes.

Options for conserving water used in icemakers include:

▣ Select ice machines to meet the calculated quantity and quality of ice. Select water- and energy-efficient machines.

▣ Retrofit single-pass water-cooled machines either by tapping into an existing air-cooled condenser or an existing recirculating chilled water system. This typically has a quick payback.

▣ Capture and reuse cooling water rather than disposing of it down the drain.

▣ Use softened water in ice cube makers, which bleed off water during the ice-making process to remove impurities and minerals.

▣ Adjust the icemaker to dispense only the amount of ice required.

▣ Maintain the seals to the ice compartment to prevent ice melting.

▣ Remind users to take only the amount of ice needed.

Other water-conserving measures in the kitchen

▣ Thaw frozen foods in the refrigerator, rather than under running water.

▣ Reduce the flow of dipper well faucets or use an alternative (for example, single servers).

▣ Install aerators, flow restrictors, or water-saving faucets. Flow rates of 1.5–2.5 gpm are appropriate for general kitchen purposes. (The federal Energy Policy Act of 1992 established maximum water usage of 2.5 gpm [at 80 psi of water pressure] for kitchen faucets.)

▣ Use air-cooled, rather than water-cooled, frozen yogurt and soft ice cream dispensers.

Laundry

Residential-sized units may be appropriate for smaller users, such as smaller hair salons. The most common type of machine used in large laundry generators, such as hospitals, hotels, and motels, is washer-extractors that typically vary in size from 25 to 400 dry pounds of laundry per load and that consume 2.5–3.5 gallons of water per dry pound. Continuous batch-washers use 1–2 gallons per dry pound.

> A study by the Multi-housing Laundry Association determined that washing machines in apartments use an average of 11,797 gallons per year per apartment, whereas coin-operated machines located in common laundry rooms use 3,270 gallons per apartment—a 72 percent lower rate of water use.

Options for conserving water used in clothes washing machines include:

▣ Reduce the amount of washing that needs to be done.

▣ Wash only full loads.

▣ Select washing machines that match the laundry requirements of the establishment. Incorporate water- and energy-conserving considerations into purchasing decision.

▣ Consult with laundry chemical supplier to calculate optimal size of loads, appropriate quantities of chemicals, and the fewest number of rinses.

▣ Reclaim rinse water for use in wash cycles.

▣ Install coin-operated machines in common laundry rooms.

Heating and Cooling

Heating and cooling systems can be substantial users of water. When the systems are improperly sized or inadequately maintained they use water inefficiently. When water-conserving measures are implemented, they often offer the added benefit of saving energy and chemicals.

General

▷ Use automatic controls that turn off units when they are not needed.

▷ Regularly check the system and repair leaks as soon as practical.

Boiler and Steam Systems

Boilers and steam generators are used in heating, as well as cooking and processes where steam or heated water is required.

▷ Evaluate the installation of a condensate return system.

▷ Install automatic blowdown control to manage the treatment of make-up water.

Cooling Towers

Cooling towers are major water consumers, losing water mostly through bleed-off (or blowdown, which is the discharge of water that has accumulated concentrations of dissolved solids that can cause scaling and corrosion) and to a lesser extent through evaporation and drift (mist carried out of cooling tower). Thus, the water-conserving measures are designed to smooth the flow of water through the systems.

Thermal efficiency of cooling towers is dependent upon balancing water quality variables: makeup water quality, water treatment, and blowdown rate. As the "concentration ratio" (the ratio of the water quality of the blowdown water relative to the quality of the makeup water) increases, the amount of blowdown and the makeup water that is needed decreases.

A guideline for water loss to evaporation is 2.4–3.0 gpm for every 100 tons of cooling. (Towers typically are between 50 and 1,000-plus tons, where a ton of cooling capacity equals 12,000 BTUs per hour.)

The principal ways of reducing water consumption in cooling towers are evaporative cooling, ozonation, and air heat exchange.[5]

Options for reducing cooling towers water use include:

▷ Minimize bleed-off by achieving a chemical balance that inhibits scale formation, corrosion, and algae and bacteria growth.

▷ Install conductivity and flow meters on makeup and bleed-off lines to allow ongoing monitoring of flows and water quality.

▷ Bleed-off continuously or at short intervals to avoid wide conductivity fluctuations and the buildup of minerals.

▷ Reduce the motor control speed to slow the air induction fans or cycle the motor on and off in low-humidity conditions—reducing water losses to evaporation and energy for the fan motor.

▷ Adjust pH to be more acidic, which inhibits the formation of mineral deposits (scale). While effective in reducing water consumption (by up to 25 percent) this process requires proper worker handling of acids and rapid injection, and may require a chemical inhibitor to counteract the corrosive effects of the acid.

- ▷ Install sidestream filtration, especially if there is a high concentration of airborne contaminants, water cloudiness, or a system configuration susceptible to clogging.
- ▷ Treat water with ozone in order to kill viruses and bacteria. (The ozonation also may limit corrosion by oxidizing inorganics and soluble ions.)
- ▷ Identify and use high-quality (but not potable) makeup water, such as reverse osmosis reject water, water used in once-through cooling, or treated municipal wastewater; and determine other uses for blow-down water.

Single-Pass (Once-Through) Cooling Systems

In these systems, water is piped through a piece of equipment, cooling it down, and then discharged into a drain. Equipment that uses this technology includes air conditioners, CAT scanners, x-ray processors, degreasers, air compressors, welding machines, vacuum pumps, and viscosity baths. Water-saving options include:

- ▷ Modify single-pass equipment to closed-loop cooling systems that recirculate the water rather than disposing of it down the drain.
- ▷ Connect the water-cooled equipment to chilled water or cooling tower circulation system.
- ▷ Replace water-cooled equipment with air-cooled equipment.

Evaporative Coolers ("Swamp Coolers")

These systems operate on the same principle as cooling towers. Air is cooled and humidified when it passes through porous, water-moistened pads. Excess water drips through the pads and then collected for either discharge or return to the system. Evaporative coolers work best when used in low-humidity—desert—conditions. Options for saving water in evaporative coolers include:

- ▷ Ensure bleed-off is limited, typically to less than one gallon per hour for every 1,000 cubic feet of airflow.
- ▷ Modify the system to recirculate water, or capture and reuse the water for other uses.
- ▷ Inspect the recirculation pump regularly to ensure optimal operation.
- ▷ Replace worn or torn pads to optimize water flow.

Cleaning and Maintenance

Opportunities for water savings may be found in cleaning and janitorial activities, depending upon the ways in which water is currently used.

Building

Start by preventing the need for cleaning by reducing the amount of dirt that enters the building or is tracked throughout the building. Then identify alternate approaches to water-based cleaning. Water-saving measures include:

- ▷ Use floor mats and transition areas to reduce tracking of dirt and waste into or throughout the facility.
- ▷ Identify and eliminate sources of recurrent spills and leaks.
- ▷ Evaluate non-toxic cleaning methods that require little or no water.

▶ Assess whether broom-swept or vacuuming would be preferable to mopping or hosing down floors, walks, drives, and parking areas.
Broom-sweeping during rains is effective for exterior surfaces.

▶ Spot mop.

▶ Don't hose down windows.
Clean windows with squeegees and water when windows are dirty.

▶ When water is needed for sanitation (for example, in commercial kitchens and medical facilities) use high-pressure, low-volume spray systems.

▶ Use spring-loaded nozzles on all manually operated hoses.

▶ Select appropriate nozzle spray patterns (fan, cone, hollow cone, air atomizing, fine spray, and foggers) for the application.

▶ Clean tanks with spray washing and rinsing instead of draining-scrubbing-refilling tanks.

▶ Dispose of discharges from power washing or carpet cleaning properly.

Vehicles

Vehicle exteriors get soiled with oil, fuel, grease, tar, road salt and de-icing chemicals, splattered bugs, and a host of other substances. Ways to reduce water consumption in vehicle cleaning include:

▶ Minimize the quantity of water consumed in car washing by using low-volume nozzles and buckets, washrags, and a little elbow grease.

▶ Use commercial car washes that collect and reuse wash water.

▶ For enterprises with larger fleets, collect and reuse wash water with a drain, sump, and storage system.

▶ Ensure that wastewater does not enter soils and especially does not enter surface waters. (This includes not disposing of wastewater into storm drains.) Wastewater that is collected and/or can no longer be used should be disposed of properly. (Contact the sewer district to determine whether the wastewater can be discharged into the sanitary sewer and/or whether pretreatment or discharge permitting is needed.)

Production Processes

Water is often a critical resource used in manufacturing and other commercial processes. The opportunities for water efficiency can be industry-specific and beyond the scope of this guide. However, certain general practices apply to many industries and can be used as guidance in considering water-saving options:

▶ Review production processes to determine whether less water can be used. It can be useful to create a process map that illustrates production processes in detail, including all resource inputs (such as water [including the quality of the water needed], energy, labor and raw materials) and outputs (such as products, wastewater, waste heat, and waste materials).

▶ Determine the need to install flow meters and sub-meters to monitor the volumes of water used in production.

▶ Determine the feasibility of substituting equipment and processes that use less water or no water, such as ultrasonic cleaners in the place of multi-tank rinsing.

▷ Evaluate the feasibility of counter-current rinsing, spray systems, flow reduction devices, solenoid, and/or timed shut-off valves, pH and/or conductivity probes, and batch processing.

▷ Regularly inspect water lines, pumps, valves, sensors, and controls to ensure proper operation.

▷ Install pressure reducers where high water pressure is not required.

▷ Use reverse osmosis and de-ionized water only where essential.

Landscaping

Landscaping is often a significant consumer of water. Xeriscaping is an approach to landscaping that combines prudent selection, placement, and maintenance of plants in order to optimize water use. The following sections address the seven principles of xeriscaping:

Landscape Planning and Design

Planning the landscape offers tremendous opportunities in conserving water, including the following:

▷ Create water-use zones: divide into high-, moderate-, and low-water-consuming planting areas.

　▷ Restrict high-water use areas, where plantings are watered regularly, to highly visible locations.

　▷ Moderate-use plantings are watered only when they begin to show signs of moisture stress.

　▷ Low-water zones typically are not irrigated once the plantings are established.

▷ Plant sun-loving plants in the sun, and shade-loving plants in the shade.

▷ Establish shaded areas that provide cooling and reduce the amount of water needed for irrigation (and that cool the area near buildings).

▷ Plant water-loving plants in low-lying areas, near water bodies and at the bottom of slopes.

▷ Construct hardscapes (walkways, parking areas, patios) of porous material that allows rainwater to percolate into the soil, enhancing overall soil moisture content.

▷ Manage the amount of drainage exiting the site (by including ponds, wetlands, and drainage swales on the property) to enhance soil moisture during dry periods and potentially serve as a source of irrigation water.

▷ Ensure plants have room to grow. Maintain adequate separation and ensure plantings under trees do not "steal" water.

Building Optimal Soils

Fertile soils require less fertilization for healthy plants, and less fertilization reduces the need for irrigation. Instead of fertilizing, build up the quality of the soil. Ensure soil conditions allow water to penetrate. Aeration and adding soil amendments (compost, mulch, manure) can provide optimal conditions for root development and reduce watering. State extension services and agriculture departments offer soil analysis services that can help determine soil conditions and the soil amendment that is needed.

Proper Selection of Plants

Plants adapted to the conditions of the area are less prone to stress and use less water. Select native plants that are adapted to the precipitation, drainage requirements, pest tolerance, air temperature, and soil conditions of the region—and property. Retain native vegetation as much as possible.

Lawns

Lawns are water hogs, needing approximately an inch of water a week (approximately 0.57 gallons of water for every square foot of lawn each week). Lawns also demand soil amendments that can result in fertilized runoff that compromises water quality. Options for reducing water for lawns include:

- ◨ Limit the amount of grass, select drought-tolerant varieties, and/or eliminate summer watering, which results in the grass going dormant.
- ◨ Maintain grass at optimal height. Shorter grass blades reduce water demand; longer grass blades promote root development and drought tolerance. Some studies show that mowing lawns at alternating heights reduces water needs by up to 30 percent.
- ◨ Mow frequently, which allows the shorter, clipped grass to fall back onto the lawn, where it acts as water-saving mulch.
- ◨ Eliminate fertilizing of lawns or limit fertilization to the late summer and fall to reduce prolonged blade growth that increases water demand.
- ◨ Aerate lawns at least once a year to promote water penetration.
- ◨ Remove thatch (when thicker than one-quarter inch) to allow water to penetrate the soil surface.

Efficient Irrigation

Irrigation that delivers the appropriate quantity of water based on the particular needs of a plant is an effective way to maintain healthy plantings. Practices for saving irrigation used for water include:

- ◨ Create an irrigation map that shows the location of all water lines, valves, sprinklers, bubblers, and emitters. Prepare an overlay of the topography, drainage, trees, major plantings, and hydrozones.
- ◨ Replace electro-mechanical clocks with more accurate and flexible electronic controls.
- ◨ Create a watering plan that reflects the seasonal needs of plants.
- ◨ Water trees and shrubs deeply and thoroughly, using slow methods (such as soaker hoses) that allow water to penetrate into the root zone.
- ◨ Use soaker hoses for larger non-turf areas. Drip irrigation is an excellent choice to deliver the optimal volume of water to individual plants. Avoid oscillating and spray-head sprinklers that lose much of the water to evaporation.

  Avoid overspray onto sidewalks and streets, or otherwise create runoff.
- ◨ Use best practices for installing and maintaining drip systems: Size the emitter to the need of the plant, place emitters around the root zone (edge of plant canopy) to foster root growth, and cap unneeded emitters.

◙ Water plantings during the early morning—shutting off near sunup—when evaporation losses are minimal. Care may be needed with some plants to ensure that conditions do not contribute to the formation of molds or mildew.

◙ Adjust the system periodically—usually monthly—to reflect the changing needs of the plants.

◙ Consult local nurseries, the water utility, or extension service for optimal timing.

◙ Create multiple zones, which allows for the precise delivery of water.

◙ Ensure proper system pressure. A pressure reduction valve may be needed, especially if there are recurrent problems with "blown" emitters.

◙ Periodically conduct a distribution uniformity test to determine how evenly water is applied when sprinklers are used to irrigate a large area.

◙ Avoid watering when the wind exceeds 10 mph. Higher winds accelerate evaporation.

◙ Rain shutoff controls prevent scheduled watering when it is raining. Rainfall sensors and soil tensiometers also help to avoid over watering when sufficient water already is present in the soil.

Mulch

Mulch is organic matter that covers the base of plants and reduces the amount of water that is evaporated from the soil. Finer mulches retain water better than coarse materials. Be careful that a thick application of too-fine mulch does not create an impervious layer that prevents water from percolating into the soil.

Proper Maintenance

Plants require more water when they are stressed. The following considerations can help reduce the need for water:

◙ Manage pests to reduce the stressing of plants.

◙ Prune plants during the spring and fall in order to reduce stress.[6]

◙ Fertilize trees once every two to three years. Most established perennials require fertilizer every other year. Annual flowers and roses require regular fertilization throughout the growing season. Don't fertilize too much.

◙ Use fertilizers with nitrogen content as low as practical. High nitrogen content (the first of the three numbers in the fertilizer analysis) promotes leaf growth at the expense of root development. Root growth is preferred because it takes up water and nutrients from the soil.

◙ Weed and thin plantings to promote lush growth and eliminate unwanted plants competing for water.

Swimming Pools, Spas, and Water Features

Swimming pools, spas, and water features (decorative fountains) can consume large volumes of water depending on the difference in temperature between the air and water, the surface area exposed to evaporation, and humidity conditions. Actions for saving water include:

◙ Inspect and ensure absence of leaks and the proper functioning of equipment.

◙ Use a cover or blanket to reduce evaporation (up to an inch of water a week in arid climates) and reduce temperature and chemical losses.

- ☒ Remove the cover to allow rainwater to fill the pool, spa, and water features.
- ☒ Clean the filter no more than necessary (yet frequently enough to maintain healthy water conditions).
- ☒ Use water-saving filters to reduce use of up to 250 gallons of water for backflushing.
- ☒ Dispose of filter-cleaning wastewater in a sanitary system. Do not drain into surface waters or storm drains, or onto the ground.
- ☒ Plug the overflow outlet when the pool is in use.
- ☒ Turn off water features—which are prone to evaporation—when not needed, or few will enjoy them.
- ☒ Use a broom, not a hose, to clean around pools and spas.
- ☒ Discourage splashing or lower the water level of the pool/spa to keep water in.
- ☒ Install fences and landscaping that divert evaporating winds away from the pool surface.

Reusing Water

Wastewater from different uses is of varying quality and should be evaluated for reuse opportunities. Water that is reused is water that is conserved.

Water reuse may require treatment in order to attain a quality necessary for its intended purpose. Treatment methods include the following:

Low water-quality treatment methods
- ▶ Recirculation of water.
- ▶ Solid settling.
- ▶ Oil skimming.
- ▶ Filtration using bag, cartridge, disk, indexing fabric, and sand.

High water-quality treatment methods
- ▶ Ultra filtration.
- ▶ Reverse osmosis (nanofiltration).
- ▶ Carbon filtration.
- ▶ Ion exchange.

Examples of Reclaimable Water Sources		
Cleaning	Heating and Cooling	Domestic
• Washdown water • Power washing water • Car wash water	• Reusable circulating water • Blowdown water	• Water fountain excess • Dishwasher and prewasher water • Laundry rinse water • Garbage disposer water • Treated wastewater
Landscaping	Pools	Production
• Irrigation water • Precipitation	• Backwash water	• Rinse water, especially final rinse tank water • Deionized water

Figure 22.4

Figure 22.4 identifies examples of water that can be reclaimed.

Rainwater can be collected from roofs via gutters and downspouts, as well as from the storm water control system, and stored in tanks, swales, and ponds for reuse.

Chapter 23

Noise

Noise is unwanted sound. The significance of noise pollution is a function of its effect on receptors, such as:

- ▶ Noise-induced hearing impairment.
- ▶ Interference with conversation.
- ▶ Disturbance of rest and sleep.
- ▶ Physiological and mental health effects.
- ▶ Interference with activities, including performance effectiveness.

Sound Levels

Sound levels typically are measured in units known as decibels (dB) that characterize sound on a logarithmic scale and weight the level based on the variability in our ability to hear different noise frequencies. (The logarithmic scale means that for every 10 dB increase, we perceive a doubling in the sound level. The sound level weighting is expressed in dBA units.) Figure 23.1 identifies the sound levels associated with common sound conditions and sources.

Sound Levels, Noise Limits[1]			
Sound Level (dBA)	Source or Condition Environmental Noise	Sound Level (dBA)	Source or Condition Environmental Noise
140	*Hearing damage risk for short exposure* *Loudest recommended exposure with hearing protection*	70	Vacuum cleaner
		60	Normal conversation
125	Pneumatic riveter at 4 feet *Threshold of pain*	50	Light traffic High volume copier, running
120	Ambulance siren		
110	Vehicle horn (within 3 feet) Circular saw, miter saw, reciprocating saw *U.S. occupational noise limit for 30 minutes/day exposure*	40	Quiet interior
		20	Whisper
		0	Threshold of Hearing
100	Grinder, hammer drill, jig saw Chain saw *U.S. occupational noise limit for 2 hours/day exposure*	Perceptions of increases of decibel level (change in dB)	
		1	Imperceptible change
90	Drill Power lawn mower, food blender *U.S. occupational noise limit for 8 hours/day exposure*	3	Barely perceptible change
		5	Clearly noticeable change
85	Orbital sander Accelerating truck or bus at 50 feet *Threshold for ear protection*	10	About twice as loud

Figure 23.1

Enterprise-generated noise comes from a variety of sources: power equipment, vehicles, office equipment, pumps, motors, hydraulics, music, kitchen appliances, and so forth.

Federal and state occupational health agencies promulgate rules and determine acceptable levels of noise in the work environment. Additionally, many local jurisdictions have regulations that govern the generation of noise: restricting the sound levels and time at which noise may be legally generated.

Noise Reduction Program

Strategies for reducing noise are reliant upon an understanding of the regulatory framework, as well as the characteristics of the noise source (sound level, frequency, duration, and time), the physical relationship of the noise source to receptors (distance, sound reflection, and absorption), and the sensitivity of the receptors.

The first step in reducing sound levels is to identify and characterize the major sources of sound, and the location of receptors, especially sensitive receptors, such as schools or medical facilities. A physical map is useful for identifying the locations of generators and receptors, and surfaces that may alter (amplify, attenuate, or reflect) the transmission of sound.

For low sound/noise levels or for remotely sited organizations the map may be limited to the confines of the enterprise, or it may extend outside the office/building/property to illustrate sound generators and receptors.

Noise measurement may be necessary to create an accurate baseline of the sound environment. Simple monitoring may be accomplished with rented sound level equipment if the enterprise does not have its own. However, loud or complex environments or sensitive receptors may require the skills of a noise control specialist.

Based on the sound audit the enterprise may wish to reduce noise levels in sensitive areas.

Reduce Generated Noise

A sampling of suggestions for reducing noise generation include:

Substitution

- Substitute mechanical equipment with non-mechanical alternatives. For example, use rakes instead of leaf blowers.
- Substitute mechanical equipment with quieter models that accomplish the same task (use vehicle immobilizers instead of car alarms).
- Restrict times of use of equipment to be a good neighbor.

Machinery and Equipment

- Turn off equipment when not in use.
- In equipment: Reduce speeds gently between forward and reverse movements, replace metal parts with plastic parts, and maintain lubrication levels.
- Use acoustic mats, rubber washers, and rubber coasters that reduce the vibration in equipment and that isolate the equipment from floor, wall, or ceiling surfaces that conduct sound.

◨ Consider installing equipment on dedicated pads that separate the machinery from the remainder of the building.

◨ Isolate equipment to unoccupied areas.

◨ Enclose noisy equipment, installing sound-absorbing materials on the interior surfaces. Muffle ventilation and exhaust openings to and from the enclosure.

◨ Determine whether mufflers are appropriate for reducing equipment noise (such as electric motors, combustion engines, air outlets for pneumatic valves, HVAC ductwork, and air compressor intakes).

Materials Handling

◨ In handling materials use cushioning to receive hard impacts.

◨ Consider installing belt conveyors, which are usually quieter than roller conveyor systems.

◨ Determine whether pipelines and conveyor systems can operate at lower speeds.

Building and Site Modifications

◨ Install insulation in (interior) walls separating noise sources and sensitive receptors.

◨ Weatherstrip around doors leading between noise-generating areas and quieter environments.

◨ Install sound-absorbing materials and surface coverings (furniture, fabrics, acoustic tiles, carpets, plants, and so forth).

◨ Use hardscapes (for example, berms and fences) to intercept or direct noise away from sensitive receptors.

◨ Use landscaping to dampen noise. (However, the benefit is typically more psychological than real.)

Change the Perception of the Noise Environment

The sound environment can be intentionally altered in order to affect the perception of low volume sounds. Consider the following:

◨ Install aquariums, water features, and other white-noise devices that mask noises.

◨ Allow music.

Hearing Protection

The principal hearing protection devices that can be used to reduce sound levels are:

▶ Expandable foam plugs that are rolled into a thin cylinder and gently placed in the ear canal, where they expand to fill the canal.

▶ Pre-molded, reusable plugs that are made from silicone, plastic, or rubber, and come in a variety of sizes.

▶ Earmuffs completely cover the outer ear with some offering additional volume that allows extra ear protection (such as foam) to be added.

The National Institute for Occupational Safety and Health (NIOSH) offers a *Hearing Protection Device Compendium* that enables users to identify suitable hearing protection based on device type, (dB) noise reduction rating, and other specifications.

Chapter 24

Air Quality

There are four categories of air quality issues generally associated with organizations:

1. Greenhouse gas emissions.
2. Heat emissions.
3. Process emissions.
4. Indoor air quality.

Greenhouse Gas Emissions

Greenhouse gases (GHGs) are atmospheric gases that warm the surface of the Earth and the adjacent water and air layers. A layer of GHGs is essential to maintaining temperatures that support life on the planet, but excess gases reduce the amount of heat that is radiated back into space, thereby increasing the amount of heat that is trapped in the atmosphere. This greenhouse effect is similar to what one experiences when a car is parked in the sun.

There are six types of GHGs:

◘ Carbon dioxide (CO_2).
◘ Methane (CH_4).
◘ Nitrous oxide (N_2O).
◘ Ozone.
◘ Chlorofluorocarbons (CFCs).
◘ Water vapor.

These gases occur in varying concentrations and are characterized by differing warming potential. In order to facilitate evaluating the effects of multiple GHGs, each GHG is related to CO_2 by its warming potential, which results in carbon equivalents (CO_2 Eq). Figure 24.1 describes the atmospheric persistence and the global warming potential of a select group of GHGs.

Figure 24.2 shows relative contributions of GHGs by source, indicating that industry releases the greatest amount of GHGs (based on CO_2 equivalent), followed by the transportation, commercial, and residential sectors. CO_2 accounts for 80 percent of the GHG emissions (primarily from the burning of fossil fuels), except in the agriculture sector, which is dominated by N_2O emissions. In this figure, GHGs from electrical generation, which accounts for one-third of the GHGs in the United States, has been distributed to the sectors based on usage.

184

Global Warming Potential of Select GHGs[1]				
Industrial Designation or Common Name	aka	Chemical Formula	Lifetime (years)	Global warming potential (over 100 years)
Carbon dioxide		CO_2	1	1
Methane		CH_4	12	25
Nitrous oxide		N_2O	114	298
HFC-23	Trifluoromethane	CHF_3	270	14,800
HFC-32	Fluroform	CH_2F_2	4.9	675
HFC-125	Difluoromethane	CHF_2CF_3	29	3,400
HFC-134a	1,1,2,2,2-pentafluorothane	CH_2FCF_3	14	1,430
HFC-143a	1,1,2,2-tetrafluorothane	CH_3CF_3	52	4,470
HFC-152a		CH_3CHF_2	1.4	124
HFC-227ea	1,1-Difluoroethane	CF_3CHFCF_3	34.2	3,220
HFC-236fa	1,1,1,2,3,3,3-Heptafluoropropane	$CF_3CH_2CF_3$	240	9,810
HFC-43-10mee		$CF_3CHFCHFCF_2CF_3$	15.9	1,640
PFC-14	Carbon tetrafluoride Freon 14	CF_4	50,000	7,390
PFC-116		C_2F_6	10,000	12,200
PFC-3-1-10		C_4F_{10}	2,600	8,860
PFC-5-1-14		C_6F_{14}	3,200	9,300
Sulfur hexafluoride		SF_6	3,200	22,800

Figure 24.1

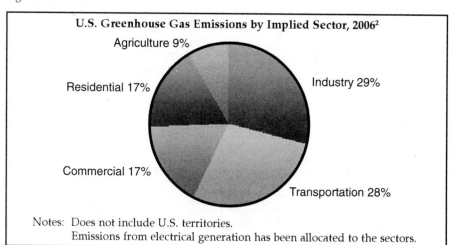

U.S. Greenhouse Gas Emissions by Implied Sector, 2006[2]

Agriculture 9%

Residential 17%

Industry 29%

Commercial 17%

Transportation 28%

Notes: Does not include U.S. territories.
Emissions from electrical generation has been allocated to the sectors.

Figure 24.2

Figure 24.3 lists detailed GHG emissions data by source for the five sectors, plus electrical generation.

U.S. Greenhouse Gas Emissions by Sector and Source[3]			
Sector/Source	GHG*	Sector/Source	GHG*
Electricity generation	2,377.8	Industry	1,371.5
CO_2 from fossil fuel combustion	2,328.2	CO_2 from fossil fuel combustion	818.6
Municipal solid waste combustion	21.3	Natural gas systems	130.9
Electrical transmission and distribution	13.2	Non-energy use of fuels	120.8
Stationary combustion	10.8	Coal mining	58.5
Limestone and dolomite use	4.3	Iron and steel production	50.1
		Cement manufacture	45.7
Transportation	1,969.5	Petroleum systems	28.7
CO_2 from fossil fuel combustion	1,856	Lime manufacture	15.8
Mobile combustion	34.1	Nitric acid production	15.6
Substitution of ozone depleting substance	69.5	HCFC-22 production	13.8
Non-energy use of fuels	9.9	Ammonia manufacture and urea consumption	12.4
Commercial	394.6	Aluminum production	6.5
CO_2 from fossil fuel combustion	210.1	Adipic acid production	5.9
Landfills	125.7	Substitution of ozone depleting substance	5.7
Wastewater treatment	23.9	Abandoned underground coal mines	5.4
Substitution of ozone depleting substance	22.4	Semiconductor manufacture	4.8
Human sewage	8.1	Stationary combustion	4.6
Composting	3.3	N_2O product uses	4.4
Stationary combustion	1.2	Limestone and dolomite use	4.3
Agriculture	533.6	Soda ash manufacture and consumption	4.2
N_2O from agricultural soil management	265	Petrochemical production	3.6
Enteric fermentation	126.2	Magnesium production and processing	3.2
Manure management	55.7	Titanium dioxide production	1.9
CO_2 from fossil fuel combustion	43.6	Carbon dioxide consumption	1.6
CH_4 and N_2O from forest fires	27	Ferroalloy production	1.5
Rice cultivation	5.9	Phosphoric acid production	1.2
Liming of agricultural soils	4.4	Mobile combustion	1
Urea fertilization	3.6	Zinc production	0.5
Field burning of agricultural residues	1.3	Lead production	0.3
Mobile combustion	0.4	Silicon carbide production and consumption	0.2
N_2O from forest soils	0.3		
Residential	344.8		
CO_2 from fossil fuel combustion	326.5		
Substitution of ozone depleting substance	12.9		
Stationary combustion	3.9		
Settlement soil fertilization	1.5		
*GHG emissions are Tg of CO_2 equivalent.			

Figure 24.3

Strategies for the reduction of GHG emissions are at the heart of this guide and are addressed throughout:

- Reduce electrical energy use   See Chapters 9–18
- Reduce industrial processing of materials See Chapters 5, 25, and 26
- Reduce packaging   See Chapter 6
- Reduce transportation requirements See Chapters 8 and 21
- Reduce space heating and water cooling See Chapters 8 and 10
- Reduce water heating   See Chapter 13
- Reduce disposal requirements See Chapter 25
- Reduce water consumption and treatment See Chapter 22

An enterprise can calculate its fuel-related GHG footprint (its carbon coefficient) by applying the following multipliers to its fuel consumption figures:

- Natural gas   0.12 lbs/cubic foot
- Fuel oil   22.29 lbs/gallon
- Electricity—coal plant generated 2.095 lbs/kWh
- Electricity—petroleum fired facility 1.969 lbs/kWh
- Electricity—natural gas fired facility 1.321 lbs/kWh
- Electricity—MSW, tires, and other fuels 1.378 lbs/kWh

Transportation-related GHG emissions can be calculated using data presented in Chapter 22.

Heat Emissions

Organizations should be aware of several categories of heat emissions:
- Heat generated from vehicle operations.
- Heat generated from processes and equipment.
- Heat generated from space conditioning equipment.
- Heat generated during the production of raw materials and products.

Heat emissions that are released are a concern because of their contribution to global warming, their potential effect on comfort, and their resultant effect on space heating and cooling. Thermal emissions can be considered as localized, remote, and/or mobile.

Localized heat emissions are those that are generated at the site of the organization. These may include heat emitted from incandescent bulbs or from equipment, such as computers; or waste heat from inefficient space conditioning that results in a portion of the usable heat "going up the stack."

Remote heat emissions occur in locations separated from the enterprise and are typically associated with electricity generation and the processing of raw materials, components, and supplies used by the organization.

Mobile source emissions are created by airplanes, trains, vehicles, and construction equipment that burn fossil fuels, dispersing air pollution into the atmosphere.

Most of the strategies to reduce heat emissions are a beneficial consequence of avoiding (electrical, virgin material, natural gas, and so forth) resource consumption; consuming materials and supplies in a more efficient manner; and reducing the amount of waste generated.

Solar radiation that is absorbed by asphalt parking surfaces becomes a "heat sink" by radiating heat energy out at a rate slower than its intake. (Site design to avoid creation of material "heat sinks" is addressed in Chapter 8.)

Process Emissions

Process emissions refer to the atmospheric releases of air contaminants that result from production processes. The complexity of production processes; their emission profiles; alternative processes and equipment; and federal, state, and local regulations precludes any rigorous analysis in the guide.

Some of the greatest concerns are nearly 200 Hazardous Air Pollutants (HAPs). HAPs are commonly used in enterprises: benzene, which is found in gasoline; perchloroethylene, which is emitted from some dry cleaning facilities; and methylene chloride, which is used as a solvent and paint stripper. Examples of other listed air toxics include dioxin, asbestos, toluene, and metals, such as cadmium, mercury, chromium, and lead compounds.[4] These chemicals are known or suspected to cause cancer or other serious health effects. The U.S. EPA has identified 175 source categories for these HAPs.[5]

In regulating these chemicals, the U.S. EPA applies its Maximum Available Control Technology (MACT). MACT requires that existing HAP sources have emission levels that meet or exceed the best-performing 12 percent of emitters their source category. For new sources, the MACT floor must equal the level of emissions control currently achieved by the best-controlled similar source.

As of August 2000, EPA had issued 45 air toxics MACT standards that affect 82 categories of major industrial sources. EPA also has issued standards to control emissions, including certain toxic pollutants, from solid waste combustion facilities.

In general, enterprises will want to consult with process engineers, regulators, and other appropriate professionals in developing production-specific approaches that avoid HAPs when possible, minimize the quantity of HAP emissions, and minimize the possibility of worker and public exposure. The eco-effective enterprise will seek to eliminate HAPs, but also other chemicals that have not been proven safe for the human and natural environments.

Indoor Air Quality

Indoor air quality refers to the characteristics of the interior air environment of a structure. Interior air quality can be an issue when the concentration of contaminants poses a threat to the health and comfort of the occupants.

Factors that affect indoor air quality include:

- ▸ The exchange of air between indoors and out.
- ▸ Concentrations of naturally occurring chemicals, such as radon.
- ▸ Concentrations of chemicals generated by occupant equipment and activities, such as cleaning products, carbon monoxide, and volatile organic compounds (VOCs).
- ▸ Microbial contaminants, such as bacteria and mold.
- ▸ Allergens, such as pollen and fragrances.

Provide for Ample Air Exchange

Indoor air quality has become more of a health issue as energy-efficiency improvement measures, particularly sealing to reduce air infiltration, reduces the air exchange between the inside and outside environments. Newer construction, especially in multi-story buildings, often has fixed windows, making it impossible for occupants to manually control their environment: Space conditioning is automated. This may result in "sick building syndrome," which describes buildings whose indoor air quality has been compromised to the extent that it poses a health risk to occupants.

Generally, an interior environment must offer its occupants an air exchange rate of the ASHRAE standard of 20 cubic feet per minute (cfm) per occupant. In the event there are releases of toxins in the space, the air exchange rate must be increased to acceptable levels.

Maintain Safe Radon Levels

Radon is an odorless, colorless gas that occurs naturally as a result of the decay of radium, which is found in rock formations. Radon can migrate into buildings through below-grade cracks and openings in the building envelope. Radon also can enter buildings through well water that releases the gas through showers, faucets, and rinse baths. Occasionally radon may be contained in stone used as building material.

Radon exposure is the second leading cause of lung cancer and the leading cause for non-smokers. Radon concentrations are site-specific, although certain geographic regions tend to have greater potential for higher radon concentrations because of the geology of the area. The U.S. EPA maintains a set of state maps of radon concentrations; however, the information is shown as the average across the entire county and, therefore, is not considered a reliable predictor of radon concentrations in a given building. Eco-friendly enterprises take steps including the following to ascertain risks associated with radon exposure:

- Test radon concentrations in buildings, either by contracting with a qualified radon inspector or by using relatively inexpensive self-assessment "radon trap" kits that are set out for several days, capped, and then mailed to independent laboratories for analysis and reporting.
- Where test results reveal concentrations in excess of acceptable levels, develop an appropriate plan for mitigating the radon problem.

The U.S. Surgeon General recommends that homeowners take remedial action at radon concentrations in excess of 4 picocuries per liter (pCi/L).

Eliminate Exposure to Unhealthy Chemicals and Odors

Commercial buildings often contain or use equipment and products that emit harmful chemicals. Commonly found office pollutants and their sources include environmental tobacco smoke; asbestos from insulating and fire-retardant building supplies; formaldehyde from pressed wood products; other organics from building materials, carpet, and other office furnishings, cleaning materials and activities, air fresheners, paints, adhesives, copying machines, and photography and print shops; biological contaminants from dirty ventilation systems or water-damaged walls, ceilings, and carpets; and pesticides from pest-management practices.

The following actions can help manage exposures to pollutants:

☒ Identify the chemicals used in the building. Evaluate their components, determine the health risk they pose, and determine whether eco-preferable substitutes are available.

☒ Where appropriate, seal plumbing chases, HVAC chases, electrical conduits, telephone and computer cable chases, compressed air lines, and other pathways for chemicals and odors.

☒ Ensure no smoking is allowed in the building.
  If there is a smoking lounge, ensure adequate exhaust (60 cubic feet per minute per smoker at maximum capacity[6]).
  If there is a designated outside smoking area, ensure that the smoke does not enter the building or require people entering or leaving the building to pass through a smoke-filled area.

☒ Use eco-friendly cleaning products. (See Chapter 8.) Ensure that cleaning staff are trained and apply best practices: proper cleaning, rinsing, and drying techniques for different surfaces and dirt; proper mixing, and disposal techniques of cleaning products; use lint-free dust cloths, and/or High Efficiency Particulate Air (HEPA) filters or high-efficiency vacuum systems that don't contribute to airborne dust.

☒ Purchase carpeting and pads certified (by the Carpet and Rug Institute) as having no or low VOC emissions.

☒ Avoid purchase of furniture made from particleboard and similar materials that have not been properly sealed and pre-ventilated.

☒ Avoid paints containing high concentrations of VOCs.
  Paint during unoccupied periods.
  Use fast drying, water-based paints rather than oil-based paints that require hazardous solvents for clean up.
  Close off areas being painted and use high volumes of exhaust air to evacuate fumes and speed drying. Continue to ventilate for some period after occupancy.

☒ Use properly designed exhaust hoods over production areas, such as painting areas, laboratory benches, and cooking stations.

☒ Consider lower-volume exhaust fans adjacent to copiers and printers, which emit both air contaminants and heat.
  Pest control starts with cleanliness. Use the proper pesticide for the pest. Avoid regular application of pesticides as a preventive measure. Ventilate for some period after occupancy.

☒ Consider air filtration systems that have HEPA filters, odor-filtering activated charcoal, and air flow rates that are capable of removing contaminants and odors.

Indoor houseplants can be an aesthetically pleasing way to increase oxygen levels and reduce pollutant concentrations. The Boston fern, Florist's mums, the Gerbera daisy, and the dwarf date palm all can help reduce formaldehyde concentrations. Areca palms, the Moth orchid, and the dwarf date palm can absorb xylene and toluene. Other beneficial plants include the bamboo palm, Chinese evergreen, English ivy, indoor dracaenas, and the snake plant.[7]

Control Mold

Moisture is a problem because it can be a breeding ground for biocontaminants, such as mold. Measures to contain moisture effects on air quality include:

▶ Eliminate standing water on the roof. Ensure there is sufficient slope to allow drainage and that drains are functional.

▶ Position air intakes away from water sources, especially cooling towers and any standing water.

▶ Fix leaks immediately. Replace any water-stained ceiling tiles; they likely can support microbial growth. Dry any wet materials immediately.

▶ Ensure that the exterior drainage system conveys rain and melted snow away from the building.

▶ If the basement leaks, install exterior waterproofing and/or proper drainage.

▶ Don't overwater plants, and clean up any spills.

▶ Monitor condensation on windows and sills, which can be a sign of leaky weatherstripping, a window with poor thermal characteristics, insufficient airflow, or high indoor humidity.

Control Allergens

The following measures should be considered for controlling allergens:

▶ Establish a fragrance-free policy.

▶ Use filters to remove allergens, fine dust particles, and other contaminants.

▶ Clean HVAC ducts.

Apply Fastidious Facilities-Maintenance Practices

Consider adopting the following maintenance practices to maintain a healthy air environment:

▶ Keep complete and accurate records on building systems, equipment specifications, and maintenance.

▶ Establish a preventive maintenance program.

▶ Periodically evaluate air intakes and outflows for proper flow volumes.

▶ Periodically measure temperature, humidity, CO, and CO_2 levels throughout the building.

▶ Be open to occupant comfort complaints and look for indicators of occupant discomfort, such as fans, heaters, air cleaners, and intentionally blocked HVAC vents.

▶ Be aware of worker health in general. Look for frequency and patterns of illnesses.

▶ Determine whether special improvements can be made for individuals with asthma or allergies.

The U.S. Environmental Protection Agency's IAQ Building Education and Assessment Model (I-BEAM) contains resources that can be used in monitoring indoor air quality.

Chapter 25

Materials and Waste Management

Our commerce system has been based on the mistaken beliefs that there is an inexhaustible supply of natural resources to fuel our economy and that when a product is no longer needed it can be discarded with little or no consequence.

Resources

Resources are the food of commerce. Our natural resources include, but are not limited to:

- Clean air.
- Clean water.
- Productive forests.
- Agricultural soils.
- Metals and minerals.
- Non-renewable energy sources: petroleum, coal, natural gas.
- Renewable energy sources: solar, wind, geothermal, hydropower.
- Aquatic and terrestrial habitat.
- Fisheries.

In 1972 the controversial book *Limits to Growth* concluded that the population explosion and the simultaneous increase in resource consumption would place a limit on the amount of economic growth that could be sustained at projected resource usage rates. Detractors argued the validity of the assumptions of the model, but in doing so missed the point: It isn't a question of *whether* many of the key resources on which commerce depends will be depleted; it is a question of *when.*

The Club of Rome, which commissioned *Limits to Growth,* also supported the preparation of the treatise *Factor Four,* which advocates doubling wealth and halving resource consumption in order to increase resource efficiency. (The book cites 50 different ways in which this can be achieved, including transport and building efficiency.) A more provocative recommendation, *Factor Ten,* proposes that developed countries slash resource efficiency tenfold in order to achieve sustainable growth.

This chapter addresses the management of common materials that are inappropriately considered waste by many organizations. Several other resources are addressed in separate chapters: paper (Chapter 26), packaging (Chapter 6), air (Chapter 24), water (Chapter 22), energy (Chapters 9–20), and transportation (Chapter 21).

Waste

In 2006 the United States generated 251 million tons of municipal solid waste (MSW), or about 1670 pounds per person.[1] Commercial and industrial establishments and institutions generated between 35 and 45 percent of all MSW.[2] Figure 25.1 profiles typical wastes from various enterprise types, revealing the differences in volumes and types of waste generated.

Commercial Waste Generation and Recycling[3]				
Enterprise Category		Daily Waste Generation Rate	Waste Types (% of generated waste by weight)	Overall Recycling Rate
Office Buildings		5.5 lbs per 1000 sq. ft.	Paper (49%) Food (17%) Plastic (12%) Cardboard (5%) Carpet (4%) Glass (2%) Metal (2%)	6.6%
Retail	Big box	21.3 lbs per employee	Cardboard (61%) Food, landscaping waste (9%) Pallets and crates (9%) Plastic (4%) Paper (6%) Metal (2%) Industrial packaging film (3%)	63.3%
	Other retail	10.1 lbs per employee	Cardboard (50%) Paper (14%) Pallets and crates (10%) Food, landscaping waste (8%) Plastic (4%) Metal (4%) Glass (3%) Industrial packaging film (3%)	53.7%
Restaurants (full-service)		17.6 lbs per employee	Food (53%) Cardboard (25%) Paper (9%) Plastic (6%) Glass (2%) Metal (2%)	31.6%
Food Stores		45.4 lbs per employee	Cardboard (57%) Food (28%) Paper (4%) Plastic (4%) Pallets and crates (4%) Glass and metal (1%)	71.3%
Note: Generated wastes don't total to 100% due to minor contributions from special wastes and mixed residues.				

Figure 25.1

Thirty-two and a half percent of the total MSW was recycled, 12.5 percent was incinerated with energy recovery (MSW burned to produce electricity [and in some cases using heat by-product for process uses]), and the remaining 55 percent was landfilled.[4]

Figure 25.2 illustrates the variability in recovery rates for different types of materials. Recycled, incinerated, and landfilled rates differ between commercial and residential sectors. Solid residues from business operations include paper and packaging, discarded electronics, various consumables, glass, aluminum cans, and landscaping waste.

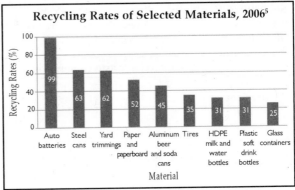

Figure 25.2

The waste of an enterprise is comprised of more than the solid wastes that are deposited in dumpsters and garbage cans. The waste extends upstream and downstream to include the amount of waste generated during each life cycle stage of the many products and services that the business uses. (See Chapter 5 for a discussion of life cycle assessment.) Thus, there may be upstream waste from resource extraction, transport of raw materials, manufacture, packaging, and distribution; and downstream waste from the use and ultimate disposal of the product.

From a product and process design perspective, waste is an indication of inefficiencies in the delivery of a product or service, whether that waste is excess heat, pollutant releases into the atmosphere, effluent discharges into waterways, or solid residues that are landfilled or incinerated. If the product or service is produced and used efficiently there should be zero waste. The concept of waste becoming food for another commercial process is a cornerstone of resource efficiency and is addressed in Chapter 5.

Materials and Waste Audit

Materials management requires an understanding of the flow of materials into, through, and out of the enterprise. A basic waste audit will identify the amount and type of waste being generated. Data for an audit can be compiled from various sources: waste haulers, purchasing records, a facility walk-through, or a waste sort. The Appendix contains the *Waste Audit Worksheet* template that can be used to record the waste profile of an enterprise.

Materials and Waste Management Strategies

Effective materials and waste management is based on four strategies:

▶ Reducing the amount of a resource that is consumed or the amount of waste that is generated—ideally resulting in zero waste.

- ◘ Reusing a resource in its original processed form—either in the same application or in a different application.
- ◘ Recycling a resource by reprocessing the material into a new feedstock (referred to as secondary material) that can be manufactured into new products of the same kind (aluminium cans to aluminium cans) or of a different kind (aluminium cans into cosmetic packaging).
- ◘ Selecting ecologically friendly final disposal methods.

Waste management requires an understanding of the implications of disposal options:

- ◘ Landfilling, which makes the deposited material uneconomic to recover and generates methane gas as materials slowly decompose.[6]
- ◘ Incineration, which may release air pollutants (some of which may be hazardous), and ash residue that is landfilled (and which also may be hazardous).

Nonetheless, zero waste is still the best option because:

- ◘ Landfilling is a sub-optimal use of land and can negatively impact or destroy specie habitats.
- ◘ Landfills, if improperly managed, can leach pollutants into soils and groundwater.
- ◘ Incineration—excepting optimized plasma gasification technologies— releases air pollution, such as CO_2, dioxins, and furans.

Figure 25.3 presents data on energy consumption and greenhouse gas (GHG) emissions for common products manufactured from virgin and recycled materials. It also shows emissions rates for two disposal options: landfilling and combustion of waste. The figure indicates that, for several materials, there are significant energy savings in manufacturing product from recycled material rather than using virgin feedstock. This is particularly the case with metals (where recycled aluminum cans offer a 93-percent energy savings; steel, 57-percent; and copper, 17-percent), plastics (95-percent savings), corrugated cardboard (54-percent savings), and office paper (46-percent savings). Similarly, there are reductions in GHG emissions as a result of using recycled feedstock as opposed to virgin materials. Variability in GHG emissions from final disposal also is a function of the latent energy content of the disposed material and how the material decomposes when landfilled.

There are two ways to recycle. *Upcycling* refers to the practice of using a recycled material so that it either maintains or increases in value. An example would be the recycling of a plastic water bottle into fiberfill that can insulate a jacket. *Downcycling*—the opposite of upcycling—is the recycling of a material so that a portion of its usefulness or value is lost. The recycling of plastic furniture into trash can liners is an example of downcycling.

Material reuse and recycling success is partly a function of locating an organization that has need for the material. Materials and waste exchanges link suppliers of waste materials with entities that can use the product.

Material Energy Content, and Changes in Energy Consumption and Greenhouse Gas Emissions for Common Base Products under 4 Materials Management Scenarios[7]

Material/ Base Product	Base energy (MMBTU/ Ton of product)		Typical recycled content (%)	Composite energy: for product with typical recycled content (MMBTU/ Ton of product)	Net Energy Consumed/Avoided from Materials Management Options (MMBTU/Ton of product [with typical recycled content])				GHG Emissions (Metric Tons of Carbon dioxide equivalent/Ton of product)			Net GHG Emissions from Materials Management Options (Metric Tons of Carbon dioxide equivalent/Ton of product [with typical recycled content])		
	100% virgin material	100% recycled material			Reduce	Recycle	Combust	Landfill	100% virgin material	100% recycled material	Reduce	Recycle	Combust	Landfill
Aluminum cans	239.41	17.60	51	126.71	-126.18	-206.42	0.42	0.53	4.27	0.30	-2.24	-3.70	0.02	0.01
Steel cans	37.02	15.81	28	31.32	-30.79	-19.97	-17.24	0.53	1.01	0.51	-0.87	-0.49	-0.42	0.01
Copper wire	123.82	103.22	5	122.84	-122.31	-82.59	0.39	0.53	2.02	1.66	-2.00	-1.34	0.01	0.01
Glass	8.62	4.66	23	8.06	-7.53	-2.13	0.38	0.53	0.18	0.09	-0.16	-0.08	0.01	0.01
HDPE	70.76	4.25	10	64.21	-63.68	-50.90	-6.37	0.53	0.54	0.05	-0.49	-0.38	0.25	0.01
LDPE	77.33	4.25	4	74.45	-73.92	-56.01	-6.37	0.53	0.64	0.05	-0.62	-0.46	0.25	0.01
PET	73.24	4.25	3	71.2	-70.67	-52.83	-3.16	0.53	0.59	0.05	-0.57	-0.42	0.30	0.01
Corrugated cardboard	26.99	12.53	35	22.13	-21.91	-15.42	-2.21	0.23	0.23	0.25	-1.52	-0.85	-0.18	0.11
Magazines/ Third class mail	33.66	32.66	4	33.62	-33.21	-0.69	-1.58	0.41	0.46	0.46	-2.36	-0.84	-0.13	-0.08
Newspaper	41.10	22.01	23	36.87	-36.45	-16.49	-2.54	0.42	0.58	0.34	-1.33	-0.76	-0.20	-0.24
Office paper	37.28	20.03	4	36.59	-36.58	-10.08	-2.13	0.01	0.28	0.37	-2.18	-0.78	-0.17	0.53
Phonebooks	40.29	NA	0	40.29	-39.87	-11.42	-2.54	0.42	0.68	0.42	-1.72	-0.72	-0.20	-0.24
Textbooks	35.34	34.59	4	35.31	-35.30	-0.53	-2.13	0.01	0.60	0.58	-2.50	-0.85	-0.17	0.53
Dimensional lumber	3.90	4.14	0	3.90	-3.53	0.59	-2.66	0.37	0.05	0.07	-0.55	-0.67	-0.21	-0.13
Medium-density fiberboard	11.88	12.26	0	11.88	-11.51	0.86	-2.66	0.37	0.10	0.12	-0.60	-0.67	-0.21	-0.13
Food waste	NA	NA	NA	NA	NA	0.58	-0.55	0.33	NA	NA	NA	-0.05	-0.05	0.20
Yard trimmings	NA	NA	NA	NA	NA	0.58	-0.70	0.41	NA	NA	NA	-0.05	-0.06	-0.06
Mixed MSW	NA	NA	NA	NA	NA	NA	-1.49	0.28	NA	NA	NA	NA	-0.03	0.12
Carpet	91.59	NA	0	91.59	-91.06	105.88	-4.78	0.53	1.09	NA	-1.09	-1.96	0.11	0.01
Personal computers	957.27	NA	0	957.27	-956.74	-43.44	-4.69	0.53	15.13	NA	-15.13	-0.62	-0.05	0.01
Clay bricks	5.66	NA	0	5.66	-5.13	-0.11	NA	0.53	0.08	0.00	-0.08	0.00	NA	0.01
Concrete	NA	NA	0	NA	NA	-4.77	NA	0.53	0.00	0.00	NA	-0.24	NA	0.01
Fly ash	NA	NA	0	NA	NA	NA	NA	0.53	0.00	0.00	NA	NA	NA	0.01
Tire (retreading)	88.70	NA	0	88.70	-88.17	-51.96	-26.71	0.53	1.09	0.45	-1.09	-0.50	0.05	0.01

Notes: MMBTU = millions of BTUs; GHG = Greenhouse gas. See Air chapter for explanation of Carbon dioxide equivalent. NA = Not available or not applicable.
For calculating energy and GHG emissions for steel, iron, other ferrous metals, use steel cans data. For non-ferrous metals, use average of copper and aluminum.
For other plastics and rubber, use average of PET, HDPE, and LDPE. For boxboard and Kraft paper, use corrugated cardboard. For coated paper, use magazines/third class mail.

Figure 25.3

Materials Management

The following discussion can help inform enterprise managers about managing various material resources.

Metals

Metals typically are produced from mined and processed ores. Some metals, such as steel, copper, aluminum, gold, and silver, historically have had high values in the secondary marketplace. Because there is a finite amount of economically and technologically retrievable ores and because the costs of production (primarily energy) are increasing, used metals are an increasingly valuable resource. Accordingly, manufacturers that incorporate metals into their products will increase their competitiveness by using as little metal as possible (while maintaining product quality) and using components manufactured from reused metals. Each ton of steel that is recycled saves 2,500 pounds of iron ore, 1,400 pounds of coal, and 120 pounds of limestone.

Various scrap dealers will pay for scrap metals (See the Resources.)

Glass

Glass has become a less-prominent component of the waste stream due to the increasing use of aluminum and plastic beverage containers.

Glass is manufactured from a melted mixture of silica (sand), soda ash, and limestone. Used glass can be reprocessed into "new" glass easily. The recycling of glass for reprocessing involves collecting, sorting, crushing the glass into "cullet," and reformulating. Because color is an important quality of glass, the marketplace applies a premium to color-separated glass (typically clear, brown, and green [amber glass usually can be mixed with brown; blue glass, with green]) over mixed-color glass, which has limited market value.

Recycled glass can be used for more than containers. Reprocessed glass can be incorporated into asphalt, Portland cement, construction aggregate, on-site wastewater treatment filters, and industrial minerals.

If the enterprise disposes of substantial quantities of glass, a commercial glass recycler should be contacted for establishing a suitable collections program. Again, *www.earth911.com* is a good resource for identifying glass recyclers.

Additional tips:

☒ Work with vendors to accept beverages in reusable containers.

☒ Set up collection containers according to the volume and types of glass being collected.

☒ Provide signage on best practices (types of glass accepted in each container; types of glass not accepted [usually broken glass and mirrors, window panes, light bulbs]) and ensure that glass has been rinsed of food or other contaminants.

Plastics

Plastics are a versatile group of synthetic materials made from polymers that achieve different material characteristics depending on the substances that are added. Plastics are widely used in the construction, packaging, electronics, and transportation industries. However, plastics production is petroleum-intensive, using an estimated 8 percent of the world's petroleum production in 2001.[8] Additionally, there are some health concerns related to the manufacture of plastics, and consumers' exposure to chemicals that may leach from plastics in certain uses and under certain circumstances. Note that leaching may occur even when plastic products are used for their intended purpose (examples include phthalates and Bisphenol A [BPA] in plastic bottles).

Recycling plastics has the benefit of saving energy and water, reducing landfill needs, and reducing greenhouse gas emissions. In order to facilitate recycling most consumer plastics are identified by a plastic resin logo. However, not all resins are recyclable in all communities.

Figure 25.4 shows there are a number of products that can be manufactured using recycled plastic. Even so, the overall recycling rate for all plastics was 6.9 percent.[9] Plastic recycling depends upon the efficient collection and separation of plastics, and a market for products made from recycled material.

In response to environmental and health impacts associated with various plastics, there is a growing new industry dedicated to the development of degradable plastics. There are two types of degradable plastic:

- ▶ Compostable plastics are materials that degrade over time, regardless of the environmental conditions to which they are exposed. The Biodegradable Products Institute certifies products as compostable.[10] (See Figure 28.1.)
- ▶ Photodegradable plastics require exposure to sunlight in order to degrade. They will not decompose if they are buried in a landfill or a compost pile.

Organizations can promote eco-friendly use of plastic resources in the following ways:

- ▣ Avoid the manufacture, sale, or use of products containing PVC, polystyrene, or polycarbonate.
- ▣ Seek alternatives to petroleum-based plastic products. Evaluate the suitability of plastic products derived from renewable feedstocks.
- ▣ Where appropriate, ensure that plastics-containing products manufactured, distributed, or sold by the enterprise incorporate best ecodesign practices.
- ▣ Apply resin identification code logos to plastic parts to facilitate responsible handling after product use.
- ▣ Create a plastics recycling program for the organization:
  - ▷ Identify which plastics are picked up by the MSW collector.
  - ▷ Determine the types of plastic waste being generated by the enterprise and their locations; place site collection bins in convenient locations.
  - ▷ Have collection bins indicate what types of plastics may be added, which plastics, if any, must be excluded, and any other restrictions (for example, separation of plastics; no food-contaminated plastics; remove caps; and so forth). If the local MSW collector does not pick up all plastics that are generated on site, use the Earth 911 directory to identify other recycling options.

Plastic Types, Their Uses, and Recyclability[11]			
Resin identification code #, abbreviation, andpolymer name	Typical uses	Comments	Recycled uses
1 PET Polyethylene terephthalate	Water bottles Soft drink bottles Boil-in-bag pouches Condiment containers	Easily recycled Recycle rate: 20.3% ———— No known health issues.	Fiberfill for sleeping bags and jackets Tote bags Furniture Carpet Paneling
2 HDPE High density polyethylene	Milk jugs Juice bottles Bleach, detergent and household cleaner bottles Personal care bottles Some trash, shopping bags Cereal box liners Some butter, yogurt tubs	Easily recycled Recycle rate: 9.6% ———— No known health issues.	Lumber Benches Fencing Picnic tables Detergent bottles Oil bottles Pens Floor tiles Fencing Outdoor furniture
3 PVC Polyvinyl chloride	Office binders Cleaning product bottles Cooking oil bottles Clear food packaging Cling wrap Siding Pipe Windows	Rarely recycled Recycle rate: 0% ———— Harmful chemicals produced in manufacturing, disposal or destruction include: lead, dioxins, ethylene dichloride and vinyl chloride	Decking Paneling Mudflaps Roadway gutters Flooring Cables Speed bumps Mats
4 LDPE Low density polyethylene	Grocery bags Dry cleaning bags Produce bags Food wrap Squeeze bottles Tote bags Clothing Furniture Carpet	Sometimes recycled Recycle rate: 4.2% ———— Many stores recycle bags No known health issues. Sometimes recycled	Trash cans and liners Compost bins Shipping envelopes Lumber Landscaping ties Floor tile

Figure 25.4 (Page 1)

Plastic Types, Their Uses, and Recyclability[11] (continued)			
Resin identification code #, abbreviation, and polymer name	Typical uses	Comments	Recycled uses
5 PP Polypropylene	Syrup, ketchup bottles Yogurt containers Drink lids Medicine containers Disposable diapers Outdoor carpet House wrap	Recycle rate: 0.5% ——————— No known health issues.	Pallets Streetlights Battery casings and cables Brooms Brushes Rakes Ice scrapers Landscape borders Bicycle racks Bins
6 PS Polystyrene	Rigid and foam packing Carry out containers Disposable plates and cups Meat trays Egg cartons Medicine containers Jewel (CD) cases Foam insulation	Sometimes recycled Recycle rate: 0.4% ——————— Styrene can leach out, over long term can act as neurotoxin. Styrene can be absorbed by food, which can lead to bioaccumulation.	Foam packing Carry out containers Egg cartons
7 Other (e.g. polycarbonate, nylon, fiberglass)	Computer and electronics cases 3 and 5 gallon water bottles "Sport" water bottles Signs and displays Nylon Food containers Some clear plastic cutlery	Problems with recycling Recycle rate: 9.5% ——————— Polycarbonates can leach bisphenol A (BPA), a known endocrine disrupter.	Plastic lumber Custom-made products
7 Bioplastics	Plastic bags Water bottles Disposable cutlery Carpet Cups Packaging Car floor mats Produce packaging Food containers	Compostable plastics rapidly decompose and are non-toxic. ——————— Biodegradable plastics may contain toxins, requiring specialized composting	

Figure 25.4 (Page 2)

▣ Employ reusable fabric bags or boxes instead of plastic (or paper) bags when receiving purchases from suppliers.

▣ If the organization distributes goods, encourage the customer to use fabric bags rather than plastic or paper bags.
Sell reusable bags made from industrial hemp or other eco-friendly material. If plastic (grocery, produce, shopping) bags are given away, employ compostable bags.

▣ Based on LCA assessments, consider the use of compostable plastics instead of plastics manufactured from virgin resins for bags, storage, and transport.

▣ Opt for products manufactured and/or packaged with at least a portion of the plastic containing recycled material.

▣ Supply reusable dishes and cutlery for the kitchen. Encourage workers to use reusable containers, dishes, and mugs.

▣ When reusable cutlery and dishes cannot be used (such as for events, meetings, and gatherings), consider using compostable plastic or recycled paper alternatives.
Also review the chapters 5 and 6 for additional ideas.

E-Waste (Computers, Printers, Cell Phones, Fax Machines, and So On)

E-waste refers to electronic waste that is discarded by consumers. This waste includes computers, monitors, printers, keyboards, input devices and other peripherals, fax machines, scanners, telephones and cell phones, PDAs, and the like. In 2005, consumers recycled about 15–20 percent of the 1.5–1.9 million tons of electronic waste that was generated.[12] Although the total weight of recycled electronics has increased, the rate over the past decade has remained fairly constant because of the increased numbers of electronics being purchased.

E-waste is a concern because of hazardous materials that are in the electronics. These substances include mercury, cadmium, and brominated flame retardants (added to plastic cases), as well as antimony, arsenic, lead, chromium, beryllium, and zinc. Improper handling of e-waste can expose individuals to these and other hazardous substances. Incineration of electronic waste can result in the release of minute quantities of the hazardous waste into the atmosphere. Landfilling can result in hazardous substances leaching out of the containment area.

Different states and municipalities have different regulations pertaining to the collection and disposition of e-waste. California, for example, considers cathode ray tubes (CRTs) in computer monitors to be hazardous waste. California and Maine ban the disposal of cell phones into the municipal solid waste stream, and require retailers to accept used cell phones for reuse, recycling, or approved disposal. Managing e-waste requires an understanding of the applicable regulations and the options available.

As the disposal of electronics becomes more regulated and costly, an unscrupulous electronics processing industry has emerged. This shadow industry collects electronic waste and transports it to poor countries, where materials are salvaged by unprotected workers who are exposed to toxics. Well-meaning organizations that are collecting the e-waste usually are unaware of the health impacts of their programs. The Basel Action Network promotes sound recycling policies and environmental justice by encouraging disposers to ensure that their e-waste is processed safely.

The following guidelines are intended to inform and should be considered in concert with federal, state, and local regulations.

Electronics Purchasing: Alternatives

▣ Before acquiring a new computer, first consider optimization of the existing device by defragmenting hard drives, reinstalling the operating system and other software, archiving files, uninstalling unused or outmoded software, and performing routine hardware maintenance (of course, first ensuring that all files are backed up).

▣ When feasible, upgrade an electronic product that is being considered for replacement (for example, acquire more memory).

▣ Assess whether purchasing a used device would meet the needs of the organization.

▣ Determine whether leasing or purchasing the service of a product is an appropriate alternative to product purchase. This may be an effective strategy for users that require high performance, or organizations that are experiencing growth or have limited capital.

Electronics Purchasing: Criteria

▣ Consider life cycle resource use and disposal implications when evaluating the procurement of electronics. Increasingly, electronics manufacturers are offering end-of-life product takeback options.

▣ Purchase electronics whose performance meets expected production requirements. Don't buy more equipment or higher performing electronics than needed.

▣ Purchase electronics that have been manufactured with fewer resources and, especially, that contain fewer hazardous substances and sensitive materials.

▣ Purchase electronics that have been produced with recycled content and designed for ease of recycling at the end of the life of a product.

▣ Purchase electronics that have been designed for easy upgrade.

▣ Purchase electronics that have been manufactured by companies with takeback programs. The *Computer TakeBack Campaign* monitors manufacturers' programs.

▣ Purchase electronics that meet ENERGY STAR guidelines.

▣ Purchase electronics that are transported in ecologically friendly packaging.

▣ Consider life cycle requirements of consumable supplies such as toner cartridges for printers (data available from product specifications of the manufacture for individual products and from Better Buys for Business for peripherals comparisons), and take energy use (ENERGY STAR program) into account.

The Green Electronics Council's *Environmental Product Environmental Assessment Tool (EPEAT)* applies 23 mandatory criteria and 28 optional criteria in evaluating desktop and notebook computers, and monitors. Their product registry is a starting point for product assessment. (See Figure 28.1.) The *Beyond EPEAT* program complements the *EPEAT* criteria with criteria that reflect stricter environmental performance, as well as labor standards and occupational health and safety standards that are not a part of the *EPEAT* criteria. The Center for Clean Products and Clean Technologies' *Electronics Environmental Benefits Calculator (EEBC)* may be a useful tool for quantitatively comparing the impacts of different computer systems.

Electronics Reuse

▣ Determine whether the electronic device can be reused in the organization in a different capacity (for example, a slow printer can be used for draft documents only, and a slower fax machine can be used as a backup for a newer machine).

▣ Determine whether the equipment can be sold or traded in. Dealtree works with several electronics manufacturers (such as Casio, Gateway, Sharp, Sony, and Toshiba) and retailers (buy.com and eBay), offering a check or gift certificate for products, as well as marketplaces for B2B transactions.

▣ Determine whether the electronic device can be donated to another organization, agency, or school. "Umbrella" organizations, such as the National Cristina Foundation or Computers for Learning, connect owners of unwanted computers with individuals and organizations in need.

▣ Determine whether the electronic device can be sold or given to employees or their families. (Care may need to be taken to ensure any transfer is treated correctly with respect to laws governing worker compensation).

▣ Determine whether manufacturer will take back the equipment for reuse or recycling.

▣ Determine whether a local retailer will accept and collect equipment for reuse and recycling.

▣ Confirm that the e-waste collector is committed to responsible disposal practices by being listed on the Basel Action Network's list of companies that have signed the *Electronic Recyclers Pledge of True Stewardship*.

> Computers often have sensitive information that must be completely wiped from hard drives before they are reused. Federal regulations, including the Health Insurance Portability and Accountability Act (HIPAA), the Gramm-Leach-Bliley Act, the Sarbanes-Oxley Act, the Identity Theft and Assumption Deterrence Act, the Fair and Accurate Credit Transactions Act, the Fair Credit Reporting Act, the Children's Online Privacy Protection Act, and other regulations may require the cleansing of data from computers before they are donated, recycled, or disposed of.
>
> Enterprises should not assume that receiving organizations clean hard drives; the computers should be fully wiped by the donor so that data cannot be recovered. See *Do the 'PC' Thing: Donate Computers* for a list of disk-cleaning software programs.

Batteries

Batteries most commonly used in business are the same as those used by individuals:

▶ Lead-acid automobile batteries.

▶ Non-automotive lead-acid batteries.

▶ Dry-cell batteries (alkaline, button-cell, and rechargeable batteries).

Batteries use an electrolyte and a metal to generate power. Their usefulness comes with an environmental cost due to mining and manufacturing of heavy metals, such as mercury, lead, cadmium, and nickel. Improper handling can expose individuals to these toxic substances. Incineration of batteries can result in metals being emitted into the atmosphere or concentrating in the residual, landfilled ash.

The life of rechargeable batteries can be extended through best practices. Figure 19.1 describes how to optimize the performance of rechargeable batteries.

Batteries are a type of hazardous waste classified as "universal waste," and should be disposed of properly.

Battery Types and Disposal Preferences[13]			
Battery type	Use	Composition	Disposal
Lead-acid automobile batteries*	Vehicles, equipment	60–80% recycled lead and plastic	Auto battery retailers collect used batteries for recycling
Non-automotive lead-acid batteries*	Industrial equipment, emergency lighting, and alarm systems		
Dry-cell batteries — Alkaline and carbon-zinc batteries	9-volt, A, AA, AAA, C, D Flashlights, small electronics, remote controls	Alkaline, carbon, zinc	Reprocessing possible
Button-cell batteries	Small appliances	Mercury, silver, cadmium, lithium, etc.	Recoverable metals
Rechargeable batteries	Flashlights, small electronics, remote controls	Nickel-cadmium (NiCad); nickel metal hydride (NiMH); lithium ion (Li-I); small sealed lead (Pb)	**Multiple: see Rechargeable Battery Recycling Corporation

*End users of lead batteries (including but not specifying Pb batteries) in AZ, AK, CA, CT, FL, HA, IN, IO, KY, LA, ME, MN, MI, MO, NE, NH, NM, NC, ND, OR, PA, SC, SD, TX, UT, VT, VA, WV, WI, and WY are prohibited from disposal except through manufacturer, distributor, retailer, or secondary lead smelter or other collection programs (such as RBRC).

**End users of Ni-Cad and Pb batteries in FL, IA, ME (commercial and other users), MD, MN, NJ, RI, and VT are prohibited from disposal except through manufacturer/distributor or other collection programs. CA and New York City require retailers to provide collection and recycling for rechargeable batteries.

Organizations subject to the Universal Waste Rule governs the disposal of Ni-Cad and Pb batteries.

Figure 25.5

Oil

Used oil includes petroleum- and synthetic-based oils that have been used in engines, transmissions, refrigeration units, compressors, metalworking, hydraulics, and other applications. Used oils are often contaminated with metal shavings, dirt, sawdust, solvents, saltwater, or halogens.

One gallon of used oil can be re-refined into 2.5 quarts of high-quality lubricating oil (42 gallons of crude oil is required to make the same volume).[14] Re-refining used oil also saves about two-thirds of the energy of refining crude oil.[15]

Resource efficient practices for managing oil include:

- Using bio-based lubricants, where suitable.
- Minimizing the volume of used oil produced (that is, change oil only when necessary).

▷ Filtering, separating, and reconditioning used oil.

▷ Purchasing re-refined oil products.

▷ Using best practices in managing used oil.

▷ Using appropriate precautions, hot-drain oil filters. (Remove the oil filter from the engine while still warm, puncture the casing, and drain for at least 12 hours.)

▷ Being prepared to manage spills.

▷ Major generators of waste oil should consider accepting oil from do-it-yourselfers.

Note that oil filters, which have a steel casing, also are recyclable.

Cooking oils also can be recycled as an additive for biofuel, and there are increasing numbers of recycling services. Restaurants can contact local biofuel processors to determine their interest in collecting used cooking oils. Consult *Earth911.com*'s database for collection and drop-off locations.

Tires

In 2005, markets for used tires were controlling 86.6 percent of the 299 million waste tires generated; an additional 16 million tires were retread. This is a dramatic increase from the early 1990s, when only 11 percent of waste tires were consumed by secondary markets. Figure 25.6 illustrates the disposition of waste tires in 2005.

Scrap Tire Markets in the United States, 2005[16]			
Disposition	Primary uses	Numbers of Tires (millions)	Percentage of Waste Tires
Tire-derived fuel	Cement industry Pulp and paper mills Electric utilities Industrial boilers	155.09	51.8
Civil engineering	Landfill construction Septic drain field media Road construction	49.22	16.5
Ground rubber	Athletic/recreational Molded/extruded products Asphalt, sealants New tires Animal bedding Horticultural	37.47	12.5
Export		6.87	2.3
Cut/punched/stamped	Hundreds of products	6.13	2.1
Agriculture/miscellaneous	Low-speed farm equipment Erosion control Cover weights	3.05	1.0
Electric arc furnaces	Steel and carbon source	1.34	0.4
Land disposed	Landfill Monofill Land reclamation	40.43	13.5
Total		299.6	100.0

Figure 25.6

Through solid maintenance practices, enterprises can ensure that the tire lifetimes on vehicles and equipment are maximized. (See Chapter 21.)

Organizations that dispose of substantial quantities of tires should investigate the secondary market through brokers and resource exchanges.

Ensure that tire disposal is compliant with federal and state laws. For enterprises located in states that have weak laws governing the disposal of tires, seek recycling alternatives.

Hazardous Waste

According to the U.S. EPA, a hazardous waste is a substance that can cause or contribute to mortality, serious irreversible illness, or incapacitating reversible illness; or pose a risk to human health or the environment when improperly treated, stored, transported, or disposed of.

The EPA has two broad categories for hazardous wastes: characteristic waste and listed waste. Characteristic waste has one or more of the following characteristics: ignitability, reactivity, corrosivity, or toxicity. Listed wastes are wastes specifically identified by the EPA as hazardous, and are categorized into the F-list (non-specific source wastes), the K-list (source-specific wastes), the P-list (acutely hazardous chemicals), or the U-list (discarded wastes).

The EPA also regulates universal wastes, which are ubiquitous wastes that are produced by many generators and generally pose less of a hazard relative to other hazardous substances. The most common universal wastes are batteries, fluorescent bulbs, cathode ray tubes, and devices containing mercury.

Federal and state regulations pertaining to hazardous wastes are complex and nuanced. Thus, our recommendations pertaining to hazardous wastes are generalized:

- Ensure compliance with federal and state regulations governing hazardous substances.
- Reduce the generation of hazardous wastes by seeking material substitutions and process alternatives.
- Identify and evaluate all substances used in business operations (including those that are not subject to federal or state regulations) and determine whether there is the potential for human and environmental health effects. Substitute benign materials for those substances of potential concern.

Construction and Demolition Debris

Construction and demolition debris includes a variety of reusable and recyclable materials that can be diverted from landfills.

In many cases a building that is being demolished or renovated is a source of materials (such as framing, doors, windows, fixtures, and rubble) that are in demand by contractors, architects, designers, and building owners. Deconstruction refers to the methodical dismantling of a structure or part of a structure such that the materials may be recovered for reuse.

Structures that offer the most amount of materials for reuse are those that contain heavy timbers, wood framing, valued fixtures, woods, moldings, multi-paned windows, and high-quality brick. (Care needs to be taken to ensure that any hazardous materials, such as lead, contaminated soils, or asbestos, are identified and properly disposed of). The following building materials are reusable:

- ▶ Asphalt.
- ▶ Brick, masonry, and tile.
- ▶ Carpet and carpet pads.
- ▶ Ceiling tiles.
- ▶ Concrete.
- ▶ Doors.
- ▶ Drywall.
- ▶ Hardware.
- ▶ Landscaping.

- ▶ Lighting fixtures.
- ▶ Metals.
- ▶ Plastics.
- ▶ Plumbing fixtures.
- ▶ Rock, stone, sand, dirt, and soil.
- ▶ Roofing.
- ▶ Store fixtures.
- ▶ Windows.
- ▶ Wood (framing, sheathing, flooring, molding, and so forth).

Deconstruction requires more time and effort than demolition, so adequate time needs to be planned for resource recovery. Preparing an inventory of the materials of a structure facilitates marketing the materials (to Habitat for Humanity and similar organizations, deconstruction specialists, architects, designers, and homeowners) and evaluating the cost savings relative to demolition/disposal. Deconstruction also should be done by those knowledgeable of best practices.

Food Waste

Restaurants, commercial kitchens, hospitals, schools, super-markets, and cafeterias generate a substantial quantity of food waste that may be categorized as pre-consumer food waste (preparatory scraps, such as vegetable trim-mings) or post-consumer-waste (plate scrapings and leftovers).

The EPA has suggested a food waste recovery hierarchy designed to show productive uses of excess food. The hierarchy reflects the following recovery strategies:

EPAs Food Waste Recovery Hierarchy

Source reduction

Feed people

Feed animals

Industrial uses

Compost

Landfill/incinerate

Figure 25.7

- ☑ Source reduction: Reduce the volume of food waste generated through accurate ordering of raw foods, proper trimming, reducing serving sizes, offering choices of side dishes (so only wanted foods are served), encouraging diners to take home (in compostable containers) uneaten foods they've ordered, and giving diners complementary dishes of excess foods that otherwise would be wasted.
- ☑ Feed people: Donate extra foods to food banks, soup kitchens, and shelters.

◘ Feed animals: Donate extra (pre-consumer and post-consumer) food waste to farmers and ranchers for their stock.

◘ Industrial uses: Provide fats for rendering, oils for biofuel production, and food discards for animal feed and fertilizer production.

◘ Compost: Convert undressed vegetable and fruit scraps, coffee grounds and filters, tea bags (without staples), eggshells, flowers, and non-greasy and non-meaty leftovers into compost.

◘ Where space exists on-site, combine compostable food wastes with landscape waste.[17] Small anaerobic digesters also can be installed to effectively "compost" waste on site.

◘ If on-site composting is not possible, identify users willing to collect or accept compostable waste, using *Earth911.com* or other searchable databases.

◘ Landfill and incineration: Plasma gasification of food waste could be beneficial as it produces energy (or in some cases, fuel) without the pollution associated with other type of incineration.

Organizations with kitchens may also want to consider eco-friendly food policies, such as purchasing organic, locally grown foods, supporting small farming operations, buying organic, offering seasonal menus, and emphasizing low-impact menus (fair catch fish, and free-range, limited meats).

Landscaping Waste

Landscaping waste is partly a function of the landscape design. (See Chapter 8.) The following tips can help manage landscape wastes:

◘ Maintain as much of the site in its natural state as possible.

◘ Select slow-growing and low-maintenance plantings.

◘ Minimize turf grasses.

◘ Chip pruned branches and other woody waste into mulch that can be used on site.

◘ Use boulders, rocks, stone, and soil on site. Place boulders to establish visual interest; use rock and stone for stone walls and drainage; reuse rich soils in planting areas; and form berms with less productive soils.

◘ When re-landscaping, donate healthy plants to other properties and organizations.

◘ Establish a composting area on site (See the previous section on food waste.) If yard waste cannot be composted on site, compost off site when possible.

◘ Compost grass clippings or leave short clippings in place where they can mulch the lawn.

◘ Compost plant prunings.

◘ Reuse or return pots, containers, planters, and bedding trays to their sources for reuse.

Chapter 26

Paper and Printing

The dawn of the information age promised that paper use would be sharply reduced. In fact, paper use has increased dramatically.

Each person in the United States consumes about 700 pounds of paper annually—more than five times the global average.[1] About half of the paper is recycled—a fivefold increase since 1990[2]—with the remainder becoming municipal solid waste (MSW). Slightly more than one third of the MSW (by weight) is paper and paperboard.[3]

Paper Types and Uses

The average office employee uses 10,000 sheets of paper annually.[4]

Business Papers

Business papers are used for letters, forms, memos, reports, documents, envelopes, and labels that are printed from copiers, and laser and ink-jet printers. Specifications are based on the customers' expectations, the use of the product, and the requirements of office machines and printing equipment. Weight, brightness, shade, coating, and texture are some of the attributes that guide paper selection choices. Additional properties that are considered include strength, stiffness, moisture content, smoothness, dimensional stability, ink/toner receptivity, and the absence of lint.[5]

Publication Papers

Publication papers include paper used in magazines, books, catalogs, direct mail, annual reports, brochures, advertising, and other commercially printed material. Lithographic offset printing is the dominant method for printing on these materials. Because of the stresses that paper undergoes in the commercial printing processes, the paper must be able to meet physical specifications for cleanliness, strength, consistency, and finishing (folding, perforating, gluing, binding, and trimming). Weight, opacity, shade, and brightness are some of the factors that affect print quality.[6]

Kraft Papers

Kraft papers are typically unbleached "brown" papers used for grocery bags, light packaging, and packing papers to fill voids in packaging boxes.

Paperboard

Paperboard is used in packaging, corrugated boxes, folding cartons (for mass-produced consumer packaging), and set-up boxes (custom-designed for liquor and jewelry). Corrugated boxes are generally used in one of two ways: Single boxes are used in the transport of product from one location to another; and bulk boxes are packed with a series of smaller, single boxes. Strength is the key characteristic of corrugated boxes; other factors include "runability" on automated packaging machines, consistency of performance, and appearance.[7]

Other Paper Products

Other paper products that an organization might use include wipes, sorbents, towels, and toilet tissues.

Paper Production and Its Ecological Impacts

The ecological impacts of paper are greatest in the manufacturing process.

Obtaining Fiber

Both collecting recycled paper and harvesting virgin pulp from forests require the expenditure of energy. Harvesting virgin pulp from forests affects the construction and maintenance of roads, erosion and water quality, and the degradation of habitat and many recreational resources.

Natural forests are one of the planet's great resources. Trees naturally improve air quality by absorbing CO_2 and producing oxygen; they capture and filter rainfall that otherwise could result in soil erosion and stream degradation; and they represent habitat for 90 percent of terrestrial plant and animal species.[8] Sustainable forestry practices reduce environmental impacts by ensuring that plantings replace harvested trees and by using best practices in managing the resource. The Forest Stewardship Council (FSC), an independent, nonprofit organization comprised of more than 500 environmental organizations, progressive companies, scientists, and community leaders, is the leader in promoting sustainable forests.

Paper does need to be manufactured from trees. Tree-free paper uses pulp stock from alternative rapid-growing sources, such as bamboo, flax, recovered cotton, agricultural residues, industrial hemp, and kenaf (an annual related to cotton and okra). Many of these sources have per-acre yields greater than that of pine (the predominant tree used in paper production), are more resistant to pests, and have low cultivation costs.

Producing Pulp

Fiber is the raw material for making pulp. The fiber source is typically whole trees or recycled paper; however, other fibrous material, such as rice, rags, or sawdust, also can be used. Using chemicals, pulp mills break down the raw materials into a slurry of fibers and chemicals, which becomes the base input for papermaking.

There are two methods for pulping wood for paper manufacture:

- **Mechanical pulping** forces the wood fibers apart to create a suspension.
- **Chemical pulping** dissolves the lignin, which bonds the wood fibers together.

Chemical pulp is stronger than mechanical pulp and does not yellow. Consequently, chemical pulping is typically used in the production of printing and writing-grade paper. Most chemical pulp is made from the Kraft process (also known as the sulfate process), which uses caustic soda and sulfur-based compounds to dissolve wood chips under heat and pressure, which results in a brown pulp. The pulp is finished by removing unwanted natural compounds, and bleached to achieve desired brightness.

The production of pulp from recycled paper requires the collection and transport of the materials to the materials recovery facility and then to the pulping mill, where paper coatings, staples, rubber bands, and inks are removed through washing, filtration, and flotation. Once washed and deinked, recycled pulp is handled the same as virgin pulp; however, because the pulp usually is produced from bleached paper, it does not go through an intensive bleaching process.

Producing pulp from virgin fiber or recycled paper consumes large quantities of energy, water, and chemicals, and results in releases of air and water pollutants and the generation of solid and hazardous waste. The ecological impacts of processing pulp from recycled papers are generally much less than those associated with the manufacture of paper from virgin fibers, because the most energy-intensive and environmentally intrusive steps are avoided.

Papermaking

To manufacture paper, the pulp slurry is spread and carried through a series of screens and rollers and dried into finished paper. The paper is then trimmed to size, with the trimmings often used as "pre-commercial" fiber input to pulp manufacture.

Recovered fiber comprises approximately 37 percent of the raw material used to produce paper products.[9] Recycled content papers are available in virtually all grades of paper; the consumer is in the position to specify the weight, appearance, and brightness of paper stock, with little apparent difference between papers made from virgin pulp or from recycled pulp.

There are a variety of impacts depending upon the application of the product. Papers used in communications have inks applied, and consume energy in the computing, word processing, printing, transport, and storage stages. Cardboards and packaging materials use inks and energy as well.

Brightness is one of the characteristics that contributes to the ecological impact of papermaking. Chlorine gas bleaching has the greatest ecological impact of all the paper bleaching processes. However, there are reduced impact processes that are alternatives to chlorine gas bleaching:

- Elemental Chlorine Free (ECF) uses chlorine dioxide or other chlorine derivatives.

- Process Chlorine Free (PCF) has no added chlorine or chlorine derivatives in the process (although chlorine may be present from the pulping process or from recycled fiber), using oxygen, ozone, and hydrogen peroxide instead.
- Totally Chlorine Free (TCF) bleaching means that no chlorine or chlorine derivatives are used at any point in the process.

Recycling

Recycling paper and cardboard entails consumption of energy in the collection of the discarded material, transport to the processing center, and the processing process. Some paper products are difficult to recycle because of being contaminated from their use in cleaning and food packaging.

Paper cannot be recycled indefinitely: The fiber begins to disintegrate and lose its strength after being recycled four to six times.

Landfilling and Incineration

Disposal of paper and cardboard impacts the environment through air and water emissions, and, in the case of incineration, the need to landfill residual ash from the combustion.

Ecological Impacts From Paper Production

There is great variability in the life cycle impacts of pulp and paper production. Some of the factors that determine the variability include:

- The makeup of the raw material (harvested trees, collected paper, or other fiber source). From a life cycle basis each ton of paper made from 100-percent recycled content saves 1.32 tons of CO_2 equivalent and uses less than half the energy of a ton of paper made from virgin pulp.[10]
- The distance between the source of the raw material and the pulp or paper mill, which entails fuel consumption for transport.
- The processing technology at the mill. (See Figure 26.1 on page 213.)
- The amount of energy generated at the mill and the fuel source of additional energy that supplements mill production.
- The pollution control technology at the mill (determined in part by state environmental regulations).
- The receiving environments (the degree to which the mill contributes to pollutant concentrations in the receiving water or airshed).

Minimum-impact mills integrate best practices throughout their operations, including such measures as:

- Maximizing lignin removal through oxygen delignification and extended delignification processes, thereby reducing the quantity of bleaching chemical used, lowering energy consumption, and improving effluent quality.
- Replacing chlorine dioxide with ozone in the first bleaching stage.

| | | Wood Use | | Total Energy (million BTUs) | Air Emissions | | | | Waste-water (gals) | Solid Waste (lbs) |
Paper Product	Post-consumer content (%)	Tons	Trees		GHGs (lbs CO$_2$ equiv.)	Particulates (lbs)	HAPs (lbs)	VOCs (lbs)		

Estimated Life Cycle Environmental Impacts Associated With One Ton of Select Paper Products[11]

Paper Product	Post-consumer content (%)	Tons	Trees	Total Energy (million BTUs)	GHGs (lbs CO$_2$ equiv.)	Particulates (lbs)	HAPs (lbs)	VOCs (lbs)	Waste-water (gals)	Solid Waste (lbs)
Uncoated freesheet (copy paper)	0	3	24	38	5,690	12	2	6	19,075	2,278
	30	2	17	33	5,058	11	2	4	16,450	1,941
	50	2	12	30	4,036	10	1	4	14,700	1,717
	100	0	0	22	3,582	7	<1	2	10,325	1,155
Coated freesheet (high-end magazine)	36	2	13	31	4,695	10	1	4	14,395	1,780
Coated groundwood (standard magazine)	36	1	9	28	5,234	9	<1	3	13,007	1,820
Uncoated groundwood (newsprint)	11	2	15	33	6,575	12	<1	4	15,146	2,277
Supercalendered (newspaper insert)	25	2	12	30	6,101	10	<1	3	14,322	2,005

Figure 26.1

▶ Improving the first stage of the bleaching process by replacing elemental chlorine with chlorine dioxide, thereby reducing the discharge of chlorinated organic compounds.

▶ Maximizing the use of pulping liquors through recovery and reuse.

▶ Using totally chlorine-free processes.

▶ Ensuring that energy consumption is minimized, that best pollution-control technologies are incorporated into on-site energy systems, and that purchases from fossil-fueled power plants are minimized.

▶ Applying environmental management systems in combination with strategic improvements in a manner that balances economic costs, quality, and productivity.

Ecological Impacts of Printing

Printing, similar to many industrial processes, employs a range of potentially hazardous chemicals, consumes energy, and generates waste.

Hazardous materials include etch baths used to make printing plates, solutions used in photographic platemaking, and mineral-based printing inks and cleaning solutions. Some of the inks that are used in printing contain hazardous metals that ordinarily are "bound" to the paper, but may be released when exposed to certain environmental conditions, including landfill.

Changes in printing technology are reducing the environmental impacts of traditional printing methods. Two of the most important technological advances are:

- Digital press technologies, which allow direct transfer of images from computer to printing plates, thereby avoiding the need for photographic plate making.
- Less-polluting inks, such as soy- and vegetable-based inks, which are substitutes for traditional inks. Traditional inks are being reformulated to reduce their content of heavy metals and volatile organic compounds.

Ecologically Preferable Paper

Ecologically friendly paper is available for just about every commercial application and, with the exception of economy grades, is often cost-competitive compared to environmentally harmful papers.[12] Moreover, the strength, runability, and appearance of papers are comparable to papers produced from virgin pulp.

Ecologically friendly paper has one or more of the following attributes:

- 50 percent or greater tree-free source material (30 percent for coated papers).
- Source material contains fibrous material—recovered cotton, denim, agricultural and manufacturing remainders—that otherwise would be landfilled or incinerated.
- Source material contains postconsumer waste.
- Tree-based pulp content is harvested from sustainably managed forests (that have not recently been converted from natural forests into tree plantations).
- The paper can be certified by the Forest Stewardship Council (FSC) or from a paper manufacturer/ supplier that can attest to sustainable paper production through the supply chain.
- Bleached paper has been produced using Totally Chlorine Free (TCF) or Processed Chlorine Free (PCF) methods.
- The pulp mill, paper mill, and/or the paper supplier apply best available pollution-control technologies and sound environmental management principles to their operations.
- Paper has been produced regionally or locally—as a way to reduce transportation-related impacts.

> The FSC certification process requires companies to be inspected by third parties annually and to meet the established criteria. To receive a Forest Management Certificate the company must meet or exceed the criteria related to tree harvesting, environmental protection, worker health, and community responsibility. For paper or printed products to be awarded a FSC certificate, it must be demonstrated that the criteria are met throughout the chain-of-custody of the product, from harvesting, to the pulp and/or paper mill, the paper merchant, and the printing company.

Paper Management

A sound paper policy is built on an understanding of paper use in the organization and considers that data in the development of an appropriate paper management plan.

The Paper Audit

The use profile quantifies the flow of paper into, through, and out of the enterprise.

A paper audit enables the organization to illustrate and quantify paper use in the organization (and is effectively integrated into an organization work flow process diagram[s]). (The Appendix contains a *Paper Audit Worksheet* that is scaled for smaller organizations with modest paper use.)

Organizations that consume large volumes of paper and enterprises that are diligently calculating their footprints will want to extend their understanding of paper use. They will collect data on the source of papers—especially the operating characteristics of the pulp and paper mills responsible for the paper manufacture, and the sources of the raw inputs to the production process (virgin pulp, virgin pulp harvested from sustainably managed forests, recycled paper, and so forth). The Natural Resources Defense Council offers a *Paper Product Fiber Verification Form* that can be used to acquire detailed information on paper sources, contents, and production processes.

The Paper Management Plan

Four principles are the foundation of an eco-friendly paper management plan:
1. Use less paper.
2. Reuse paper.
3. Recycle paper
4. Use ecologically preferable paper.

The following general measures should be considered when preparing and implementing the paper management plan:

- Create a paper-management plan that specifies what types of paper can be reused, what can be recycled, and what must first be shredded before recycling. The management plan also should identify paper specifications for purchasing paper.
- Distribute guidelines and post reminder signs.
- Establish a corporate purchasing policy that clearly expresses the goals and preferences of the organization for paper buying.
- Spread the word: On stationery, collateral materials, proposals, reports, and other documents, incorporate a statement about the ecologically friendly characteristics of the paper being used.

Use Less Paper

A list of actions for using less paper is identified in the following broad categories.

General Communications

The principal strategies for reducing paper use in communications are based on selecting alternate media for communications, reducing copies of printed documents, and simplifying forms.

Consider the following for both internal and external communications:

▶ Spell-check, proof, and preview documents on screen before printing.

▶ Set the document display to oversize text so that it's easier to read on-screen (for example, 125 percent on a size 14 font).

▶ Set the document font color to contrast with the background (such as bright blue text on a white background).

▶ Use collaborative software that allows multiple authors to contribute to a shared document.

Alternatively, use the Track Changes, Edit, and/or Comment features incorporated into word-processing software.

If a printed document is to be reviewed by several individuals, circulate a single document and request reviewers to expedite their examination and to initial their comments.

▶ Eliminate unnecessary forms.

Collect only the minimum amount of information.

Design forms to be filled in online and submitted electronically.

Redesign paper forms to be two-sided (duplex) printed. Or repeat forms on a single sheet that can be cut to multiple individual forms.

▶ If you receive a document that has been printed on a single page, contact the author and request that future submittals be duplexed.

▶ Encourage e-mail recipients to not print the document.

In-House Communications

▶ Use e-mail or voice mail instead of paper documents.

▶ Establish a local area network (LAN) that provides an easily accessible, shared database of enterprise documents, such as personnel policies, instruction manuals, meeting minutes, and company newsletters/memoranda.

▶ If the communication can't be distributed or posted electronically, post a printed copy or circulate memos, documents, periodicals, and reports, rather than distributing individual copies.

▶ Create a house style in the word-processing program that uses narrower margins and smaller fonts for brief documents. (Balance against the need to avoid eyestrain by using slightly wider margins and larger fonts.)

▶ Accept final in-house documents with hand corrections.

▶ Use reusable mailers (such as interoffice envelopes for internal mailings).

▶ Use narrow-ruled notebooks.

▶ Make scratch pads or print draft documents (if only one side has been used) from used paper or outdated documents.

External Communications
▶ Use e-mail and electronically distributed documents (such as invoices) instead of paper or faxes whenever practical.

▶ Query customers and external stakeholders about preferred means of communications.

▶ Establish a secure local area network that can be used to establish a database of project files, with suitable internal and client/vendor access controls and security.

Printers, Copiers, Scanners, and Fax Machines
▶ Set computers, printers, and copiers to default to double-sided printing.

▶ Set computers to default to "draft" or "normal" quality printing; use higher-quality printer settings for final documents.

▶ Use network printers instead of personal printers to discourage unnecessary printing.

▶ Send and receive faxes directly from your computer without printing out a hard copy.

▶ Use a removable-adhesive fax transmittal label.

Or create a fax memorandum template or incorporate fax headers into documents.

Or use one-third of a sheet of paper for a cover sheet, and then reuse the back.

Document Formatting, Production, and Storage
▶ When printing multiple copies of a document, electronically preview the document. Then print a single sample document to ensure the document is acceptable for mass printing.

▶ Use central files for hard copies, rather than distributing personal documents.

▶ Track the causes of production errors and develop methods to reduce their occurrence.

▶ When printing brochures, annual reports, promotional materials, and so on, print only what is needed, plus a reasonable margin for insurance.

▶ Develop a system for electronically archiving and retrieving documents. Scan and save documents on electronic media instead of printing hard copies.

Incoming Mail
▶ Opt for e-mailed invoices, newsletters, newspapers, and magazines.

▶ Reduce the number of hard-copy periodical subscriptions that are received.

▶ Donate old publications to the local library or other beneficiary.

▶ Call, e-mail, or mail postcards to senders of unwanted junk mail and ask that your organization be removed from their mailing lists.

▶ Request that organizations not provide the mailing address of your enterprise to others without authorization.

▶ Only list the name of the organization, the telephone number, and/or the generic e-mail address (such as *info@nameoforganization.com*) in Yellow Pages and other directories.

Outgoing Mailings
- ▣ Consolidate mailing databases to avoid duplicate mailings.
- ▣ Keep mailing lists current to avoid duplications.
- ▣ Make it easy for recipients to opt out of mailings by calling a toll-free number, e-mailing, or sending in a postcard.
- ▣ Ensure purchased outside mailing lists are current.
- ▣ Stop receiving catalogs, bulk mail, and magazines addressed to former employees by submitting their names to the free service offered by the EcoLogical Mail Coalition.

Kitchen and Restrooms
- ▣ Instead of paper towels, paper napkins, and paper plates, provide "real" plates and mugs, reusable hand towels, and cloth napkins.
- ▣ If paper towels are used, opt for those with high postconsumer content.
- ▣ Encourage workers who bring their own meals to use lunch boxes, reusable paper bags, and/or reusable containers.

Reuse and Recycle Paper

Paper reuse refers to using the paper again—either for its original or similar purpose. Reuse is preferable to recycling because it generally consumes less energy and resources. A paper reuse and recycling policy must balance ecological responsibility with prudent record retention and the protection of confidential, sensitive, and private information.

Consider the following measures for reusing and recycling the paper of the organization:

- ▣ Create and publicize a paper reuse and recycling policy, and then make it easy to reuse and recycle paper.
- ▣ Reuse paper that is consistent with the reuse guidelines of the organization.
- ▣ Collect 8.5 × 11–inch paper that has been printed on a single side, restack it neatly (with the printed side facing in one direction), and reuse the collected stock in draft printers, draft trays in multi-tray printers and copiers, and fax machines.
- ▣ Establish paper collection stations at appropriate locations, such as next to printers, copiers, and fax machines, and at workstations where there is a high volume of paper flow.

  Label separate collection bins for reuse and recycling, and post instructions. Instruct the cleaning crew not to dispose of the collected paper.
- ▣ Don't overstock preprinted items incorporating information that may become outdated (such as stationery, business cards, envelopes, brochures, and collateral material).

  If a change to preprinted items occurs, purchase labels with the new information in order to use up the old stationery.

Consider keeping only blank stationery paper and envelopes in stock, and create word-processing templates to print out letterhead, memoranda, transmittal forms, invoices, and similar documents as the correspondence is created. (There may be a tradeoff, however, in the cost-effectiveness due to the cost of printer toner cartridges versus the cost of outside printing.)

▣ In multi-tray printers, dedicate one tray for previously used paper and print draft documents from that tray.

▣ Designate specific printers as draft printers and stock them with previously used paper.

▣ As printers and copiers are replaced, acquire multi-tray, duplexing units that allow users to select which paper tray to use (which allows for the designation of a tray of previously used paper for draft documents).

▣ Make scratch pads from used paper.

▣ Use outdated letterhead for in-house memos.

▣ Reuse oversized envelopes and boxes.

▣ Determine the disposition of collected recycled paper. The paper should be transported to a nearby mill for reprocessing.

If the collected paper is being shipped overseas or hauled an unreasonable distance, encourage the collector to change practices or change the collector.

Use Ecologically Preferable Paper

Consider the following measures for using ecologically preferable paper:

▣ Always avoid paper produced from 100-percent virgin pulp.

▣ Use suitable paper with the highest percentage of postconsumer content. If possible, use stock with a minimum of 50 percent for uncoated paper or 30 percent for coated stock.

▣ After maximizing postconsumer recycled content, give preference to paper that contains other recovered materials, such as preconsumer recycled fiber or bamboo, flax, recovered cotton, agricultural residues, industrial hemp, or kenaf.

▣ If paper contains virgin fiber content, be sure that the virgin fiber comes from sustainably managed forests; that the fiber is not from "paper plantations" that recently converted diverse forest ecosystems; or that the paper is certified by the Forest Stewardship Council. If FSC paper is unavailable, ask the paper supplier to document the "chain of custody" of the paper content and production process.

▣ Specify a minimum acceptable brightness.

If the paper must be bleached, specify Totally Chlorine Free (TCF) paper. Accept Processed Chlorine Free (PCF) paper, if TCF is unavailable. Chlorine-free paper, though, may necessitate a higher percentage of virgin pulp content.[13]

▣ Specify lighter weight paper for jobs such as newsletters, brochures, and reports.

Ecologically Preferable Printing

This section addresses out-of-house printing choices for reducing ecological impacts. Printed materials are an expression of the image of the enterprise, and they convey the values of the organization. Organizations can create powerful documents without compromising ecological principles.

Apply Paper-Efficient Design Principles

A "green" designer and/or printer should be aware of and suggest product options so that paper-efficient design and less environmentally damaging laminates, coatings, foils, adhesives, labels, glues, bindings, and other components can be used.

The following design principles should be considered when planning paper-based projects:

- Combine jobs to reduce paper, ink, and press-cleaning impacts.
- Work with the graphic designer, paper vendor, printer, and/or mill to ensure that the project design specifications are based on standard parent paper sizes, thereby reducing waste from cutting.

  Oversized and irregular sizes, and complex folds and pockets, can use greater amounts of paper than needed to achieve the design objectives of the project.
- Consider embossing and die-cutting as alternatives to foil stamping or labeling.
- Use digital photographs instead of film-based sources.
- Reduce ink coverage.

  Specify environmentally friendly inks, such as vegetable-based inks that use soybean, corn, walnut, coconut, linseed, or canola oil. Less ink is needed for printing, it's easier to de-ink the paper when recycled, and these inks generally contain less VOCs than petroleum-based inks. Some vegetable-based inks contain 25-percent VOCs and should be avoided.

  Avoid metallic and fluorescent inks.

  Consider ultraviolet inks and coatings that release no VOCs or solvents. (Proper protection is needed for the press workers.)

  (An excellent description of inks and their ecological impacts are contained in the report, *EcoStrategies for Printed Communications.*)
- Consider aqueous-based varnishes instead of petroleum-based varnishes in order to reduce VOCs, eliminate the need for solvents, and enhance recyclability.
- Use aqueous-based glues as an alternative to perfect-bound documents that require petroleum-based adhesives.
- Consider metal staples (corner, side, or saddle stitched), which can be recycled, as can wire and plastic comb bindings.
- Describe the attributes of the environmentally preferable paper and printing processes used in order to raise awareness and demonstrate accountability.

Use Ecologically Preferable Printing and Printers

Consider the following measures in selecting eco-friendly printing processes and printers:

☒ When feasible opt for biodegradable toner-based digital printing, "print on demand," which eliminates chemicals used in film processing and plate making.

☒ Evaluate waterless printing, which uses a silicone rubber, multi-layered plate, and special ink, instead of traditional ink and fountain solution. This faster and cleaner printing reduces VOCs and provides excellent resolution and color saturation.[14] There may be questions, however, about the efficacy of aqueous-based solvents in their ability to bind heavy metals contained in petroleum-based inks.[15]

☒ Visiting and careful interviewing helps in identifying commercial printers who are applying best management practices with respect to:

  ▷ Air emissions.

  ▷ Chemical use and discharges.

  ▷ Recycling and solid waste generation.

  ▷ Energy use.

☒ When evaluating printers, determine:

  ▷ Is the printer FSC-certified?

  ▷ Does the printer's mission statement address environmental responsibility?

  ▷ Is the printer a member of a green printing trade association?

  ▷ Has an independent environmental audit been conducted? If so, can the document be reviewed?

  ▷ Does the printer have an environmental management plan in place?

  ▷ Have there been any complaints registered with regulatory agencies that oversee air emissions, effluents, hazardous waste, or worker safety?

Chapter 27

Marketing the Green Enterprise

The media are replete with self-proclamations that organizations are green, are sustainable, and are caring about the well being of future generations. Yet, how can a company that is claiming to be green on the one hand, also be fighting regulators so that it is allowed to dump more pollution into a lake on the other? It's enough to make a cynical marketplace question the veracity of *any* company claims.

If an organization is taking deliberate and legitimate actions to green its operations, how can it capitalize on that goodwill by publicizing its deeds in a manner that doesn't generate skepticism? The answer lies in understanding the market and the values of the customer base, and then translating that information into a message that resonates with target customers.

This chapter considers two perspectives of green marketing: marketing green products and services; and promoting an organization that is becoming greener, but isn't necessarily producing a green product or service.

The Marketplace

In this guide, we consider that there are two marketplaces: business-to-business (B2B) and business-to-consumer (B2C).

Why Consumers Buy

There are many reasons why consumers buy products and services. Figure 27.1 lists the principal 50 reasons that marketing expert Geoff Ayling identified. The reasons are shown in no particular order.

Two of the 50 reasons for purchasing are directly relevant to a green marketing perspective: buying in order to conserve energy, and buying in order to protect the environment. Other reasons are indirectly related to eco-friendly products (such as efficiency).

Why Organizations Buy

Organizations also have different motivations for buying, as shown in Figure 27.2.

Even with the application of specific criteria for making purchasing decisions in the organizational environment, it's individuals who are making the purchasing decision—people with a variety of values, aspirations, and conscious and subconscious beliefs.

Why Consumers Buy[1]

1. To make more money.	12. To become more efficient.	25. To be accepted.	37. To satisfy an impulse.
2. To become more comfortable.	13. To buy friendship.	26. To save time.	38. To save money.
3. To attract praise.	14. To avoid effort.	27. To become more fit and healthy.	39. To be cleaner.
4. To increase enjoyment.	15. To escape or avoid pain.	28. To attract the opposite sex.	40. To be popular.
5. To possess things of beauty.	16. To protect their possessions.	29. To protect their family.	41. To gratify curiosity.
6. To avoid criticism.	17. To be in style.	30. To emulate others.	42. To satisfy their appetite.
7. To make their work easier.	18. To avoid trouble.	31. To protect their reputation.	43. To be individual.
8. To speed up their work.	19. To access opportunities.	32. To feel superior.	44. To escape stress.
9. To keep up with the Joneses.	20. To express love.	33. To be trendy.	45. To gain convenience.
10. To feel opulent.	21. To be entertained.	34. To be excited.	46. To be informed.
11. To look younger.	22. To be organized.	35. To communicate better.	47. To give to others.
	23. To feel safe.	36. To preserve the environment.	48. To feel younger.
	24. To conserve energy.		49. To pursue a hobby.
			50. To leave a legacy.

Figure 27.1

Why Organizations Buy[2]

1. To make money.	10. To make sales more easily.	18. To build teamwork.	25. To enhance worker health.
2. To save money.	11. To acquire new customers.	19. To reduce risk.	26. To be environmentally responsible.
3. To attract investment.	12. To improve service to customers.	20. To increase safety.	27. To enhance image among peers.
4. To increase the value of the company.	13. To retain customers.	21. To increase the value of products or services.	28. To return something to the community.
5. To increase efficiency.	14. To increase sales to customers.	22. To increase the *perceived* value of products or services.	29. To be unique.
6. To enhance their image.	15. To make the purchasing process more smooth.	23. To enhance communications.	30. To be a greater resource to customers.
7. To improve performance.	16. To attract new vendors.	24. To reduce stress.	
8. To retain qualified workers.	17. To change the organization's culture.		
9. To attract qualified workers.			

Figure 27.2

Consumer Attitudes and Behaviors Related to Green Purchasing

Researchers start with market segmentation to understand how important "green" is to the (B2C) buying public. Various marketing companies and businesses engaged in marketing green goods to consumers have crafted different segments.

GfK Roper Consulting has been conducting Green Gauge surveys in the United States since 1990, using the following segments defined by attitudes:

- ☐ **True Blue Greens:** the most engaged environmental leaders, demonstrating their commitment through activism and/or green purchasing (11, 30 percent).
- ☐ **Greenback Greens:** those individuals who are willing to pay higher prices for green products (8, 10 percent.)
- ☐ **Sprouts:** novice green consumers (33, 26 percent).
- ☐ **Grousers:** individuals uninvolved or uninterested in environmental issues (14, 15 percent).
- ☐ **Apathetics** (formerly Basic Browns): unengaged individuals who believe that environmental indifference is the norm (33, 18 percent).

Within the parentheses are estimates of the surveyed population fitting into the segment in 2005 and in 2007, respectively. (It's unclear whether the percent differences are a reflection of meaningful changes in green attitudes or a result of the shift in survey methodology from online to in-person interviews).[3]

Yankelovich segments the population differently and concludes that there is a disconnect between stated attitudes and actual behaviors:

- ▶ **Greenthusiasts:** concerned, ardent environmental supporters (13 percent).
- ▶ **Green speaks:** talk the environmental talk, but don't walk the walk (15 percent).
- ▶ **Greensteps:** concerned and aware, these folks are taking a few eco-friendly steps (25 percent).
- ▶ **Greenbits:** not concerned and doing a few things (19 percent).
- ▶ **Greenless:** unconcerned (29 percent).

The 2007 Yankelovich study, "Going Green," also resulted in other findings:

- ▶ "The vast majority of people don't have very well-articulated views of the environment."
- ▶ Thirty-seven percent of consumers are "highly concerned" about the environment; however, only 25 percent believe they are highly knowledgeable about environmental issues.
- ▶ In trying to change behaviors of the Greenless and Greenbits segments, increasing the consumer's knowledge isn't as important as "making it personally relevant."[4]

The Natural Marketing Institute (NMI) has identified an activist green segment: Lifestyles of Health and Sustainability (LOHAS) refers to a segment—the "Cultural Creatives"—who are progressive, well-informed, meticulous consumers of green products and services that are manufactured and sold by virtuous companies. This segment comprises 17 percent of the population, and they actively communicate their experiences with organizations—whether good or bad. Other segments identified by NMI include:

- ▶ **Naturalites** are concerned about their wellness and use many natural products. They are not politically motivated and less sure of what they personally can do to protect the environment. However, they believe that companies should be environmental stewards and they reward that stewardship with loyalty. (17 percent)
- ▶ **Drifters** aren't highly concerned about the environment as evidenced by their buying practices, but they do have good intentions. The trendiness of green may appeal to them. (24 percent)
- ▶ **Conventionals** are practical and likely to reduce their energy use and recycle. They would prefer that companies do the right thing, although they may not be willing to change brands to reward or punish companies. (26 percent)
- ▶ **Unconcerned** know little about green products, and would buy them only if they happened to fit their requirements with respect to price, quality, convenience, or value. (23 percent)[5]

These data suggest that there is no correct market segmentation, but rather impressions to be considered from the different segment characterizations and from various surveys.

Consumer Expectations About Company Ecological Responsibility

The Cone Consumer Environmental Survey conducted in 2007 reported the following attitudes about how Americans think of corporate activities that affect the natural environment:

- ▶ 93 percent of those surveyed believe that companies have a responsibility to help preserve the environment.
- ▶ 71 percent believe companies should take action to reduce pollution in manufacturing and office operations.
- ▶ 69 percent believe companies should design products and packaging with environmentally friendly contents and minimal packaging.
- ▶ 69 percent believe products should be transported and distributed more efficiently.[6]

Survey respondents also believed that companies should:

- ▶ Communicate with consumers and employees about their environmental programs so that these groups can support greening initiatives. (62 percent)
- ▶ Donate money to environmental causes. (59 percent)
- ▶ Lobby for environmentally friendly policies. (57 percent)[7]

25 Principles to Guide Green Marketing

The following principles are intended to help marketers develop green marketing programs. These principles are inspired by green business expert Joel Makower's "Lessons from the Leaders" (see the Bibliography for complete information), and are drawn from some of the previously stated survey results, general marketing best practices, and observations.

1. Be aware of the ecological impacts of your organization, including the life cycle costs of the products and services that are being delivered and used.
2. Communicate the ecological story of the organization effectively. Proactively tell its history, its current efforts, and where it intends to be. (See Chapter 28.)
3. Monitor what's being said of the organization in various media.
4. Learn about stakeholders' interests and concerns, and how they possibly could affect the ecological policies and programs of the organization.
5. Frame ecological benefits in terms that resonate with the buyer's core values, attitudes, and beliefs. Fear tactics, pessimism, and guilt are not effective ingredients of a green marketing menu.
6. Use terms that consumers can relate to: energy conservation, not greenhouse gas emissions or climate change; recycled content, not reduced packaging; human health, not indoor air quality or volatile organic compounds.[8]

7. Express ecological benefits in terms of decision-making criteria that are meaningful to the audience (such as cost-effectiveness, durability, quality, safety, health, and security).

8. Consider green as an extension of organizational strategy—not the only strategy.

9. Ensure that the overall performance is comparable or superior to competing products and services.

10. State performance claims prominently and accurately. Do not greenwash. (See the sidebar.)

11. Verify performance claims with credible third-party verifiers and certifiers.

12. Encourage consumers, environmental organizations, and other stakeholders to offer ideas and suggestions for products and operational improvements.

13. Demonstrate how product improvements benefit the environment and how ecological initiatives lead to higher quality products.

14. Capitalize on rich images of the natural environment.

15. Be a green enterprise advocate and thought leader in industry, technical, academic, and public forums.

16. Explain with pride and purpose how ecological programs fit into the vision, mission, and strategic plans of the organization.

17. Be able to describe how individual ecological programs in the organization fit into a larger commitment to ecological responsibility.

18. Take managed risks. Experiment publicly. Acknowledge and convey successes, failures, and lessons learned.

19. Educate customers, prospects, and other stakeholders.

20. Thank customers and other collaborators for green choices, feedback, and engagement. Explain how their actions make a difference.

21. Integrate eco-friendly features throughout product and service offerings. Green is not an option with a price premium.

22. Name green products and services to induce affiliation with non-green values, qualities, and benefits that resonate for the target audience.

23. Clarify that price premiums (relative to competitor products) are justified by quality, durability, and other non-ecological factors.

24. Guarantee the product performance.

25. Use a blend of media tailored to reach target segments.

TerraChoice Environmental Marketing's *The Six Sins of Greenwashing™*

1. **Sin of the Hidden Trade-Off:** Environmental claims based on limited aspects of a product, while ignoring the product's impacts that are environmentally harmful.

2. **Sin of No Proof:** Environmental claims that cannot be substantiated.

3. **Sin of Vagueness:** Environmental claims that are defined so broadly as to be meaningless.

4. **Sin of Irrelevance:** Environmental claims that may be truthful but are not connected to the product.

5. **Sin of Fibbing:** False environmental claims.

6. **Sin of the Lesser of Two Evils:** Environmental claims that may be factual for the product category, but ignores the greater adverse impacts of the category when taken as a whole.

Chapter 28

Eco-Labels

What is natural? What is organic? What is green? What is sustainable?

In this guide we've addressed some of these terms. However, consumers often are confused about whether products that are represented as being ecologically friendly are in fact what they are claimed to be.

The confusion is warranted. There are many products promoted with assurances that they are natural or green, and many of them are. Unfortunately, many of them are not. Manufacturers may assert that their product is green, even if the package it comes in is oversized relative to the volume of the product, or the packaging is derived from timber harvested from old forest, or if the dyes used to color the package are made from toxic chemicals. Of course, whether a product is green or not has to do with more than just its packaging attributes: It is the sum of its ecological impacts from each of the stages of its life cycle, including its use and ultimate disposal.

There are unscrupulous manufacturers who deliberately claim to be producing green products when they know they are not. The marketplace has come up with a descriptive term for these opportunists: greenwashers. (See the sidebar in Chapter 27.)

Consumers are becoming increasingly aware of the greenwashing problem. In part this is a consequence of consumer activists who expose greenwashers. Activists are blogging, posting manufacturers' misleading ads on Websites, and encouraging consumer boycotts. Their efforts may not have a significant effect on profits; however, it is conceivable that some manufacturers whose greenwashing has been exposed will have tarnished brands for years to come.

Consumers who are intent upon purchasing and using environmentally friendly products may find themselves confused by claims, cynical because of greenwashing, and at a loss as to how to make environmentally correct purchasing decisions.

Eco-labels are a way for diligent enterprises to communicate to the marketplace that their products meet or exceed environmental performance guidelines or standards. A survey of procurement specialists noted that there is an increasing reliance on eco-labels.[1]

Eco-Label Types

There are more than 300 eco-labels that are currently being applied to products and services worldwide. Eco-label programs have been developed by a variety of government agencies, non-governmental organizations, and private companies.

Eco-Label Examples			
	Eco-label	Comments	Contact
No eco-label	Audubon Green Leaf™ Eco-Rating Program	Self-evaluation followed by audit for hotels.	Kevin Gallagher, TerraChoice Environmental Marketing, Inc., at Enquiries@terrachoice.com or call (613) 247-1900 ext. 222 www.auduboninternational.org/programs/greenleaf/
COMPOSTABLE	The Biodegradable Products Institute's Certification Program	Applies American Society for Testing and Materials Specifications (D6400 or D6868) to approve products.	Biodegradable Products Institute 331 West 57th Street, Suite 415 New York, NY 10019 (888) 274-5646 www.bpiworld.org/
EcoLogo	Canada's Environmental Choice EcoLogo™ Program	Certification of wide variety of products based on application review and audit by third party.	The EcoLogo™ Program c/o TerraChoice Environmental Marketing 171 Nepean Street, Suite 400 Ottawa, Ontario K2P 0B4 Canada (800) 478-0399 www.ecologo.org/
CERTIFIED NATURALLY GROWN	Certified Naturally Grown	Alternative to USDA's organic certification, geared to small farmers.	Certified Naturally Grown POB 156 Stone Ridge, NY 12484 (877) 211-0308 www.naturallygrown.org/
CERTIFIED cradletocradle	Cradle to Cradle℠ Certification	Four rating levels awarded based on use of healthy and recyclable/ biodegradable materials, renewable energy, water stewardship, and social responsibility.	McDonough Braungart Design Chemistry 1001 E. Market Street, Suite 200 Charlottesville, VA 22902 (434) 295-1111 www.mbdc.com www.C2Ccertified.com
energy ENERGY STAR	Energy Star	Energy use performance-based certification program for energy-consuming appliances and products, and houses.	U.S. EPA 1200 Pennsylvania Avenue, NW Washington, D.C. 20460 (888) 782-7937 www.energystar.gov/ EPEAT®
EPEAT	Electronic Product Environmental Assessment Tool (EPEAT®)	Manufacturer-declared computer or monitor performance (at three levels) related to 23 required and 28 optional criteria embodied in IEEE 1680. Independent post-declaration surveillance and verification.	Green Electronics Council 1(503) 574-3346 (802) 479-0317 www.epeat.net/
FSC	Forest Stewardship Council Certification	Seven different certifications address sustainable forestry, use of recycled forest products, and chain of custody.	Forest Stewardship Council 11100 Wildlife Center Dr., Suite 100 Reston, VA 20190 (703) 438-6401 www.fsc.org/

Eco-Label Examples (continued)

	Eco-label	Comments	Contact
Green-e.org	Green-e Certification of renewable energy and carbon offset products	Organizations and events that purchase qualifying amounts of Green-e Energy certified, renewable energy (or generate themselves) can license the Green-e logo for use in promotion and communications.	Green-e Marketplace Center for Resource Solutions 1012 Torney Ave. San Francisco, CA 94129 (415) 561-2100 *www.green-e.org/marketplace*
GREENGUARD Indoor Air Quality Certified	GREENGUARD Certification programs by the GREENGUARD Environmental Institute	ANSI-designated standards developer with product certifications related to indoor air quality and low chemical emissions.	GREENGUARD Environmental Institute 2211 Newmarket Parkway, Suite 110 Marietta, GA 30067 (800) 427-9681 *www.greenguard.org*
GREEN SEAL	Green Seal	Application and audit reviewed against standards for 27+ categories of products and services.	Green Seal 1001 Connecticut Ave., NW, Suite 827 Washington, D.C. 20036 (202) 872-6400 *www.greenseal.org*
SCS SCIENTIFIC CERTIFICATION SYSTEMS	Scientific Certification Systems: standards development, environmental certification, and life-cycle assessment	Third-party assessment and certification services for flooring, furniture, wood products, textiles, cleaning products, and paints. Certifications include: Recycled Content, Biodegradable, Indoor Air Quality, FSC and EPP.	Scientific Certification Systems 2200 Powell Street, Suite 725 Emeryville, CA 94608 (510) 452-8000 *www.scscertified.com*
U.S. GREEN BUILDING COUNCIL LEED USGBC	The Leadership in Energy and Environmental Design (LEED®) Green Building Rating System™	Promotes the construction and operation of green building systems through LEED certification.	US Green Building Council 1800 Massachusetts Ave, NW, Suite 300 Washington, D.C. 20036 (800) 795-1747 *www.usgbc.org*
USDA ORGANIC	US Department of Agriculture's National Organic Program Certification	Accredited certifying agents examine source and packaged products for certification.	USDA Agricultural Marketing Service (202) 720-8998 *www.ams.usda.gov/*

Note: All logos produced with permission.

Forest Stewardship logo © 1996 FSC A.C.

LEED® and the related logo is a trademark owned by the U.S. Green Building Council and is used by permission.

Cradle to Cradle Certified^CM is a certification mark of MBDC.

Listing of certifying organizations and their logos does not imply endorsement.

Figure 28.1

Eco-labels also may be national (such as Canada's EcoLogo^CM program, which has certified more than 7,000 products, and Germany's Blue Angel), multinational labels (for example, EU-label, awarded to several hundred products), industry specific labels, or single-issue certification (including certified organic cotton, fair trade coffee, dolphin-safe tuna, and sustainable forestry).

There is considerable variability among the individual labeling programs. One difference is the types of products and services that are covered by a given eco-labeling program. Another difference is the range of ecological (and other) topics that are considered as part of the certifying process. The depth of analysis of the topics also varies, with some organizations using guidelines, some using required and optional criteria, and others using standards developed by independent third parties. The process by which the product or service is examined also is not uniform: Some eco-labels allow the applying enterprise to self-report (with or without verification); others require an independent third party to conduct the evaluation.

Two international entities are involved in the development of standards designed to create a consistent framework for eco-labels: the International Organization for Standardization (ISO) and the Global Ecolabelling Network (GEN). Their work recognizes three label categories:

Type I Standard:	A voluntary program that uses objective, certifying third parties who apply multiple criteria to examine life-cycle impacts of a product within a particular category.
Type II Standard:	A self-declaration by a manufacturer, importer, or distributor that uses unjuried assessment considerations that are not independently verified.
Type III Standard:	A quantitative presentation of the impacts of the life cycle of a product, in which the performance indicators are established by a business sector or independent entity. Similar to the familiar food nutrition labels.

The ISO has developed a series of standards for eco-labeling.[2]

Type II standards reflect labels that often apply one or few environmental considerations in their assessments. Type II standards are the least credible of the three. In the United States, Energy Star and Green Seal—both Type I standards—are the most familiar to consumers.

Some of the eco-labels that are commonly used in the United States are displayed in Figure 28.1. A survey of U.S. and Canadian procurement specialists conducted by TerraChoice revealed that ENERGY STAR was the most trusted eco-label (cited by 60 percent of respondents), followed by EcoLogo (27 percent) and GreenSeal (26 percent).[3]

Eco-Label Selection

Businesses that manufacture products should consider certifying the ecological performance of their product and having that certification displayed on the product packaging. The rationale is that many buyers and procurement specialists view eco-labels as reliable indicators of environmental performance that reduce the need for verification of supplier claims.[4]

There is no single label that is suited to all products or all companies. With so many eco-labels being used, it can be daunting to select one that best meets the particular needs of the enterprise that wishes to label the environmental performance of its product.[5] The determination of which label, declaration, or certification that is best suited to the organization must balance various considerations, such as:

- ▶ Does the eco-label use a set of meaningful and verifiable standards that have been developed through an open process engaging stakeholders (including the public)?
- ▶ Does the evaluation weigh environmental performance criteria?
- ▶ Which label is respected within the industry?
- ▶ Which label is recognized and respected by the customer base?
- ▶ Which label provides credibility in geographic and/or industry categories that the organization wants to market to?
- ▶ What is the cost for application, assessment, and consideration?
- ▶ How long will the process take?
- ▶ If modifications in product specifications and performance are made during the certification process (either independent or as a result of the environmental analysis), will the assessing and/or certifying body adjust the fee and/or process for certification?
- ▶ Is the certifying organization independent and free of conflict of interest?
- ▶ Does the certifying organization demonstrate transparency by providing information on the board, advisors, and financial condition (including sources of funds)?

Chapter 29

Certification of Green Enterprises

Ecologically friendly business certification helps enterprises to promote their organization as a green enterprise. In this guide we differentiate between eco-labeling (see Chapter 28), applied to individual or categories of products and services, and eco-certification, which considers the broader range of ecological impact.

A variety of public and private entities are promoting eco-certification and environmental business networks. Certifying organizations, some of which are shown in Figure 29.1, differ in their guidelines and in the design of their programs. Credible certifying entities use guidelines and standards (such as ISO 14020, 14021, 14024, 14025, and 14040 [See Chapter 28]) that have been created through open, inclusive processes, and rely on objective third parties to assess or verify compliance with the developed standards.

Business environmental certification is becoming increasingly important for several reasons. Major purchasers regard their suppliers as essential partners in transforming their businesses to be more ecologically efficient. Consequently, if an enterprise wants to conduct business with an organization that requires its suppliers to meet or exceed a standard of ecological performance, the business needs to comply with the certification process required to document that standard. Wal-Mart and Ikea, for example, require their respective suppliers to support the environmental goals they have established for themselves.

As described in Chapter 27, an increasing number of customers consider environmental performance factors when making decisions about which businesses to patronize. The 2008 *Cone Green Gap Survey* reported that 63 percent of the 1,080 American adults surveyed viewed certification as influential in purchasing a product or service that claimed an environmental benefit.[1]

Eco-certification helps the organization to validate the ecological intent and performance to the community. Regional and local agencies support green certification programs as an economic development and environmental management strategy, providing a mechanism for consumers to recognize which enterprises in their community are going green.

For some organizations the eco-certification process provides a framework for the greening of the enterprise. Guidelines prepared by certifying agencies serve as a blueprint for how to go about reducing energy, water, and materials consumption, and the amount of generated waste. Organizations may wish to explore more comprehensive certification schemes that extend past ecological responsibility and into economic and equity, such as the Sustainable Business Institute's "SBI Seal of Sustainability" or the Global Reporting Initiative framework.

Examples of Eco-Business Certification Programs

	Eco-label	Comments	Contact
No eco-label	American Consumer Council's Green C Certification	Three-tiered application addresses seven key areas related to organizational issues and environmental compliance and is followed by site visit.	Green C Certification Program American Consumer Council POB 503016 San Diego, CA 92150 (760) 787-0414 *www.americanconsumercouncil.org/green/*
Certified **(B)** **Corporation**	Certified B Corporation	Certification based on responses to approximately 80–170 questions followed by B Lab-administered audit. B Corporations required to adopt legal framework to incorporate stakeholder interests.	B Lab 8 Walnut Avenue Berwyn, PA 19312 (610) 296-8283 *www.bcorporation.net/index.cfm*
Green America **APPROVED** **FOR PEOPLE AND PLANET**	Green America's Green Business Network	Screening process enables organizations to be listed in *National Green Pages*. Green America was formerly known as Co-op America.	Green America 1612 K Street NW Washington, D.C. 20006 (800) 584-7336 *www.coopamerica.org/*
EARTHRIGHT® **GREEN**	EarthRight Green Business Certification	Three rating levels awarded based on environmental impact and level of performance relative to peers.	EarthRight Business Institute 2965 Telemark Drive Park City, UT 84060 (800) 750-4380 *www.earthrightinstitute.com*
GREENIFIED **2009**	Green Business Alliance's Greenity	Applicant commits to complying with guidelines covering six categories of environmental performance.	Green Business Alliance 925 South Federal Hwy, Suite 750 Boca Raton, FL 33432 (561) 361-6766 *www.greenbusinessalliance.com*
(Green Business Certified logo)	Institute for Green Business Certification, Inc.'s Green Business Certification	Uses proprietary checklist (audit) for certifying small, medium, and large businesses. Six locations throughout the U.S.	Institute for Green Business Certification, Inc 227 Barker Road, Suite 203 Michigan City, IN 46360-7415 (219) 221-6262 (877) 780-4733 *www.gbcertified.com/*

Examples of Regional and Local Green Business Programs

Bay Area (California) Green Business Program
Chicago Sustainable Business Alliance
Jefferson County, WA Green Business Program
Maine Department of Environmental Protection Green Business Certification

Puget Sound Green Business Certification Program—Envirostars
Santa Barbara County, CA Green Business Program
Santa Monica, CA Green Business Certification Program
Washington, D.C.—Skustainable Business Network of Washington

Note: See also the list of eco-labeling organizations in Figure 28.1. A number of those certifiers examine the environmental performance of companies (and not only the environmental performance of individual products and services). Listing of certifying organizations and their logos does not imply endorsement.

Figure 29.1

Chapter 30

Communications and Reporting

As described in Chapter 4, stakeholders can be valuable partners in greening an organization. Successful engagement with these stakeholders is dependent upon organizing and applying a purposeful, well-executed communications plan.

This chapter addresses three elements of communications and reporting:

- ▶ Determining the desired outcomes of communications with stakeholder groups.
- ▶ Selecting appropriate communications channels.
- ▶ Delivering communications.

Determining Desired Outcomes in Communicating With Stakeholders

At the outset, it is important to identify stakeholders who may be involved in, be affected by, or otherwise have an interest in the ecological program of the organization. (See Chapter 4.)

Stakeholder communications depend on an appreciation for the value of engaging with the party. Having goals for stakeholder communications is the essential framework for an effective communications plan. Refer to Figure 4.4 for examples of outcomes that organizations might have for communicating with internal and external stakeholders.

Determining Appropriate Levels of Communication

It stands to reason that an organization will want to have a greater level of communication with those stakeholders whose actions may have the greatest impact on the enterprise.

The Levels of Communication

The *Stakeholder Engagement Manual* identifies five levels of stakeholder communication, which are described in order of increasing engagement.

- ▶ **Acquisition of information** is intended to manage risks by ensuring compliance with existing regulations and monitoring regulations being proposed.
- ▶ **One-way communication** without response typifies a variety of communications, such as product labels, product specification sheets, advertisements, posted responses to FAQs, and environmental and sustainability reports.

Memoranda, balanced scorecards, and white papers also can be used to inform internal stakeholders about green goals and programs. These representations of facts can be effective in informing and building trust with stakeholders.

▶ **Dialogue** is a powerful tool for exchanging information and experiences. Actively soliciting comments on environmental reports extends the utility of that otherwise-unilateral communiqué. Formal gatherings (staff meetings, meetings with external stakeholders, conferences, and workshops) also are forums for exchanging information. Suggestion boxes, follow-up calls to customers, customer service lines, and blogs are additional avenues for opening communications in order to solicit feedback.

▶ **Ongoing consultation** takes the forms of partnerships, alliances, and networks of participants collaborating to achieve a common goal. For example, product development teams working with materials and components suppliers create products with minimal life cycle footprints.

▶ **Collaboration** is the most sophisticated and challenging communication level. Collaboration extends ongoing consultation through shared decision-making. For example, public-private partnerships are used extensively to rehabilitate contaminated properties and redevelop them in productive uses. Other examples include businesses cooperating to develop a carpooling program for their combined employee base.

Framework for Planning Stakeholder Communication Levels							
Stakeholders		Potential impact (L, M, H)	Communication Emphasis				
			Acquire	One-way	Dialogue	Consult	Collaborate
Owners/Investors		*					
Board							
Management							
Staff							
Customers	Wholesalers	M			X		
	Retailers	H					X
	End users	H				X	
Suppliers	Vendors	H					X
	Banks, insurers	M			X		
Industry associations							
Competitors							
Media							
Environmental organizations							
Governmental agencies							
Educational institutions							
Local community							
Employee families and friends							
General public							

Figure 30.1

Selecting Communications Strategies for Stakeholders

Figure 30.1 presents a framework for connecting the level of interaction to the communication of stakeholder significance. (See Figure 4.5 and the accompanying discussion of stakeholder identification, assessment, and engagement in Chapter 4.) Figure 30.1 shows several examples of stakeholder engagement for a hypothetical greening organization. Note that when the potential impact of a stakeholder is determined by the organization to be high, a deeper level of engagement is planned for.

Following a determination of the communication level, the organization can plan the types of communications that will occur during the greening program, as shown in the examples embedded in Figure 30.2. (The Appendix contains both a *Stakeholder Communications Scheduling Worksheet* and a *Stakeholder Communications Level Worksheet*.)

Framework for Planning Stakeholder Engagement							
Stakeholders		Planning Stage Involvement					
		Audit	Goals	Strategic	Action	Monitor	Calibrate
Owners/Investors							
Board							
Management							
Staff							
Customers	Wholesalers	Survey, meet: solicit input	Inform	Solicit feedback on strategic steps	Solicit feedback on action steps	Survey, solcit input	Solicit feedback, inform
	Retailers	Survey, focus group: solicit input	Solicit feedback on draft goals	Help define strategic initiatives	Help define action steps	Inform, survey, solicit	Help define refinements
	End users	Survey, focus group: solicit input	Solicit feedback on draft goals	Help define strategic initiatives	Help define action steps	Inform, survey, solicit	Inform
Suppliers	Vendors						
	Banks, insurers						
Industry associations							
Competitors							
Media							
Environmental organizations							
Governmental agencies							
Educational institutions							
Local community							
Employee families and friends							
General public							

Figure 30.2

Selecting Communication Channels

There are a variety of communication channels available to organizations. (See the *Marketing Tools Checklist: Channels for Delivering Your Marketing Message* in the Appendix.) The organization can choose the appropriate communications channel based on balancing key criteria: the communication emphasis, the stage of the greening program, the budget of the organization, and other considerations.

Delivering Communications

General Principles

There are general principles that guide effective communications with stakeholders:

- **Proactive** communications are effective in preventing misunderstandings and building relationships with stakeholders. It's preferable to be ahead of the curve in delivery of information than to be defensively responding to questions and challenges.
- **Listening** is the most important aspect of communicating. Listening helps one to understand the issues the speaking party is concerned about, making it easier to craft communications that are relevant to the needs of the stakeholder.
- **Accurate** information is required in order to be credible and build trust. When unsure of information, the organization should say so.
- **Tailor** the message so that it is easily comprehended. Not everyone "gets" the numbers. Explain incomprehensible numbers in equivalents that people can relate to. For example, express energy savings as the equivalent to removing "X" cars from the road. Use or define terms.
- **Impactful** communications tell stories that engage the senses and connect with audiences. Use impactful words, graphics, photographs, colors, and fonts in reports, Websites, and presentations. Use demonstrations and tours to transform concepts into reality for the audience.
- **Teachable moments** are opportunities to elevate understanding of unfamiliar concepts, thereby increasing the audience's comfort with ecological topics.

Key Reports

There are two key reports that greening organizations are likely to produce:
- Eco-indicator reports.
- Status reports.

Eco-indicator reports

Eco-indicator reports express the ecological impacts of the enterprise. The reporting usually is introduced by explaining the general limits of the disclosure (such as the geographic scope of the reporting or to what degree life cycle impacts are addressed). Eco-indicator reports are effectively snapshots of ecological performance and lend themselves to straightforward reporting for the benefit of board, management, and staff; explanatory narrative can be minimized.

The following are the categories of ecological impacts that are typically addressed in indicator-type disclosures:

- Energy use.
- Fuels used (conventional and renewable).
- Energy generated.
- Water used.
- Water reused.
- Water releases (volume, contaminant load, thermal loads—related to receiving waters).
- Land used.
- Natural resources used.
- Natural resources reused and recycled.
- Volume of toxic, non-renewable materials used.
- Waste generated.

- Air emissions (GHGs, criteria pollutants, ozone-depleting pollutants, acids, and other contaminants of concern related to air sheds).
- Noise.
- Light pollution.
- Transportation.
  - VMT, passenger-miles, ton-miles.
  - Vehicle operational energy efficiency.
  - Vehicle energy intensity.
  - Vehicle life cycle energy cost.
  - Vehicle emissions.
- Organizational programs.
- Offsets.

These impacts are identified, quantitatively described, and related to the receiving environment. There also may be comparison descriptions, such as impact per revenue $, impact per "widget," or impact relative to similar enterprises.

Trends are easily conveyed using graphs and overall status of an impact category can be summarized by colors (green, yellow, red) or arrows (up, neutral, down). Impacts also may be related to the measurable goals of the organization.

Ecological Status Reports

Status reports build upon the information conveyed by eco-indicators. They amplify quantitative information with narrative, and descriptive graphics and images. The narrative often may describe the approaches of the enterprise to addressing the impacts that are described.

These reports typically are used as internal reports for medium-sized enterprises or are generated by those businesses required to disclose their impacts to external parties (such as to major supply chain customers or governmental entities). Large organizations also generate these reports for investors, environmental organizations scrutinizing their activities, and/or the public.

Larger organizations may structure their disclosures using formats such as those created by the Global Reporting Initiative.

Appendix

This Appendix contains blank templates that have been referenced throughout this book. These forms can be filled out by organizations during the planning of ecological improvements.

For additional templates visit the author's Website (*www.ravenbusiness.com*).

The author welcomes suggestions for additional worksheets as well as any other ideas that will advance the greening of organizations.

All forms except the *Energy Consumption Calculator Worksheet* are copyright Raven Business Group. The *Energy Consumption Calculator Worksheet* comes from *Putting Energy into Profits*. (See the Bibliography for more information.)

Action Plan Worksheet

Date	Lead person	Action	Goal area	Cost	Estimated performance improvement	Staff time	Resources	Comments

☐ ☐ ☐ ☐ ☐ ☐ ☐ ☐ ☐ ☐ ☐ ☐ ☐ ☐

Page ____ of ____

Prepared by _____

Door Energy-Efficiency Improvement Worksheet

Door	Location	Description	Existing R-value	Improvement option	Installed Cost	Estimated Savings	Payback

1. Inventory and characterize doors.
2. Calculate *Existing R-value* of doors based on the R-value of that insulating type of unit:

Wood, hollow core flush 1 ¾"	2.17
Wood, solid core flush 1 ¾"	3.03
Storm door wood, 50% glass)	1.25
Insulating door, metal (2" w. urethane)	15.00

Prepared by: _____
Date: _____

Energy Efficiency Measure Evaluation Worksheet

Potential Measure

Description _____ Locator _____

Location _____ Ops _____ hrs/yr

Maintenance _____ Lifetime _____ yrs

Effective Cost

Planning	$ _____	_____
Purchase	$ _____	_____
Install	$ _____	_____
Rebate	$ _____	_____
Total [A]	$	

Annual Energy Savings

Annual Energy Savings		Energy Cost			Annual Energy Cost Savings	
Electricity	_____ kwh	$	/kwh	>	Electricity	
	_____ kW	$	/kW			$ _____
Petroleum	_____ gals	$	/gal	>	Petroleum	$ _____
Natural gas	_____ ccf	$	/ccf	>	Natural gas	$ _____
Steam	_____ Mlb	$	/Mlb	>	Steam	$ _____
Propane	_____ gals	$	/gal	>	Propane	$ _____
Other	_____			>	Other	$ _____
					Total [B]	$

Other Annual Savings / Other Costs

Type	Amount	Value		Type	Value
Maintenance		$		Training	$ _____
Water		$		Maintenance	$ _____
Sewer		$		Equipment	$ _____
Disposal		$			$ _____
GHGs		$			$ _____
		$			$ _____
Total [C]		$		*Total [D]*	$

Payback: A+D/(B+C) = _____

Net Present Value: $ _____

Internal Rate of Return: _____

_____

_____

Comments & _____

Notes _____

Energy Efficiency Measures Summary Worksheet

Measure	Locator	Effective cost ($)	Annual Energy Savings (BTUs)	Payback (yrs)	Performance Improvement (L, M, H)	Resource Cost (L, M, H)	Comments

Comments & Notes

Prepared by _____ Date _____

Energy Consumption Calculator Worksheet

Energy Type	Annual consumption	Energy unit	Multiplier	Normalized consumption (kBTU/year)
Electricity		kwh	3.4	
Natural gas		therm or ccf	100	
Fuel oil, #2		gallons	140	
Fuel oil, #6		gallons	150	
Steam		Mlb	1040	
Propane		gallons	91	
		lbs	22	
Total				

Instructions:
1. Total all bills by energy type and place that sum in cell under *Annual consumption* column.
2. Multiply each fuel source's *Annual consumption* total by the *Multiplier* for that energy type and enter the product in the *Normalized consumption* column.
3. Total all figures entered into *Normalized consumption* column. That total is the energy consumption total for the year.
Note: If there is variability in production, numbers of employees, hours of operation, or weather then assemble data for several years.

Notes   _____

                        _____

                        _____

                        _____

                        _____

                        _____

Prepared by: _____

Date: _____

Energy Consumption Worksheet (for energy producers)

Energy Type	Quantity	Energy unit	Multiplier	Normalized consumption (kBTU/year)
Energy purchased				
Electricity		kwh	3.4	
Natural gas		therm or ccf	102.6	
Fuel oil, #2		gallons	139	
Fuel oil, #6		gallons	150	
Steam		Mlb	1040	
Propane		gallons	91	
		lbs	22	
Energy produced by facility				
Electricity		kwh	3.4	
Steam		Mlb	1040	
Hot water		gallons	Note 1	
Energy sold				
Electricity		kwh	3.4	
Steam		Mlb	1040	
Hot water		gallons	Note 1	
Energy consumed				
Electricity		kwh	3.4	
Natural gas		therm or ccf	102.6	
Fuel oil, #2		gallons	139	
Fuel oil, #6		gallons	150	
Steam		Mlb	1040	
Propane		gallons	91	
		lbs	22	
Total				

Directions: Energy consumed = Energy purchased + Energy produced - energy sold (if any).

Note 1: Energy content of hot water (in kBTUs) = (gallons) x (8.34) x (Output temperature (F) - Input temperature) x 1000

Note 2: There may be conversion losses in energy production. Energy produced by the facility should incorporate a determination of those losses.

End Use	Energy consumption (in MBTU/time)				Comments
	Fuel oil	Natural gas	Electricity	% of Total	
Lighting					
interior					
exterior					
Office equipment					
computers					
printers					
copiers					
scanners					
telephone system					
fax machines					
misc					
Kitchen appliances					
ovens					
stoves					
fryer					
dishwasher					
coffee maker					
refrigerator					
walk-in					
misc					
Space conditioning					
heating					
cooling					
ventilation, fans					
Water heating					
Refrigeration					
Swimming pool, spa					
People movers					
Equipment					

Energy Consumption by End Use Worksheet

Fuel Consumption Profile Worksheet

Month	Year 1	Year 2	Year 3	Year 4	Average	Comments
January						
February						
March						
April						
May						
June						
July						
August						
September						
October						
November						
December						
Annual Total						

Fuel type _____

Notes _____

Prepared by: _____

Date: _____

Green Measures Economic Summary Worksheet

Measure	Locator	Effective Initial Cost ($)	Annual Net Cash Flow ($)	Payback (yrs)	Net Present Value ($)	Internal Rate of Return (%)	Comments

Comments & Notes

Prepared by _____   **Date** _____

Green Measures Summary Worksheet

Measure	Locator	Effective cost ($)	Annual Energy Savings (BTUs)	Payback (yrs)	Performance Improvement (L, M, H)	Resource Cost (L, M, H)	Comments

Comments & Notes

Prepared by _____ Date _____

Insulation Improvement Worksheet

Surface being analyzed	Attic	Wood frame wall cavity	Floor	Crawl space wall	Basement wall interior
Goal R-value					

Surface	Location	Description	Existing R-value	Insulation Improvement	Installed Cost	Estimated Savings	Payback

1. Determine *Goal R-values* from:
   Oak Ridge National Laboratory, Building Energy Research Division. *R-Value Recommendations for Buildings* software. Accessible from *www.ornl.gov/cgi-bin/cgiwrap?user=roofs&script=ZipTable/ins_fact.pl*

2. Using following multipliers, calculate *Existing R-value* based on thickness of the existing insulation material by the R-value of that insulating material:

Fiberglass batt	3.14 – 4.30/inch	Cellulose blown (wall)	3.70/inch
Rock wool batt	3.14 – 4.00/inch	Vermiculite	2.13/inch
Rock wool blown (attic, wall)	3.10 – 4.00/inch	Urea terpolymer foam	4.48/inch
Cellulose blown (attic)	3.13/inch	Expanded polystyrene	4.00/inch

3. Calculate *Additional R-value needed* for each location by subtracting *Existing R-values* from the *Goal R-values*.
4. *Insulation improvement* can be identified based on suitability of insulating option for location and the option's R-value.

Prepared by: _____

Date: _____

© Raven Business Group, LLC, 2009

Marketing Tools Checklist
Channels for Delivering Your Marketing Message

- ☐ Adopt-a-Highway
- ☐ Advertising, print
  - ○ Newspapers
  - ○ Trade journals
  - ○ Magazines
  - ○ Church bulletins
  - ○ School yearbooks
  - ○ Shoppers
  - ○ TV guides
- ☐ Advertising, misc.
  - ○ Bulletin boards
  - ○ Bumper stickers
  - ○ Calendars
  - ○ Movie theaters
  - ○ Public transit
  - ○ Restaurant mats
  - ○ Sports venues
  - ○ Specialties; gifts
- ☐ Articles
- ☐ Audio tapes
- ☐ Billboards
- ☐ Books
- ☐ Brochures
- ☐ Business cards, stationery, logo
- ☐ Case studies
- ☐ Catalogs
- ☐ Client appreciation program
- ☐ Community service; charities
- ☐ Conferences
  - ○ Attendance
  - ○ Exhibitor
  - ○ Panel host
  - ○ Panel participant
  - ○ Presentation
  - ○ Sponsor
- ☐ Contests
- ☐ Coupons
- ☐ Customer affinity (loyalty) programs
- ☐ Demonstrations

- ☐ Directory listing
- ☐ Direct mail
  - ○ Post card
  - ○ Post card decks
  - ○ Standard (#10 envelope)
  - ○ Dimensional mailing
  - ○ Internal list
  - ○ Outside target list
- ☐ Direct marketing
- ☐ Donations
- ☐ Door hangers
- ☐ Elevator speech
- ☐ Fairs
- ☐ Flyers
- ☐ Gift certificates
- ☐ Grand openings
- ☐ Guarantees/ warrantees, written
- ☐ Inserts
- ☐ In-store displays
- ☐ Internet
  - ○ Blog
  - ○ Cross-linking
  - ○ Email
  - ○ E-zine
  - ○ Pay-per-click
  - ○ RSS
  - ○ SEO
  - ○ Website
- ☐ Mail order
- ☐ Message-on-hold
- ☐ Networking
- ☐ Newsletter
- ☐ Packaging
- ☐ Personal notes, contacts
- ☐ Point of purchase display
- ☐ Portfolio of work
- ☐ Presentations
- ☐ Press conference
- ☐ Press release

- ☐ Public service announcements
- ☐ Radio
  - ○ Commercial
  - ○ Infomercial
  - ○ Interview
  - ○ Program sponsor
- ☐ Rack card
- ☐ Referrals
- ☐ Reports
- ☐ Resume
- ☐ Samples, free
- ☐ Seminars and workshops
- ☐ Service organizations
- ☐ Signs and Banners
  - ○ Place of business
  - ○ Vehicles
- ☐ Slogan/tag line
- ☐ Space donation
- ☐ Speaking
- ☐ Strategic alliances
- ☐ Success stories
- ☐ Surveys, customer
- ☐ Telemarketing
- ☐ Television
  - ○ Commercial
  - ○ Infomercial
  - ○ Interview
  - ○ Program sponsor
- ☐ Testimonials/reference letters
- ☐ Toll-free numbers
- ☐ Trade association
- ☐ Trade shows
- ☐ Trial, free
- ☐ Video tapes
- ☐ White papers
- ☐ Window displays
- ☐ Yellow Pages
  - ○ Bold listing
  - ○ Display ad

MET Matrix Worksheet

Life cycle stage	Impact Category					
	Material		Energy use		Toxic emissions	
	(Input)	(Output)	(Input)	(Output)	(output)	
Materials and component production						
Manufacturing						
Distribution						
Use — Operation						
Use — Service						
End-of-Life — Recovery						
End-of-Life — Disposal						

Product: _____

Prepared by: _____

Date: _____

© Raven Business Group, LLC, 2009

Paper Audit Worksheet

Paper	Size	Color	Bright	Recycled content	Supplier	Manufacturer	Location	Purpose	Amount	Comments

Period:
Prepared by:
Date:

Stakeholder Communications Level Worksheet

Planning stage

Stakeholders			Potential Impact (L, M, H)	Communications Emphasis				
				Goals	Strategies	Action	Monitor	Calibrate
Internal		Owners/Investors						
		Board						
		Management						
		Staff						
External	Customers	Wholesalers						
		Retailers						
		End users						
	Suppliers	Vendors						
		Banks, insurers						
		Industry associations						
		Competitors						
		Media						
		Environmental organizations						
		Governmental agencies						
		Educational institutions						
		Local community						
		Employee families & friends						
		General public						

Stakeholder Communications Scheduling Worksheet

	Stakeholders		Audit	Goals	Strategies	Action	Monitor	Calibrate
Internal	Owners/investors							
	Board							
	Management							
	Staff							
External	Customers	Wholesalers						
		Retailers						
		End users						
	Suppliers	Vendors						
		Banks, insurers						
	Industry associations							
	Competitors							
	Media							
	Environmental organizations							
	Governmental agencies							
	Educational institutions							
	Local community							
	Employee families & friends							
	General public							

(Planning stage: Audit, Goals, Strategies, Action, Monitor, Calibrate)

Transportation Audit Worksheet

Commuting

Mode	# of workers	Worker-days	% of worker-days	VMT	GHGs	Comments
SOV/LOV						
Carpool/vanpool						
Public transit						
Bike						
Walk						
Work at home						
Other offsite						
Other						
Total			100%			

Offsite travel

Purpose	# of trips	Principal mode	VMT	GHGs	Comments
Meetings					
Visit to suppliers					
Service call					
Other					
Total					

Goods

Purpose	# of trips	Principal mode	VMT	GHGs	Comments
Incoming materials					
Outgoing freight					
Delivery product					
Takeback product					
Total					

Customers

Travel	# of customers	Principal mode	VMT	GHGs	Comments
Store visit					
Store purchase					
Web visit					
Web purchase					
Total					

Total VMT   _____

Total GHGs   _____

Prepared by: _____

Date: _____

Waste Audit Worksheet

	Material	Description	Quantity	Unit	Comments
Paper	Computer				
	Office				
	Colored				
	Cardboard	Uncompacted			
		Compacted			
		Baled			
	Newspaper	Uncompacted			
		Compacted/baled			
	Other				
Glass	Refillable bottles	Refillable beer			
		Refillable soft drink			
		Other refillable			
	Non-refillable bottles	Whole			
		Crushed			
		Manually broken			
Plastic	1 - PET	whole bottles, uncompacted			
		whole bottles, compacted			
		granulated			
	2 - HDPE	whole bottles, uncompacted			
		whole bottles, compacted			
		baled			
	3 - PVC	loose			
		granulated			
	Mixed	loose			
		granulated			
Metals	Aluminum				
	Brass				
	Cast iron				
	Chromium				
	Cobalt				
	Copper				
	Lead				
	Magnesium				
	Nickel				
	Steel				
	Zinc				
Organics	Grass	Uncompacted			
		Compacted			
	Leaves	Uncompacted			
		Compacted			
	Veg/Fruit				
	Other				
Misc	Construction waste				
	Oil - cooking				
	Oil - petroleum				
	Oil - synthetic				
	Pallets, wood				
	Rubber				
	Tires				

Water Balance Worksheet

Category	Amount	%	Comments
Water purchased			
Water pumped from onsite wells			
Water recovered			
TOTAL WATER SUPPLIED		*100*	
Boiler, cooling tower make-up			
Process use			
Once-through cooling			
Domestic			
General washing & maintenance			
Laundry			
Kitchen			
Pool, spa			
Landscaping			
Leaks (detected)			
TOTAL WATER USED			
WATER UNACCOUNTED FOR			

Period: _____
Notes:

Prepared by: _____
Date: _____

Water Conservation Worksheet

Fixture	Location	Measure	Water savings			Cost			Comments
			Per use savings	Use per day	Days per year	Annual water savings	Mtls	Labor	Total	
Annual Total										

Notes:

Prepared by: _____
Date: _____

Water Consumption Worksheet

	Year 1	Year 2	Year 3	Average	Comments
January					
February					
March					
April					
May					
June					
July					
August					
September					
October					
November					
December					
Annual Total					

Notes:

Prepared by: _____
Date: _____

Window Energy-Efficiency Improvement Worksheet

Window	Location	Description	Existing R-value	Improvement option	Installed Cost	Estimated Savings	Payback

1. Inventory and characterize windows.
2. Calculate *Existing R-value* of windows based on the R-value of that type of unit:

Glass single pane	0.91
Glass single pane w storm	2.00
Glass, double pane w. ¼" airspace	1.69
Glass, double pane w. ½" airspace	2.04
Glass, double pane w. ½" airspace and Low-E	0.20 3.13
Glass, triple pane w. ¼" airspace	2.56
Glass, triple pane w. ½" airspace	3.23

Prepared by: _____
Date: _____

Chapter 1

1. That is to say that when we burn fuel in our vehicles, we pay for the price of extracting, refining, and transporting the fuel to our vehicles. But the purchaser doesn't pay for any indirect costs that result from burning the fuel: the effects of air pollution and smog creation, the absenteeism and medical costs of treating respiratory illness, or climate change and its consequences. Economists call these external costs. They may be external costs to the fuel purchase transaction; but they are internal costs to the health of the planet and its inhabitants!

2. The United States is the third largest country. China, with a 2008 population of 1.3 billion, and India, with a population of 1.1 billion, are home to more than a third of the Earth's people.

3. "Projections of the Population and Components of Change for the United States: 2010 to 2050." Retrieved from *www.census.gov*.

4. Meadows, Randers, and Meadows, *Limits to Growth*, p. 105.

5. Hansen, "Global Warming."

6. Ibid.

7. Lovins, *The Business Case*, p. 7.

Chapter 4

1. *Business Analysis*, p. 7.

2. Based on data presented in *Business Analysis*, p. 8.

3. *Business Analysis*, p. 8.

4. *Putting Energy into Profits: ENERGY STAR ® Guide for Small Business*, p. 3.

Chapter 5

1. Van Rooijen and Udo de Haes, "Life Cycle Approaches," pp. 72–74.

2. McDonough and Braungart, *Cradle to Cradle*. Retrieved from *www.mbdc.com/ref_protocol.htm*.

3. Ibid., p.76.

4. Anastas and Warner, *Green Chemistry*.

5. Lewis and Gertsakis, *design + environment*, p. 31.

6. The project team should be assembled from inside and outside the organization, including product development, production, distribution, finance, purchasing, sales and marketing, waste managers, recyclers, raw material suppliers, component suppliers, consumers, producers, retailers, and transporters.

7. The 1, 2, 3 classification was originally determined with help from EU directives on the marking of chemicals (EU directive 67/548/EEG, European Commission 1967) and Danish lists created in 2000 by Miljøstyrelsen as cited in Hochschorner and Finnveden *Evaluation*.

8. White, Belletire, and St. Pierre, *Okala*.

9. Bare, Norris, Pennington, and Kone, "TRACI," p. 51.

10. Lewis and Gertsakis, *design + environment*, p. 37.

11. Remmen, Landfield, Saur, and Jensen, "Introduction to Sustainability," p. 10.

Chapter 6

1. Based on Envirowise et al, *Packaging Design*, Table 1: "Key Considerations for Packaging Eco-design."

2. Environmental impact estimates were made using the Environmental Defense Fund Paper Calculator. For more information, visit *www.papercalculator.org*.

3. Saphire, *Case Reopened*.

4. *Definition of Sustainable Packaging, Version 1.0*. Sustainable Packaging Coalition, October 2005.

5. Shorr, *How To Use*.

6. Shorr, *Reducing Corrugated Consumption*.

7. Ibid.

8. Shorr, *How To Use*.

9. *How to Select*.

10. Envirowise, et al. *Packaging Design*, p. 23.

Chapter 7

1. The Appendix to *Eco-S.A.T: A Green Purchasing Self-Assessment Tool (Draft)* also contains a directory of green purchasing programs.

2. *GRIP Purchasing*, pp. 29–30.

3. Ibid., pp 24–28.

Chapter 8

1. Olgyay, *Design with Climate*, p. 22.

2. Ibid.

3. *General Purpose Cleaners*, p. 3.

4. Ibid.

5. Ibid.

Chapter 9

1. Note that, in calculating sector consumption, the primary energy used in the electric generating sector was allocated to the sector in which the energy was used.

2. *Annual Energy Review 2007*.

3. *Annual Energy Outlook 2008*.

4. Note that in calculating sector consumption, the primary energy used in the electric generating sector (40.6 quadrillion BTUs in 2007) was allocated to the sector in which the energy was used.
5. *Annual Energy Review 2007.*
6. Ibid., Table 2, p. 7.
7. *Annual Energy Review 2007.*
8. Ibid.
9. Ibid.
10. Pernick and Wilder. *Solar Utility Assessment,* p.4.
11. *Carbon Dioxide Emissions,* Table 4 ("Estimated Carbon Dioxide Emissions Rates from Generating Units at U.S. Electric Plants by Census Division, 1998 and 1999") accessed May 21, 2008, from *www.eia.doe.gov/cneaf/electricity/page/co2_report/co2report.html#table_4.*
12. However, steam delivery is reported to be diminishing. See *Geysers Loosing Steam: A Finite Capacity After All* by Paul Gipe (available from *www.wind-works.org/articles/Geysers.html*).
13. *Distributed Energy Resource Guide.*
14. Wiser and Bolinger. *Annual Report,* p. 21.
15. *AWEA Small Wind,* p. 9.
16. Estimate from solardirect, manufacturer of various solar systems.
17. U.S. Department of Energy Web page: Solar Swimming Pool Heaters, *apps1.eere.energy.gov/consumer/your_home/water_heating/index.cfm/mytopic=13230.*
18. Pernick and Wilder, *Solar Utility,* p. 4.
19. "A Quick Guide."
20. Pernick and Wilder, *Solar Utility,* p. 8.
21. *Putting Energy Into Profits: ENERGY STAR® Guide for Small Business,* pp. 97–98.
22. *U.S. Climate Zones.*
23. "End-Use Consumption."
24. *Putting Energy Into Profits: ENERGY STAR® Guide for Small Business,* pp. 14–15.
25. "End-Use Consumption."
26. *Green Manufacturing,* p. 11.

Chapter 10

1. *Improving Motor and Drive,* p. 87.
2. *Putting Energy Into Profits: ENERGY STAR® Guide for Small Business,* p. 97.
3. *Industrial Energy Efficiency.*

Chapter 11

1. *Advanced Energy Design Guide for Small Warehouses; Advanced Energy Design Guide for Small Office; Advanced Energy Design Guide for Small Retail; Putting Energy into Profits; Rea, IESNA Lighting Handbook;* and *Building Upgrade Manual.*
2. "Brightness and Color of Light."
3. Ibid.
4. *A Consumer's Guide to Energy Efficiency and Renewable Energy.* LED data and efficacy data for incandescents, compact and linear fluorescents, metal halide, and LEDs from the

U.S. Department of Energy's Building Technologies Program.
5. Raven Business Group, LLC.
6. Bullough, "LED Lighting."
7. All data from *The NLB Guide* except value of energy savings computed by assuming 4,000 hours of operation, electricity costs of $.0971 per kWh, and monthly demand charges of $8.00/kW.
8. Ibid.
9. Ibid.
10. *LED Basics,* p. 1.
11. *LED Basics,* p. 2.
12. *Energy Estimates.*
13. Ibid.
14. *Building Upgrade Manual,* Lighting Chapter, p. 8.
15. *The NLB Guide,* p. 18.
16. Ibid., p. 11.
17. *Design Brief.*
18. Color-corrected sodium bulbs reduce the yellowish color of an uncorrected sodium lamp.
19. *Putting Energy into Profits: ENERGY STAR ® Guide for Small Business,* p. 45.
20. "Fact Sheet."
21. "FAQs: Information on Compact."

Chapter 12

1. OSHA Standards are presented on the Website: *www.osha.gov/SLTC/ventilation/standards.html.*
2. *A Consumer's Guide to Energy Efficiency and Renewable Energy.* Table 1: Common Weatherstripping.
3. Ibid.
4. All values from "R-Value Table" except Foam insulated sheathing value, which is from "Wall Insulation Technology."
5. *R-Value Recommendations.*
6. Modified from Carter, "New Insultation."
7. *Putting Energy into Profits: ENERGY STAR Guide for Small Business,* p. 74.
8. *Putting Energy into Profits: ENERGY STAR Guide for Small Business,* p. 74.

Chapter 13

1. *Putting Energy into Profits: ENERGY STAR ® Guide for Small Business,* p. 58.

Chapter 14

1. *Putting Energy into Profits: ENERGY STAR ® Guide for Restaurants,* p. 3.
2. Westphalen, Zogg, Varone, and Foran. *Energy Savings Potential,* pp. 4 and 22.
3. Ibid., p. 64.
4. *Boosting Restaurant Profits,* p. 15.
5. Westphalen, Zogg, Varone, and Foran. *Energy Savings Potential,* pp. 1–2.
6. Ibid., p. 65

Chapter 15

1. Scheihing, "DOE Data Center," p. 2.
2. "Thermal Guidelines."
3. Hydeman, "HVAC and Control."
4. Ibid., p. 16.
5. Ibid., p. 18

Chapter 16

1. Westphalen, Zogg, Varone, and Foran. *Energy Savings Potential*, pp. 45.
2. Ibid., p. 55.
3. *Putting Energy into Profits: ENERGY STAR ® Guide for Restaurants*, p. 3.
4. Ibid.

Chapter 17

1. *Improving Motor and Drive*, p. 69.
2. *Improving the Energy Efficiency.*
3. *Improving Compressed Air*, p. 3.
4. Ibid., pp. 17 and 59.

Chapter 19

1. Cost data for combined heat and power and fuel cells from California Energy Commission's Web-based Distributed Energy Resource Guide.
2. The U.S. Department of Energy's National Renewable Energy Laboratory has a series of maps that can be consulted to assess order of magnitude viability of renewable resources. These maps can be accessed at *www.nrel.gov/gis/maps.html.*
3. Bird, Kreycik, and Friedman, *Green Power Marketing*, p. 1.
4. Ibid., p. 3.
5. Ibid., p. 9.

Chapter 20

1. Battery University. *www.batteryuniversity.com/partone-14A.htm*. Retrieved August 15, 2008.
2. California Energy Commission, *Distributed Energy Resource Guide.*

Chapter 21

1. U.S. Department of Energy, Energy Information Administration, Monthly Energy Review, March 2007, Washington, D.C., Table 2.1.
2. Davis, Diegel, and Boundy. *Transportation Energy*, pp. 1–17.
3. Ibid., Table 1-13.
4. *Inventory of U.S. Greenhouse.*
5. Ibid., p. 8.
6. Davis, Diegel, and Boundy, *Transportation Energy*, Table 1-38.
7. Based on *National Household Travel.*
8. Ibid.
9. Ibid.
10. Moore, "National Transportation Statistics."
11. Davis, Diegel, and Boundy, *Transportation Energy*, Table 8-8.
12. Moore, "National Transportation Statistics," Table 4-20, and Davis, Diegel, and Boundy, *Transportation Energy*, Table 2-13.

13. Energy-efficiency data for rail and water from Davis, Diegel, and Boundy, *Transportation Energy*, Table 2-16.
14. Truck data based on OTA data cited in *Washington State Action Plan*, retrieved from "Truck to Train."
15. U.S. EPA original data cited in Moore, "National Transportation Statistics," tables 4-38 and 4-39.
16. Campbell, Kassel, Mark, and Robinson. "Diesel-Electric Hybrid."
17. Facanha and Horvath, "Environmental Assessment," p. 236.
18. Facanha and Horvath, "Environmental Assessment."
19. Corbett and Fischbeck. *Commercial Marine Emissions*, pp. A-9–A-12.
20. Argonne National Laboratory's GREET Website: The Greenhouse Gases, Regulated Emissions, and Energy Use in Transportation (GREET) Model: *www.transportation.anl.gov/modeling_simulation/GREET/index.html*
21. *Tires and Passenger*, p. 46.
22. "Drive Smart."
23. "Advanced Vehicle Components."
24. "Push Less Air."
25. "Improvements in Large Truck."
26. Ogburn, "Profitable GHG Reduction."
27. "Improvements in Large Truck."
28. Ogburn, "Profitable GHG Reduction."
29. *A Glance at Clean.*
30. *Saving Energy in U.S.*
31. Ogburn, "Profitable GHG Reduction."

Chapter 22

1. Vickers, *Handbook of Water Use*, p. 240. Data based on 1995 information from the U.S. Geological Survey's Circular 1200, Estimated Water Use in the United States in 1995. The USGS did not report commercial use in its five-year update in 2000, and is in the process of compiling *Estimated Water Use in the United States in 2005*. The USGS has concluded that there has been relatively little variation in total consumption since 1985.
2. Adapted from Vickers, *Handbook of Water Use*, p. 234.
3. *A Water Conservation Guide.*
4. *Texas Industrial Water Use Efficiency Study*, by Pequod Associated, Inc. Cited by Vickers, p. 241.
5. "How to Conserve."
6. Some plantings, such as maple trees, are best pruned in the summer. Consult your local nursery or extension agent to determine optimal pruning times.) Some summer pruning—to remove dead, damaged, or diseased limbs and branches—is appropriate. Emergency survival pruning may be necessary if a plant has severe drought stress. (Seek professional guidance.)

Chapter 23

1. University of Cincinnati, University Health Services' Hearing Conservation Program; Reliability Direct's Sound Level Decibel Loudness Comparison Chart: NIOSH Power Tools Database.

Chapter 24

1. *Climate Change 2007*, Table 2.14.
2. *Inventory of U.S. Greenhouse.*
3. Ibid., *Table 2-12. Annex 2, Table A-30 and U.S. EPA Power Profiler.*
4. The U.S. EPA's original list of hazardous air pollutants may be retrieved from *www.epa.gov/ttn/atw/188polls.html.*
5. For a list of categories, see the National Emission Standards for Hazardous Air Pollutants; Revision of List of Categories of Sources and Schedule for Standards Under Section 112 of the Clean Air Act, plus any revisions or amendments: *www.epa.gov/fedrgstr/EPA-AIR/ 1998/February/Day-12/a3446.htm.*
6. "IAQ Building Education."
7. Karlstrom, *How to Grow.*

Chapter 25

1. *Municipal Solid Waste*, p. 1.
2. Ibid., p. 2.
3. *Targeted Statewide.*
4. *Municipal Solid Waste*, p. 3.
5. Ibid., Figure 3, page 3.
6. Methane can be captured from landfills and used for energy generation, as can heat from incineration processes.
7. *Solid Waste Management.*
8. "Plastics Recycling."
9. *Municipal Solid Waste*, Table 7.
10. There is some controversy over the chemical agents used to enable biodegradability. If stipulating biodegradable products, consider precautionary principles to ensure all substances have been proven to cause no harm.
11. Howard, "What Do Recycling"; "Back to the Future"; "Smart Plastics Guide"; and *Municipal Solid Waste*, p. 1.
12. "General Information."
13. "Recycling Laws."
14. *Managing Used Oil.*
15. Ibid.
16. *Scrap Tire Markets.*
17. Composting options include:
    - Unaerated static pile: Organic discards are mixed with a bulking material. Suitable for small operations (e.g. employee lunch room).
    - Aerated windrow piles: Organics are piled in long rows and aerated passively or mechanically. Suitable for large operations—provided there is suitable space.
    - In-vessel composting: Manual or mechanized mixing (aerating) in vessel located inside or out. Time- and space-efficient option for processing medium quantities (although smaller vessels are marketed).
    - Vermicomposting: Worms rapidly break down organic materials into high quality compost.

Chapter 26

1. Paper consumption data retrieved May 27, 2008 from *www.tappi.org/paperu/all_about_paper/faq.htm.*
2. Ibid., p. 4.
3. *Municipal Solid Waste*, p. 4.
4. *Choose Green Report: Alternative*, p. 1. Data for 2005 confirmed in *City of Portland.*
5. *Paper Task Force*, p. 37.
6. Ibid., p. 38.
7. Ibid.
8. Forssander, *Responsible Printing.*
9. *Field Guide*, p. 6.
10. *Environmental Benefits.*
11. Environmental impact estimates were made using the Environmental Defense Fund Paper Calculator. For more information, visit *www.papercalculator.org.*
12. Forssander, *Responsible Printing*, p. 48.
13. McDonough and Braungart, *Cradle to Cradle*, p. 167.
14. *Field Guide*, p. 13.
15. McDonough and Braungart, *Cradle to Cradle*, p. 166.

Chapter 27

1. Ayling, *Rapid Response.*
2. Bachman, *Marketing.*
3. Makower, *Strategies for the Green*, p. 42.
4. Ibid., pp. 44–45.
5. Ibid., p. 47, with percentages from "2008 LOHAS Consumer Trends."
6. *2007 Cone Consumer.*
7. Ibid.
8. *Ecomarkets 2008*, p. 9.

Chapter 28

1. *Ecomarkets 2008*, p. 11.
2. The ISO standards for eco-labeling are:
    - ISO 14020: 2000 Establishes nine general principles that apply to labeling and environmental claims.
    - ISO 14021: 1999 Establishes criteria for Type II self-declared environmental claims.
    - ISO 14024: 1999 Establishes principles and procedures for Type I labeling.
    - ISO 14025: 2006 Establishes principles and procedures for Type III Standard.
    - ISO 14040: 2006 Establishes principles and framework for life cycle analyses, a key component of the Type III Standard.
3. *Ecomarkets 2008*, p. 11.
4. Ibid.
5. Retrieved August 28, 2008, from *ecolabelling.org/.*

Chapter 29

1. *2007 Cone.*

Bibliography

Advanced Energy Design Guide for Small Office Buildings: Achieving 30% Energy Savings Over ANSI/ASHRAE/IESNA Standards 90.1-1999. American Society of Heating, Refrigerating and Air-Conditioning Engineers, Inc. (ASHRAE), The American Institute of Architects, Illuminating Engineering Society of North America, New Buildings Institute, and the U.S. Department of Energy. Atlanta, Ga.: ASHRAE, 2008.

Advanced Energy Design Guide for Small Retail Buildings: Achieving 30% Energy Savings Toward a Net Zero Energy Building. American Society of Heating, Refrigerating and Air-Conditioning Engineers, Inc. (ASHRAE), The American Institute of Architects, Illuminating Engineering Society of North America, U.S. Green Building Council, and the U.S. Department of Energy. Atlanta, Ga.: ASHRAE, 2008.

Advanced Energy Design Guide for Small Warehouses and Self-Storage Buildings: Achieving 30% Energy Savings Toward a Net Zero Energy Building. American Society of Heating, Refrigerating and Air-Conditioning Engineers, Inc. (ASHRAE), The American Institute of Architects, Illuminating Engineering Society of North America, U.S. Green Building Council, and the U.S. Department of Energy. Atlanta, Ga.: ASHRAE, 2008.

"Advanced Vehicle Components Increase Fuel Economy." Clean Car Campaign, 2008. Retrieved May 15, 2008, from *www.cleancarcampaign.org/advtech.shtml.*

Anastas, Paul, and John Warner, in *Green Chemistry: Theory and Practice.* New York: Oxford University Press, 1998.

Annual Energy Outlook 2008: With Projections to 2030. Washington, D.C.: DOE/EIA-0383 (2008). Washington, D.C.: U.E. Energy Information Agency, June 2008.

Annual Energy Review 2007. DOE/EIA-0384 (2007), Washington, D.C.: U.S. Energy Information Administration, June 2008. Retrieved September 9, 2008, from *www.eia.doe.gov/aer/pdf/aer.pdf.*

"Appendix G: Planning Template" in *Environmental Packaging Guideline For the Electronics Industry.* University of California, Santa Barbara. Accessible from *www.deq.state.or.us/lq/pubs/docs/sw/packaging/toolsappendixg.pdf.*

AWEA Small Wind Turbine Global Market Study 2008. Washington, D.C.: American Wind Energy Association (AWEA), May 2008. Available from *www.awea.org/.*

Ayling, Geoff. *Rapid Response Advertising.* Warriewood, Australia: Business & Professional Publishing, 1999.

Bachman, Glenn. "30 Reasons Why Organizations Buy," delivered as part of a workshop: "Marketing: The Profile... The Pursuit... The Payoff." San Rafael, Calif.: The Business Renaissance, November 21, 2003.

"Back to the Future: Plants Made from Plants Instead of Toxic Chemicals." Center for Health, Environment and Justice. Available at *www.besafenet.com/pvc/bioplastics.htm.*

Bare, Jane C., Gregory A. Norris, David W. Pennington, and Thomas Kone. "TRACI—The Tool for the Reduction and Assessment of Chemical and Other Environmental Impacts." *Journal of Industrial Ecology.* Volume 6, Number 3–4 (2002): 49–78.

"Basement Insulation Technology Fact Sheet." DOE/GO-102002-0776. Oak Ridge, Tenn.: U.S. Department of Energy's Office of Building Technology, January 2002.

Batteries for IT Systems: Environmental Issues. GreenIT™. 2005.

Benyus, Janine M. *Biomimicry: Innovation Inspired by Nature.* New York: Harper Perennial, 2002.

Biofuels: An Important Part of a Low-Carbon Diet. Cambridge, Mass.: UCS (Union of Concerned Scientists) Publications, 2007. Retrieved May 13, 2008, from *www.ucsusa.org/clean_vehicles/vehicles_health/biofuels-low-carbon-diet.html.*

Bird, Lori, Claire Kreycik, and Barry Friedman. *Green Power Marketing in the United States: A Status Report (11th edition).* Golden, Colo.: U.S. National Renewable Energy Laboratory, October 2008.

Boosting Restaurant Profits with Energy Efficiency: A Guide for Restaurant Owners and Managers. Efficiency Partnership. San Francisco: August 2006.

Brezet, H., et al. *PROMISE Manual.* Delft, The Netherlands: Delft University of Technology, TME Institute and TNO Product Centre, 1996.

Brezet, J.A., S.A. Bijma, J. Ehrenfeld, and S. Silvester. *The Design of Eco-Efficient Services; Method, Tools and Review of the Case Study Based "Designing Eco-efficient Services" Project.* Delft, The Netherlands: Delft University of Technology. Retrieved from *www.score-network.org/files//806_1.pdf.*

"Brightness and Color of Light." Retrieved September 20, 2008, from the Environmental Defense Fund Website: *www.edf.org/page.cfm?tagid=630.*

Building Upgrade Manual. Washington, D.C.: U.S. Environmental Protection Agency. Retrieved September 18, 2008, from *www.energystar.gov/index.cfm?c=business.bus_upgrade_manual.*

Bullough, John D. "LED Lighting Systems." *Lighting Answers*, Volume 7, Issue 3, May 2003. Troy, N.Y.: National Lighting Information Program, Rensselaer Polytechnic Institute.

Business Analysis for Energy-Efficiency Investments. EPA–430–B–97–002. Washington, D.C.: U.S. Environmental Protection Agency, June 1998.

Butz, Amanda, Steve Ponce de Leon, Natasha Stevens-Sattin, and Zach Vieth. *Developing a Supplier Survey for Springs Window Fashions.* Madison, Wisc.: University of Wisconsin Student Project, 2007.

Cairncross, Frances. *Costing the Earth: The Challenge for Governments, The Opportunities for Business.* Boston: Harvard Business School Press, 1987.

Campbell, Todd, Richard Kassel, Jason Mark, and Michelle Robinson. "Diesel-Electric Hybrid Buses: Addressing the Technical and Public Health Issues." 1999. Retrieved May 10, 2008, from *www.nrdc.org/air/transportation/pd-ebus.asp.*

Cannon, Sandra. *The Competitive Advantage: Eco-Purchasing, Executive's Vision/Purchaser's Handbook.* Columbus, Ohio:: Battelle Press, 2006.

Carbon Dioxide Emissions from the Generation of Electric Power in the United States. U.S. Department of Energy and U.S. Environmental Protection Agency, 2000.

Carter, Joe. "New Insulation Options." Retrieved from This Old House Website: *www.thisoldhouse.com/toh/article/0,,1130563,00.html.*

Chemical Use in the Production of Recycled Paper. Waste & Resources Action Programme. Available from *www.wrap.org.uk/downloads/5._Chemical_use_A4.9517eebc.2714.pdf.*

Choose Green Report: Alternative Fiber Papers. Washington, D.C.: Green Seal, April/May 1998.

Choose Green Report: Copy Paper. Washington, D.C.: Green Seal, January/February 2000.

Choose Green Report: Low Rolling Resistance Tires. Washington, D.C.: Green Seal, 2003.

Clarke, A., and J. K. Gershenson. "Design for the Life-Cycle" in *Handbook of Environmentally Conscious Mechanical Design.* M. Kutz (ed.). Hoboken, N.J.: John Wiley & Sons, 2007.

Climate Change 2007: The Physical Science Basis. Intergovernmental Panel on Climate Change, Working Group I to the Fourth Assessment. Cambridge, England: Cambridge University Press, 2007.

A Comprehensive Analysis of Biodiesel Impacts on Exhaust Emissions: Draft Technical Report. EPAA420-P-02-001. Washington, D.C.: U.S. EPA, 2002.

A Consumer's Guide to Energy Efficiency and Renewable Energy. Accessible from the U.S. Department of Energy Website: *apps1.eere.energy.gov/consumer/your_home/insulation_airsealing/index.cfm/mytopic=11280.*

A Consumer's Guide to Energy Efficiency and Renewable Energy. Types of Lighting. Retrieved September 21, 2008, from the U.S. Department of Energy Website: *apps1.eere.energy.gov/consumer/your_home/lighting_daylighting/index.cfm?mytopic=12030.*

Corbett, James J., and Paul S. Fischbeck. *Commercial Marine Emissions Inventory for EPA Category 2 and 3 Compression Ignition Marine Engines in the United States Continental and Inland Waterways.* EPA420-R-98-020. Washington, D.C.: prepared for U.S. EPA, August 1998.

Crafting a Green IT Action Plan. London, Ontario, Canada: Info-Tech Research Group, April 2008.

Crul, M.R.M., and J.C. Diehl. *Design for Sustainability: A Practical Approach for Developing Economies.* Paris, France: UNEP, 2007. Downloadable from *www.d4s-de.org/.*

Culver, Alicia, Marian Feinberg, David Klebenov, Judy Musnikow, and Lara Sutherland. *Cleaning for Health: Products and Practices for a Safer Indoor Environment.* New York: INFORM, Inc., 2002.

Davis, Stacy C., Susan W. Diegel, and Robert G. Boundy. *Transportation Energy Data Book.* Oak Ridge, Tenn.: Oak Ridge National Laboratory, 2008.

Deru, M., N. Blair, and P. Torcellini. *Procedure to Measure Indoor Lighting Energy Performance.* Golden, Colo.: U.S. DOE National Renewable Energy Laboratory, Report No. NREL/TP-550-38602, October 2005.

Design Brief: Outdoor Lighting & Title 24. Architectural Energy Corporation. Calif., energy design resources, December 2006.

Design Guidelines for Sustainable Packaging. Charlottesville, Va.: Sustainable Packaging Coalition (SPC), 2008.

Di Costanzo, Diane. "Paper: Certified Recycled." *Green Guide 99*, November/December 2003. Accessed from *www.thegreenguide.com/doc/99/paper.*

Distributed Energy Resource Guide. California Energy Commission. Accessible from *www.energy.ca.gov/distgen/equipment/equipment.html.*

Dolliver, Mark. "Deflating a Myth: Consumers Aren't as Devoted to the Planet as You Wish They Were." *AdWeek*, May 12, 2008.

"Drive Smart: Fuel Savings Add Up." Retrieved April 16, 2008, from Best Driving Practices from the Environmental Defense Fund's Flight Global Warming Website: *www.edf.org/page.cfm?tagID=268.*

Ecological Footprint Standards 2006. Oakland, Calif.: Global Footprint Network, June 6, 2006. Accessible from *www.footprintstandards.org.*

Ecomarkets 2008—Summary Report. Philadelphia, Pa. and Ottawa, Ontario: TerraChoice Environmental Marketing, Inc., July 2008.

EcoStrategies for Printed Communications. Seattle, Wash.: Partners in Design, 1996. Accessible from *www.pidseattle.com.*

Eco-S.A.T: A Green Purchasing Self-Assessment Tool (Draft). North American Green Purchasing Initiative, Winter 2004.

Elizabeth, Lynn, and Cassandra Adams (eds.). *Alternative Construction: Contemporary Natural Building Methods.* New York: John Wiley & Sons, 2000.

"End-Use Consumption for Natural Gas, Electricity, and Fuel Oil, 1999 (Preliminary Estimates)." Retrieved September 9, 2009, from *www.eia.doe.gov/emeu/cbecs/enduse_consumption/intro.html.*

Energy Estimates of Light Emitting Diodes in Niche Lighting. Washington, D.C.: Navigant Consulting, Inc., prepared for Building Technologies Program of the U.S. Department of Energy, October 2008.

Environmental Benefits of Recycling Paper. Waste & Resources Action Programme. Undated information sheet. Available from *www.wrap.org.uk/downloads/Is_Recycled_better_than_virgin_3.bee37190.3143.pdf.*

"Environmentally Preferable Purchasing Guidance." Supplement to *A Common Vision for Transforming the Paper Industry: Striving for Environmental and Social Sustainability.* Ratified at the Environmental Paper Summit held in Sonoma County, Calif., November 20, 2002.

Envirowise, EROTEC Research & Consulting Ltd., Giraffe Innovation Consultants, Barry Overton, and Enviros. *Packaging Design for the Environment: Reducing Cost and Quantities.* Oxfordshire, UK: 2008. Download from *www.envirowise.gov.uk.*

Eshel, Gidon, and Pamela A. Martin. "Diet, Energy and Global Warming." *Earth Interactions. Volume 10, Paper number 9, 2006.*

"Estimating Luminance and Illuminance With Reflection-Type Exposure Meters and an 18% Neutral Test Card." Retrieved September 22, 2008, from the Kodak Company Website: *www.kodak.com/cluster/global/en/consumer/products/techInfo/am105/am105kic.shtml.*

Evaluation of Environmental Impacts in Life Cycle Assessment: Meeting Report Brussels 29–30 November 1998, and Brighton 25–26 May 2000. Paris, France: United Nations Environment Program in collaboration with U.S. Environmental Protection Agency, Center of Environmental Science at Leiden University, and Environmental Analysis and Management Group, 2003.

Facanha, Cristiano, and Arpad Horvath. "Environmental Assessment of Freight Transportation in the U.S." *Journal of Life Cycle Assessment,* 11 (4), 2006.

Facility Manager's Guide to Water Management. Prepared by AMWUA Regional Water Conservation Committee with assistance from Black & Veatch. Arizona Municipal Water Users Association, 2003.

"Fact Sheet: Mercury Use in Lighting." Northeast Waste Management Officials' Association. Updated August 2008. Retrieved September 22, 2008, from *www.newmoa.org/prevention/mercury/imerc/FactSheets/lighting.cfm.*

"FAQs: Information on Compact Fluorescent Light Bulbs (CFLs) and Mercury." U.S. Environmental Protection Agency, June 2008. Retrieved September 22, 2008, from *www.energystar.gov/ia/partners/promotions/change_light/downloads/Fact_Sheet_Mercury.pdf. Field Guide to Eco-Friendly, Efficient and Effective Print.* Brattleboro, Vt.: Monadnack Paper Mills, 2006.

Financing Your Energy-Efficiency Upgrade. EPA-430-B-97-003. Washington, D.C.: U.S. Environmental Protection Agency, June 1998.

Fishbein, Bette K., John Ehrenfeld and John Young. *Extended Producer Responsibility: A Materials Policy for the 21st Century.* New York, N.Y.: Inform, Inc., 2000.

Foreman, Stacey Stack. *City of Portland Sustainable Paper Use Policy 2005 Annual Report.* Portland, Oreg.: Bureau of Purchases, January 2006.

Forssander, Carol. "Responsible Printing in the Environmental Age." *Forum,* April 2008. Retrieved June 6, 2008, from *www.associationforum-digital.com/associationforum/200804/.*

Franks, John R., Mark R. Stephenson, and Carol J. Merry (eds.). *Preventing Occupational Hearing Loss—A Practical Guide.* U.S. Department of Health and Human Services, National Institute for Occupational Safety and Health, October 1996. Available at *www.cdc.gov/niosh/96-110.html.*

"A Fresh Look at Packaging" in *WasteWi$e Update.* EPA530-N-95-004. Washington, D.C.: U.S. Environmental Protection Agency, 1995.

Frey, H. Christopher, and Po-Yao Kuo. *Best Practices Guidebook for Greenhouse Gs Reductions in Freight Transportation: Final Report.* Raleigh, N.C.: North Carolina State University, October 2007.

Friedman, Thomas L. *Hot, Flat and Crowded: Why We Need a Green Revolution—and How It Can Renew America.* New York: Farrar, Straus and Giroux, 2008.

"General Information on E-Waste." Retrieved August 18, 2008, from the U.S. EPA Website: *www.epa.gov/epaoswer/hazwaste/recycle/ecycling/faq.htm#howmuch.*

General Purpose Cleaners. Washington, D.C.: Green Seal, Inc. 1998.

Gipe, Paul. *Wind Power for Home, Farm, and Business: Renewable Energy for the New Millennium.* White River Junction, Vt.: Chelsea Green Publishing Company, 2004.

A Glance at Clean Freight Strategies: Low Viscosity Lubricants. U.S. EPA, SmartWay^{SM} Transport Partnership. EPA 420-F- 04-006, February 2004.

Gore, Al. *An Inconvenient Truth: The Planetary Emergency of Global Warming and What We Can Do About It.* New York: Rodale Books, 2006.

Grama, Sorin, Elizabeth Wayman, and Travis Bradford. *Concentrating Solar Power—Technology, Cost and Markets.* Boston, Mass.: Prometheus Institute for Sustainable Development and Greentech Media, 2008.

Green Manufacturing: Adoption and Implementation: Summary and Analysis of EFT's Survey. Eye for Transport, August 2008.

Greening Your Purchase of Cleaning Products: A Guide For Federal Purchasers. U.S. Environmental Protection Agency. Available at *www.epa.gov/epp/pubs/cleaning.htm.*

GRIP Purchasing, An Environmentally Efficient Purchasing Procedure for: Lower Totals Costs, a More Efficient Covering of Functional Needs, the Development of Competitive and Creative Suppliers: A Guide for the Project Manager/Purchasing Officer. Oslo, Norway: GRIP Centre—Norwegian Centre for Sustainable Production and Consumption, 1996.

"Guide to Ecological Papers." Celery Design Collaborative. San Francisco: American Institute of Graphic Artists. Available from *www.greenbiz.com/files/document/O16F7331.pdf.*

Guide to Purchasing Green Power: Renewable Electricity, Renewable Energy Certificates, and On-Site Renewable Generation. U.S. Environmental Protection Agency, World Resources Institute and the Center for Resource Solutions, September 2004. Downloadable from *www.epa.gov/greenpower/documents/purchasing_guide_for_web.pdf.*

Hansen, James. "Global Warming Twenty Years Later: Tipping Points Near." Briefing delivered to the House Select Committee on Energy Independence & Global Warming. June 23, 2008.

Hawken, Paul, Amory Lovins, and Hunter Lovins. *Natural Capitalism: Creating the Next Industrial Revolution.* Boston: Back Bay Books, 2000.

Hochschorner, Elisabeth. *Assessment of Tools for Environmentally Preferable Procurement with a Life Cycle Perspective—The case of acquisition in Swedish Defense.* Stockholm, Sweden: Royal Institute of Technology, 2004.

Hochschorner, Elisabeth, and Goran Finnveden. *Evaluation of Two Simplified Life Cycle Assessment Methods.* Stockholm, Sweden: Royal Institute of Technology, April 2003.

How to Buy Better Computers: Going Beyond EPEAT. Basel Action Network, Center for Environmental Health, Clean Production Action, Green Purchasing Institute, Silicon Valley Toxics Coalition and Texas Campaign for the Environment, 2007.

"How to Conserve Water and Use it Effectively." Retrieved from *www.epa.gov/nps/chap3.html.*

"How to Pick a Better Bulb." Retrieved September 21, 2008, from the Environmental Defense Fund Website: *www.edf.org/page.cfm?tagid=608.*

"How to Press Printers to Reduce Waste, Emissions, and Costs." GreenBiz, August 9, 2004. Retrieved May 27, 2008, from *www.greenbiz.com/resources/resource/how-press-printers-reduce-waste-emissions-and-costs.*

How to Select Shipping Containers. Milford, Ohio: Buckhorn, Inc., 1991. Cited in U.S. EPA's "A Fresh Look at Packaging" in *WasteWi$e Update.* EPA530-N-95-004. 1995.

Howard, Bryan Clark. "What Do Recycling Symbols on Plastics Mean? A Guide to Recycling Codes." Retrieved August 20, 2008, from the Daily Green: *www.thedailygreen.com/green-homes/latest/recycling-symbols-plastics-460321?click=main_sr.*

Hydeman, Mark. "HVAC and Control System Design for Improved Energy Performance in Data Centers." Presentation delivered at EPA Conference on Data Centers, February 1, 2006. Retrieved from *www.energystar.gov/ia/products/downloads/HVAC_and_Control_System_Design.pdf.*

"IAQ Building Education and Assessment Model." Retrieved September 7, 2008, from the U.S. EPA Website: *www.epa.gov/iaq/largebldgs/i-beam/visual_reference/chapter_2/02_04.html.*

"Improvements in Large Truck Aerodynamics Could Save U.S. Nearly One Billion Gallons of Fuel Annually." Green Car Congress, November 14, 2006. Retrieved April 29, 2008, from *www.greencarcongress.com/2006/11/study_improveme.html.*

Improving Compressed Air System Performance: A Sourcebook for Industry. Washington, D.C.: U.S. Department of Energy, Industrial Technologies Program, Lawrence Berkeley National Laboratory and Resource Dynamics Corp., 2003. Available from *www1.eere.energy.gov/industry/bestpractices/pdfs/compressed_air_sourcebook.pdf.*

Improving Fan System Performance: A Sourcebook for Industry. Washington, D.C.: U.S. Department of Energy, Industrial Technologies Program, Lawrence Berkeley National Laboratory and Resource Dynamics Corp., 2003. Available at *www1.eere.energy.gov/industry/bestpractices/pdfs/fan_sourcebook.pdf.*

Improving Motor and Drive System Performance: A Sourcebook for Industry. Washington, D.C.: U.S. Department of Energy, Industrial Technologies Program, Lawrence Berkeley National Laboratory and Resource Dynamics Corp., 2008. Available at *www1.eere.energy.gov/industry/bestpractices/pdfs/motor.pdf.*

Improving Process Heating System Performance: A Sourcebook for Industry. Washington, D.C.: U.S. Department of Energy, Industrial Technologies Program, Lawrence Berkeley National Laboratory and Resource Dynamics Corp., 2008. Available at *www1.eere.energy.gov/industry/bestpractices/pdfs/process_heating_sourcebook2.pdf.*

Improving Pumping System Performance: A Sourcebook for Industry. Washington, D.C.: U.S. Department of Energy, Industrial Technologies Program, Lawrence Berkeley National Laboratory and Resource Dynamics Corp., 2006. Available at *www1.eere.energy.gov/industry/bestpractices/pdfs/pump.pdf.*

Improving Steam System Performance: A Sourcebook for Industry. Washington, D.C.: U.S. Department of Energy, Industrial Technologies Program, Lawrence Berkeley National Laboratory and Resource Dynamics Corp., 2004. Available at *www1.eere.energy.gov/industry/bestpractices/techpubs_steam.html.*

Industrial Energy Efficiency: Using New Technologies to Reduce Energy Use in Industry and Manufacturing. Washington, D.C.: Environmental and Energy Study Institute, May 2006.

Industrial and Institutional Cleaners. Washington, D.C.: Green Seal, Inc., 1999.

Inventory of U.S. Greenhouse Gas Emissions and Sinks: 1990–2006. EPA 430-R-08-005. Washington, D.C.: U.S. Environmental Protection Agency, April 15, 2008.

Jones, E., D. Harrison, and J.McLaren. "Managing Creative Eco-innovation: Structuring Outputs from Eco-Innovation Projects." *The Journal of Sustainable Product Design*, Volume 1, Number 1, 2001, pp. 27–39.

Jones, E., N.A. Stanton, and D. Harrison. "Applying Structured Methods to Eco-Innovation. An Evaluation of the Product Ideas Tree Diagram." *Design Studies*, Volume 22, No. 6, November 2001, pp. 519–42.

Karlstrom, Solvie. "How to Grow Clean Air." *The Green Guide*, April 17, 2007. Retrieved September 7, 2008, from *www.thegreenguide.com/blog/tow/792*.

Kibbey, David (ed.). *Architectural Resource Guide and Database*. Berkeley, Calif.: Northern California Chapter of Architects/Designers/ Planners for Social Responsibility, 2001.

Krick, Thomas, Maya Forstater, Philip Monaghan, and Maria Sillanpää. *The Stakeholder Engagement*. Cobourg, Ontario, Canada: Stakeholder Research Associates Canada, Inc., United Nations Environment Programme, and AccountAbility. July 2005.

Krupp, Fred, and Miriam Horn. *Earth: The Sequel—The Race to Reinvent Energy and Stop Global Warming*. New York: W.W. Norton & Company, 2008.

Kunstler, James Howard. *The Long Emergency: Surviving the End of Oil, Climate Change, and Other Converging Catastrophes of the Twenty-First Century*. New York: Atlantic Monthly Press, 2005.

The Lean and Green Supply Chain: A Practical Guide for Materials Managers and Supply Chain Managers to Reduce Costs and Improve Environmental Performance. EPA 742-R-00-001. Washington, D.C.: US EPA Environmental Accounting Project, January 2000.

LeClair, Kim, and David Rousseau. *Environmental By Design: A Sourcebook of Environmentally Aware Material Choices: Volume 1: Interiors*. Vancouver, B.C.: Hartley & Marks Ltd., 1992.

LED Basics. PNNL-SA-58429. Richland, Wash.: Pacific Northwest National Laboratory, U.S. Department of Energy, Building Technologies Program, January 2008.

Lewis, Helen, and John Gertsakis. *design + environment: a global guide to designing greener goods*. Sheffield, UK: Greenleaf Publishing Limited, 2001.

Life Cycle Inventory of Packaging Options for Shipment of Retail Mail-Order Soft Goods: Final Peer Report. Prairie Village, Ks.: Franklin Associates, Inc., April 2004.

Lorenz, Peter, Dickon Pinner, and Thomas Seitz. "The Economics of Solar Power: Don't Be Fooled by Technological Uncertainty and the Continued Importance of Regulation: Solar Will Become More Economically Attractive." *The McKinsey Quarterly*, June 2008.

Lovins, L. Hunter. *The Business Case for Climate Protection*. Eldorado Springs, Colo.: Natural Capitalism Solutions, 2005.

Life Cycle Assessment: Principles and Practice. Science Applications International Corporation. Prepared for National Risk Management Laboratory, Reston, Va. May 2006.

Makower, Joel. "Lessons from the Leaders." From Joel Makower's blog: two steps forward, September 21, 2005. Retrievable from *makower.typepad.com/*.

———. *Strategies for the Green Economy: Opportunities and Challenges in the New World of Business*. New York: McGraw Hill, 2008.

Managing Used Oil: Advice for Small Business. Retrieved August 15, 2008, from U.S. EPA Website: *www.epa.gov/epaoswer/hazwaste/usedoil/ usedoil.htm*.

Manzini, Ezio, and Carlo Vezzoli. *Product-Service Systems and Sustainability*. Paris, France: United Nations Environmental Programme. Retrieved from *www.score-network.org/files//820_12.pdf*.

McDonough, William, and Michael Braungart. *Cradle to Cradle: Remaking the Way that We Make Things*. New York: North Point Press, 2002.

Meadows, Donella, Jorgen Randers, and Dennis Meadows. *Limits to Growth: The 30-Year Update*. White River Junction, Vt.: Chelsea Green Publishing Company, 2004.

Mendler, Sandra, William Odell, and Mary Ann Lazarus. *The Guidebook to Sustainable Design*. Hoboken, N.J.: John Wiley & Sons, Inc., 2006.

Moore, William H. (ed.). "National Transportation Statistics." Washington, D.C.: U.S. Dept. of Transportation, Research and Innovative Technology Administration, Bureau of Transportation Statistics, 2008.

Municipal Solid Waste Generation, Recycling, and Disposal in the United States: Facts and Figures for 2006. Washington, D.C.: U.S. Environmental Protection Agency. Retrieved August 18, 2008, from *www.epa.gov/epaoswer/non-hw/muncpl/pubs/msw06.pdf*.

National Household Travel Survey, Long Distance Business Travel Quick Facts. U.S. Department of Transportation, Bureau of Transportation Statistics. Retrieved May 4, 2008, from *www.bts.gov/programs/national_household_travel_survey/ long_distance_business_travel.html*.

"1999 Preliminary End Use Estimates" in *1999 Commercial Buildings Energy Consumption Survey*. Washington, D.C.: U.S. Energy Information Administration. Retrieved September 9, 2008, from *www.eia.doe.gov/emeu/cbecs/detailed_tables_1999.html*.

The NLB Guide to Energy-Efficient Lighting Systems. Silver Spring, Md.: National Lighting Bureau, no date.

Noise Control: A Guide for Workers and Employers. U.S. OSHA. Washington, D.C.: U.S. Department of Labor, 1980. Retrieved September 9, 2008, from *www.nonoise.org/hearing/noisecon/noisecon.htm.*

Ogburn, Michael. "Profitable GHG Reduction Through Fuel Economy: Off-the-Shelf Technologies That Bring Savings to Your Bottom Line." Presentation, Rocky Mountain Institute (Boulder, Colo.), 2007.

An Office Building Occupant's Guide to Indoor Air Quality. EPA-402-K-97-003. Washington, D.C.: U.S. Environmental Protection Agency, October 1997.

Olgyay, Victor. *Design with Climate: Bioclimatic Approach to Architectural Regionalism.* Princeton, N.J.: Princeton University Press, 1963.

120 Tips on Reducing Packaging Use and Costs. Oxfordshire, UK: Envirowise and WSP Environmental Ltd., 2002.

Ottman, Jacquelyn. "The Five Simple Rules of Green Marketing." November 20, 2007. Retrievable from the MarketingProfs Website: *www.marketingprofs.com.*

———. *Green Marketing: Opportunity for Innovation.* New York: BookSurge Publishing, 1998.

———. "The Power of Green Lies in Marketers' Hands." September 16, 2008. Retrievable from the MarketingProfs Website: *www.marketingprofs.com.*

———. "The Rules of 'Green' Marketing." January 31, 2006. Retrievable from the MarketingProfs Website: *www.marketingprofs.com.*

Packaging Evaluation: Redesign Box Geometry. Portland, Oreg.: Oregon Department of Environmental Quality, 2005.

Packaging Evaluation: Packaging Waste Reduction Checklist. Portland, Oreg.: Oregon Department of Environmental Quality, 2005.

Paper Task Force Recommendations for Purchasing and Using Environmentally Preferable Paper: Final Report of the Paper Task Force. New York: Environmental Defense Fund, 1995.

Partridge, Katherine, Charles Jackson, David Wheeler, and Asaf Zohar. The Stakeholder Engagement Manual: Volume 1—The Guide to Practitioners' Perspectives on Stakeholder Engagement. Cobourg, Ontario, Canada: Stakeholder Research Associates Canada, Inc., United Nations Environment Programme, and AccountAbility, July 2005.

Pernick, Ron, and Clint Wilder. *Solar Utility Assessment Study: Reaching Ten Percent Solar by 2025.* Washington, D.C.: Clean-Edge Inc. and Co-op America Foundation, June 2008.

"Plastics Recycling Information Sheet." Retrieved August 21, 2008, from Waste Online Website: *www.wasteonline.org.uk/resources/ InformationSheets/Plastics.htm.*

Public Transportation Fact Book. Washington, D.C.: APTA, 2007.

"Push Less Air Pull More Profit: A Guide to Increasing Fuel Economy." Paccar, Inc. Retrieved April 30, 2008, from the Kenworth Website: *www.kenworth.com/brochures/FuelEfficiency.pdf.*

Putting Energy into Profits: ENERGY STAR ® Guide for Small Business. Washington, D.C.: U.S. Environmental Protection Agency, Energy Star for Business.

Putting Energy into Profits: ENERGY STAR® Guide for Restaurants. Washington, D.C.: U.S. Environmental Protection Agency, May 2007.

"A Quick Guide to Solar Electricity." Rocky Mountain Power. Retrieved October 23, 2008 from *portal.ecosconsulting.com/rmp_solar/ guide_to_solar.html.*

R-Value Recommendations for Buildings software. Oak Ridge National Laboratory, Building Energy Research Division. Accessible from *www.ornl.gov/cgi-bin/cgiwrap?user=roofs&script=ZipTable/ins_fact.pl.*

"R-Value Table." ColoradoENERGY.org. Accessible from *cloradoenergy.org/procorner/stuff/r-values.htm.*

Rea, Mark Stanley (ed.). *IESNA Lighting Handbook, 9th Edition.* New York: Illuminating Engineering Society of North America, July 2000.

Recommendations for the Design of Plastic Bottles. Institute of Scrap Recycling Industries. Accessible from *www.epa.gov/epaoswer/non-hw/ reduce/epr/docs/guidelns.pdf.*

"Recycling Laws." Accessible from the Rechargeable Battery Recycling Corporation Website: *www.rbrc.org/community/ recycling_laws.shtml.*

Remmen, A., and A. Jensen (eds.). *Background Report for a UNEP Guide to Life Cycle Management—A bridge to sustainable products.* Paris, France: United Nations Environmental Programme (Revised), 2005.

Remmen, Arne, Anne Landfield, Konrad Saur, and Allan Astrup Jensen. "Introduction to Sustainability and Life Cycle Thinking" in *Background Report for a UNEP Guide to Life Cycle Management* (ed. Jensen & Remmen). Paris, France: United Nations Environmental Programme, March 2005.

Remmen, Arne, Allan Astrup Jensen, and Jeppe Frydeddal. *Life Cycle Management: A Business Guide to Sustainability.* Paris, France: United Nations Environmental Programme, 2007.

A Resource Guide for Environmentally Preferable Products. Alameda County, California Environmentally Preferable Purchasing Program. March 2006. *stopwaste.org.*

"Review of Combined Heat and Power Technologies." ONSITE SYCOM Energy Corporation, prepared for California Energy Commission, October 1999. Available from *www.eere.energy.gov/de/pdfs/chp_review.pdf.*

Rooks, John. "The Green Market Niche: Being Green, Going Mainstream." March 20, 2007. Retrievable from the MarketingProfs Website: *www.marketingprofs.com.*

Royster, Julia, and Larry Royster (ed. by Sydney Cheryl Sutton). *A Guide to Developing and Maintaining an Effective Hearing Conservation Program.* North Carolina Department of Labor, Division of Occupational Safety and Health. Retrieved September 9, 2008, from *www.nonoise.org/hearing/hcp/hcp.htm#checklistfornoisecontrols.*

Ruck, Nancy Øyvind Aschehoug, Sirri Aydinli, Jens Christoffersen, Gilles Courret, Ian Edmonds, Roman Jakobiak, Martin Kischkoweit-Lopin, Martin Klinger, Eleanor Lee, Laurent Michel, Jean-Louis Scartezzini, and Stephen Selkowitz. *Daylight in Buildings: A Source Book on Daylighting Systems and Components.* Berkeley, Calif.: Lawrence Berkeley National Laboratory, 2000.

Saphire, David. *Case Reopened: Reassessing Refillable Bottles.* New York: Inform, Inc.: 1994.

Sakreski, Sheldon, and Carl Gagliardi. *The Paper Consumer's Guide to Climate Change: How to Reduce Greenhouse Gases with Smarter Paper Choices.* Metafore (Portland, Oreg.) and The Gagliardi Group, 2007.

Saving Energy in U.S. Transportation. OTA-ETI-589. Washington, D.C.: U.S. Government Printing Office. U.S. Congress, Office of Technology Assessment, 1994.

Scheihing, Paul. "DOE Data Center Energy Efficiency Program." May 8, 2008, presentation, p. 2. Retrieved from *www1.eere.energy.gov/industry/saveenergynow/pdfs/doe_data_centers_presentation.pdf.*

Scrap Tire Markets in the United States, 2005 Edition. Washington, D.C.: Rubber Manufacturers Association, November 2006.

Shorr, Brad. *4 Ways to Replace Packing Peanuts.* Retrieved June 9, 2008, from Salazar Packaging Website: *www.salazarpackaging.com/4WaystoReplacePackingPeanuts.html.*

———. *How To Use Less Plastic Box Sealing Tape Or None At All.* Retrieved June 9, 2008, from Salazar Packaging Website: *www.salazarpackaging.com/HowToUseLessPlasticSealingTape.html.*

———. *Reducing Corrugated Consumption—4 Ways to Get More From Less.* Retrieved June 9, 2008, from Salazar Packaging Website: *www.salazarpackaging.com/ReducingCorrugatedConsumption.html.*

———. *Stretch Film—Why Do We Use So Much?* Retrieved June 9, 2008, from Salazar Packaging Website: *www.salazarpackaging.com/StretchFilmWhySoMuch.html.*

Simple Ways to Reduce Office Paper Waste and Make Better Use of the Paper You Need. Natural Resources Defense Council. "Green Living Guide." Retrievable from *www.nrdc.org/cities/living/paper/strategies.asp.*

The Six Sins of Greenwashing™ A Study of Environmental Claims in North American Consumer Markets. Philadelphia, Pa.: TerraChoice Environmental Marketing, Inc., 2008. *www.terrachoice.com/greenwashing*

Small Wind Electric Systems: A Consumer's Guide. U.S. Department of Energy and National Renewable Energy Laboratory. July 2004.

"Smart Plastics Guide." Sea Studios Foundation. Retrieved August 20, 2008, from *www-tc.pbs.org/strangedays/pdf/StrangeDaysSmartPlasticsGuide.pdf.*

Solid Waste Management and Greenhouse Gases: A Life-Cycle Assessment of Emissions and Sinks, 3rd Edition. U.S. Environmental Protection Agency.

A Sourcebook: Good Practice in Freight Transport. European Commission, 2000.

Stegink, Lisa. Edited by Jed Mendell. "Law Review: Reuse Paper with Caution." *Forum,* April 2008. Retrieved June 5, 2008, from *www.associationforum-digital.com/associationforum/200804/.*

Steinfeld, Henning, Pierre Gerber, Tom Wassenaar, Vincent Castel, Mauricio Rosales, and Cees de Haan. *Livestock's Long Shadow: Environmental Issues and Options.* Rome, Italy: Food and Agriculture Organization of the United Nations, 2006.

Stretch Wrap Recycling: A How to Guide. American Plastics Council, Inc. Arlington, Va.: 1997. Retrieved June 26, 2008, from *www.americanchemistry.com/s_plastics/bin.asp?CID=1211&DID=4594&DOC=FILE.PDF.*

Stephenson, Carol Merry. "Choose the Hearing Protection That's Right for You." Retrieved September 9, 2008, from *www.cdc.gov/niosh/topics/noise/abouthlp/chooseprotection.html.*

Stock Packaging Evaluation: Packaging Waste Reduction Checklist. Portland, Oreg.: Oregon Department of Environmental Quality, 2005.

Subramaniam, Usha. "Reverse Logistics Strategies and Implementation: A Pedagogical Survey." *Journal of Academy of Business and Economics,* 2004.

Targeted Statewide Waste Characterization Study: Waste Disposal and Diversion Findings for Selected Industry Groups. Sacramento, Calif.: Cascadia Consulting Group, June 2006. Report to the California Integrated Waste Management Agency.

"Thermal Guidelines for Data Processing Environments." ASHRAE. Cited in Wikipedia. Retrieved October 5, 2008. from *en.wikipedia.org/wiki/Data_center#cite_note-2.*

Thompson, J. William, and Kim Sorvig. *Sustainable Landscape Construction: A Guide to Green Building Outdoors.* Washington, D.C.: Island Press, 2007.

Tires and Passenger Vehicle Fuel Economy. Washington, D.C.: Transportation Research Board. National Research Council of the National Academies, 2006.

"Truck to Train Mode Shifts." In *Washington State Transportation System Efficiency–State Action Policies* (EPA policy summary).

20% Wind Energy by 2030: Increasing Wind Energy's Contribution to U.S. Electricity Supply. DOE/GO-102008-2567. Oak Ridge, Tenn.: U.S. Department of Energy, July 2008.

2007 Cone Consumer Environmental Survey. Boston, Mass.: Cone LLC. Accessible from *www.coneinc.com/*.

2008 Green Gap Survey Fact Sheet. Boston, Mass.: Cone LLC. Accessible from *www.coneinc.com/*.

"2008 LOHAS Consumer Trends Data Base™. Retrieved from the NMI Website: *www.nmisolutions.com/lohasd_segment.html*.

Understanding the Renewable Power Options for Your U.S. Operations: An Issue Brief. Business for Social Responsibility and GreenBiz.com, October 2007. Available from *www.bsr.org/research/reports-by-category.cfm?DocumentID=2*.

U.S. Climate Zones for 2004 Commercial Building Energy Consumption Survey. Retrieved from the U.S. Energy Information Agency Website: *www.eia.doe.gov/emeu/cbecs/climate_zones.html*.

U.S. Solar Industry Year in Review, 2007. Washington, D.C.: Solar Energy Industries Association, Prometheus Institute for Sustainable Development, 2006. Available at *www.prometheus.org/*.

Van Hemel, Carolien G. "The IC EcoDesign Project: Results and Lessons from a Dutch Initiative to Implement Ecodesign in Small and Medium-Sized Companies." *Journal of Sustainable Product Design*, Issue 2, July 1997, pp. 7–18. Retrieved from *www.cfsd.org.uk/journal/archive/97jspd2.pdf*.

Van Rooijen, Martijn, and Helias A. Udo de Haes. *Life Cycle Approaches: The Road from Analysis to Practice.* Paris, France: United Nations Environmental Programme, 2005.

Ventilation for Acceptable Indoor Air Quality. Atlanta, Ga.: ASHRAE, Inc., ANSI/ASHRAE Standard 62.1-2007.

"Ventilation Standards." U.S. Department of Labor, Occupational Safety & Health Administration. Accessible from *www.osha.gov/SLTC/ventilation/index.html*.

Vickers, Amy. *Handbook of Water Use and Conservation.* Amherst, Mass.: WaterPlow Press, 2001.

"Wall Insulation Technology Fact Sheet." DOE/GO-102000-0772. Oak Ridge, Tenn.: U.S. Department of Energy's Office of Building Technology, October 2000.

WasteWi$e Update—Environmentally Preferable Purchasing. EPA530-N-01-002. Washington, D.C.: U.S. Environmental Protection Agency, July 2001.

A Water Conservation Guide for Commercial, Institutional and Industrial Users. Prepared by Schultz Communications, Albuquerque, N. Mex.: New Mexico Office of the State Engineer, 1999.

Water-Efficient Landscaping: Preventing Pollution and Using Water Wisely. Washington, D.C.: EPA Water Resources Center, 1999.

Weather and Soil Moisture Based Landscape Irrigation Scheduling Devices: Technical Review Report—2nd Edition. Temecula, Calif.: U.S. Bureau of Reclamation, Southern California Area Office and Technical Service Center, Water Resources Planning and Operations Support Group, August 2007. Specifications (including price) and performance data on a comprehensive range of sophisticated irrigation system controls may be retrieved from: *www.usbr.gov/waterconservation/docs/SmartController.pdf*.

Westphalen, Detlef, Robert Zogg, Anthony Varone, and Matthew Foran. *Energy Savings Potential for Commercial Refrigeration Equipment: Final Report.* Prepared for U.S. Department of Energy, Office of Building Technologies, Building Equipment Division. Cambridge, Mass: Arthur D. Little, Inc., June 1996.

"What to Look for in an Eco-friendly Printer." GreenBiz, December 14, 2005. Retrieved May 27, 2008, from *www.greenbiz.com/resources/resource/what-look-eco-friendly-printer*.

Whelan, Tensie. "Beyond Recycling: Responsible Paper Purchasing." Published on the GreenBiz Website: *www.greenbiz.com/print/24021*. Retrieved May 12, 2008.

White, Chad, Emma Stewart, Ted Howes, and Bob Adams. *Aligned for Sustainable Design: An A-B-C-D Approach to Making Better Products.* San Francisco, Calif.: Business for Social Responsibility (with IDEO), May 2008. Downloadable from *www.bsr.org/reports/BSR_Sustainable_Design_Report_0508.pdf*.

White, Philip, Steve Belletire, and Louise St. Pierre. *Okala: Learning Ecological Design.* Phoenix, Ariz.: Industrial Designers Society of America, 2007.

Wimmer, Wolfgang, Rainer Zust, and Kun-Mo Lee. *Ecodesign Implementation: A Systematic Guidance on Integrating Environmental Considerations into Product Development.* Dordrecht, The Netherlands: Springer, 2004.

Wiser, Ryan, and Mark Bolinger. *Annual Report on U.S. Wind Power Installation, Cost, and Performance Trends: 2007.* Berkeley, Calif.: Lawrence Berkeley National Laboratory, May 2008.

Wolsey, Robert, and Naomi Miller. *Task Lighting for Offices*, Volume 1, Number 3. Troy, N.Y.: Rensselaer Polytechnic Institute Lighting Research Center, 1994.

Zimmerman, Julie B. "Sustainable Design through the 12 Principles of Green Engineering." Presentation to the 1st International Conference on Sustainability Engineering and Science, Auckland, New Zealand, July 6–9, 2004.

Chapter 5

Center for a New American Dream's Responsible Purchasing
Network
www.responsiblepurchasing.org/
Green Seal
Has a series of reports, fact sheets, recommendations and
criteria to guide green product purchasing.
www.greenseal.org
King County, WA, Model Purchasing Policy
www.metrokc.gov/procure/green/policy.htm
No Harm
Has sample purchasing policies for recycled content, recycled
products, reusable products, and mercury-free products:
www.noharm.org/us/greenPurchasing/materialsmanagers
U.S. EPA Database of Environmental Information for Products
and Services
yosemite1.epa.gov/oppt/eppstand2.nsf
U.S. Environmental Protection Agency's Green Purchasing
Guides
www.epa.gov/epp/pubs/greenguides.htm

Ecodesign

The Biomimicry Institute
www.biomimicryinstitute.org
Clean Production
www.cleanproduction.org/Home.php
Centre for Sustainable Design
An information clearinghouse on sustainable design, and
includes free access to the *Journal of Sustainable Design.*
www.cfsd.org.uk/index.html
Entirely Sustainable Product Design—strategies checklist
www.espdesign.org/StrategiesMain.htm
GreenBlue
www.greenblue.org/index.html
Industrial Design Society of America
www.idsa.org/
International Standards Organization (ISO) Standards Related to
Product Systems
Environmental declarations and claims: 14020, 14021, 14024
and 14025.
Life cycle assessments: 14040, 14041, 14042, 14043, 14047,
14048, 14049.
General: 14000 series.
Guidelines on audit procedures, communications, and the like.
www.iso.org/iso/iso_catalogue.htm

Quality Function Deployment Institute (customer assessment)
www.qfdi.org/

Risk Assessment—Human

European Chemicals Agency's (ECHA) Registration, Evaluation,
Authorisation and restriction of Chemicals (REACH) software
reach.jrc.it/public-2/navigator_setname.htm]
Society of Environmental Toxicology and Chemistry (SETAC)
A nonprofit, worldwide professional society.
www.setac.org/node/1
U.S. Environmental Protection Agency's National Center for
Environmental Assessment—
Integrated Risk Information System (IRIS) Chemical database
cfpub.epa.gov/ncea/iris/index.cfm
Toxic Substances data bank
sis.nlm.nih.gov/enviro.html
Consolidated List of Chemicals Subject to the Emergency
Planning and Community Right-to-Know Act (EPCRA) and
Section 112(r) of the Clean Air Act
www.epa.gov/ceppo/pubs/title3.pdf
Ecological Risk
www.epa.gov/superfund/programs/risk/ecolgc.htm
Aquatic and Terrestrial Risk
www.epa.gov/oppefed1/ecorisk/

Life Cycle Assessment

Links List
www.doka.ch/lca.htm
The Society for the Promotion of Life-Cycle Assessment
www.spold.org
American Center for Life Cycle Assessment
www.life-cycle.org

Chapter 6

Packaging Design Magazine's Resource Guide
www.packagedesignmag.com/issues/2006.11/resources.shtml
Reusable Packaging Association
www.choosereusables.org/

Package Design

American Society for Testing and Materials
www.astm.org/

Package Reuse

The State of Minnesota
Maintains a directory of enterprises and organizations
offering expertise and products for reusable packaging.
www.pca.state.mn.us/oea/transport/index.cfm

Assessment Software	Overview	Assessment Software	Overview
Ecodesign PILOT	Online tool to increase the environmental performance of existing products www.ecodesign.at/pilot/ONLINE/ENGLISH/	MIET 3.0	Missing Inventory Estimation Tool is an Excel-based program designed to estimate emissions and resource consumption information that is missing from site-specific LCA analyses. MIET 2.0 may be downloaded. Incorporated into PRé's SimaPro software and as standalone (Comprehensive Environmental Data Archive (CEDA)). www.leidenuniv.nl/cml/ssp/software/miet/index.html
ecoinvent	The Swiss Centre for Life Cycle Inventories has a database of more than 4000 units that are used as inputs for several software programs. www.ecoinvent.ch/		
ECO-it	PRé Consultants' software to model product's performance using a life cycle approach, uses weighted criteria contained in Eco-indicator 99. Windows-based; operates on Mac with Windows emulator www.pre.nl/eco-it/eco-it.htm#ecoindicator		
		SimaPro 7	PRé Consultants professional LCA software is a sophisticated tool used in modeling complex products and services. www.pre.nl/simapro/simapro_lca_software.htm
Eio-lca	Carnegie Mellon's Green Design Institute's database facilitates comparison of production impacts of some 500 products using $-impact as comparison basis. www.eiolca.net/	TEAM	Ecobilan's Tool for Environmental Analysis and Management www.ecobilan.com/uk_team.php
		TRACI	LCA method developed by EPA www.epa.gov/nrmrl/std/sab/traci/
GaBi	GaBi 4 is universal professional tool for life cycle assessment and reporting. GaBi lite is simple software. www.gabi-software.com/	UMBERTO	Models, calculates, and illustrates material and energy flows. www.umberto.de/en/
IdeMat	A commercial environmental database on materials and processes. www.idemat.nl/Product/pi_frame.htm	US Life-Cycle Inventory Database	Created by the National Renewable Energy Laboratory for LCA, includes common materials, products, and processes, but not full life-cycle assessments. www.nrel.gov/lci/
KCL-ECO 4.0	Life cycle assessment software developed by pulp/paper industry leader www.kcl.fi/page.php?page_id=166		

Additional software directory: www.p2pays.org/ref%5C01%5C00047/00047d.htm

Container Recycling Institute
   www.container-recycling.org/

Pallets
National Wood Pallet and Container Association (refurbish, sourcing)
   (703) 527–7667
The International Association of Pallet Recyclers (directory of pallet refurbishers)
   (703) 908–4880

Common LCA Software Tools
EcoIndicator 99
IdeMat (materials database)
PEMS (inventory analysis and impact assessment)
EcoPackager (comparison of life-cycle impacts of alternative packaging designs)
   SimaPro5
   EcoScan
   Eco-IT
SPC's comparative packaging assessment tool, COMPASS™, will be available in 2009.

Packaging Materials
Minnesota Pollution Control Agency's Reusable Transport Packaging Directory
   www.pca.state.mn.us/oea/transport/index.cfm
Plastic Loosefill Council
   Maintains a listing of companies that accept polystyrene peanuts for recycling.
   (800) 828–2214

Packing tips
FedEx® How to Pack
   images.fedex.com/us/services/pdf/How_To_Pack.pdf
UPS
   www.ups.com/content/us/en/resources/prepare/guidelines/prepare_package1.html

Chapter 8
Green Clean
CleanGredients™
   Maintains an online database of institutional and industrial cleaning ingredients.
   www.cleangredients.org

Searchable Cleaner and Solvent Substitution Databases
www.cleanersolutions.org

Green Design
Green Globes
  An online analysis tool.
  www.greenglobes.com
U.S. Environmental Protection Agency's *Target Finder* software
  www.energystar.gov/
  index.cfm?c=new_bldg_design.bus_target_finder
U.S. Environmental Protection Agency's Building Life Cycle Cost (BLCC) Program
  www1.eere.energy.gov/femp/information/download_blcc.html

Green Materials
Convention on International Trade in Endangered Species
  Endangered Woods database *www.unep-wcmc.org/citestrade/trade.cfm*
Ecospecifier
  A database of sustainable products and resources for identifying substitute materials.
  www.ecospecifier.org/
Green2Green^SM
  A free, online resource for comparing building products.
  www.green2green.org
Green Seal–Certified Paints
  greenseal.org/findaproduct/paints_coatings.cfm
Tree Talk, Inc.'s Woods of the World Database (Compact Disk) for identifying alternative wood species.
  Tree Talk, Inc.
  P.O. Box 426, 431 Pine Street
  Burlington, VT 05401
  (800) 858–6230
  E-mail: *wow@together.net*
U.S. Department of Commerce's *Building for Environmental & Economic Sustainability (BEES)* building materials LCC analysis software
  www.bfrl.nist.gov/oae/software/bees/

Green Landscape
Invasive Species Database
  www.issg.org/database/welcome/
Non-Toxic Pest Control: Northwest Coalition for Alternatives to Pesticides
  www.pesticide.org/factsheets.html#alternatives

Chapter 9
Biomass
U.S. Department of Energy, National Renewable Energy Laboratory. Solar, wind, biomass atlases
  www.nrel.gov/gis/maps.html#resource_atlas

Cogeneration
Cogeneration and On-Site Power Production, Buyer's Guide, and Resources
  pennwell.365media.com/cogenerationonsitepowerproduction/search.html

Commercial Energy Efficiency
U.S. Environmental Protection Agency's *Portfolio Manager* software
  www.energystar.gov/istar/pmpam/#%23

Emissions
U.S. Environmental Protection Agency emissions data:
  PowerProfiler
  www.epa.gov/cleanenergy/energy-and-you/how-clean.html
  eGRID
  www.epa.gov/cleanenergy/energy-resources/egrid/index.html

Fuel Cells
Fuel Cell Store
  www.fuelcellstore.com

Geothermal
Southern Methodist University Geothermal Laboratory
  smu.edu/geothermal/

Green Energy
U.S. Department of Energy's Green Power search engine
  www.dsireusa.org/index.cfm?EE=1&RE=1

Hydroelectric Power
Directory of Dams and Reservoirs in the United States
  en.wikipedia.org/wiki/
  List_of_reservoirs_and_dams_in_the_United_States
Hydro Research Foundation
  www.hydrofoundation.org/index.html
Low Impact Hydropower Institute
  www.lowimpacthydro.org/

Renewable Energy
American Council On Renewable Energy (ACORE)
  www.acore.org/
U.S. Department of Energy's National Renewable Energy Laboratory's *HOMER* software
  analysis.nrel.gov/homer/

Solar
American Solar Energy Society
  www.ases.org
Find Solar
  A quick estimator for space conditioning, water heating, swimming pool heating, and electric generation for business; and a contractors' directory.
  www.findsolar.com/index.php?page=rightforme

Energy Planning
National Renewable Energy Laboratory, Solar Radiation Data Manual for Flat-Plate and Concentrating Collectors
  rredc.nrel.gov/solar/pubs/redbook/#maps
National Renewable Energy Laboratory, Solar Radiation Resource Maps (Database)
  rredc.nrel.gov/solar/old_data/nsrdb/redbook/atlas/Table.html
NREL'S PVWATTS PV performance calculator
  Allows for quick calculation of value.
  rredc.nrel.gov/solar/calculators/PVWATTS/
Solar Energy Industries Association
  www.seia.org

Solarbuzz
www.solarbuzz.com
U.S. Department of Energy, Calculator: Estimating Your Solar
Water Heater System's Cost *apps1.eere.energy.gov/consumer/
your_home/water_heating/index.cfm/mytopic=12910*
U.S. Department of Energy's Solar Energy Technology Program
www1.eere.energy.gov/solar/

Statistics
International Energy Agency, World Energy Outlook
www.iea.org/

Wind
U.S. Department of Energy, Wind Energy Program
www.eere.energy.gov/windandhydro/windpoweringamerica/

Chapter 10
Database of State Incentives for Renewable & Efficiency (DSIRE)
www.dsireusa.org/
U.S. Energy Information Agency, Cost of Energy
tonto.eia.doe.gov/state/SEP_MorePrices.cfm
U.S. Department of Energy, ENERGY STAR Program List of
Resource Partners
www.energystar.gov/index.cfm?c=spp_res.pt_spps
U.S. Department of Energy, ENERGY STAR Financial Calculators
www.energystar.gov/index.cfm?c=assess_value.financial_tools
U.S. Environmental Protection Agency *PowerProfiler*, Fuel Source by
Utility Lookup
www.epa.gov/cleanenergy/energy-and-you/how-clean.html
U.S. Environmental Protection Agency, *eGRID*
A detailed inventory of power and emissions data for U.S.
generating facilities.
www.epa.gov/cleanenergy/energy-resources/egrid/index.html
Zip Code–Based Description of Sulfur Dioxide, Nitrogen Oxide,
and Carbon Dioxide Emissions From Electricity-Generating
Facilities
oaspub.epa.gov/powpro/ept_pack.charts

Chapter 11
International Association of Lighting Management Companies
(NALMCO™)
www.nalmco.org/
Lighting Research Center at Rensselaer Polytechnic Institute
www.lrc.rpi.edu/
U.S. Department of Labor, Occupational Safety and Health
Administration. Computer Lighting Website
*www.osha.gov/SLTC/etools/computerworkstations/
wkstation_enviro.html#lighting*
U.S. Department of Energy. *Solid-State Lighting* Web portal
*www.netl.doe.gov/ssl/usingLeds/
general_illumination_efficiency_luminous.htm*

Chapter 12
U.S. Department of Energy, Commercial Energy Performance
Resources
*www1.eere.energy.gov/buildings/commercial/
apps1.eere.energy.gov/buildings/tools_directory/subjects_sub.cfm*

U.S. Department of Labor, Occupational Safety & Health
Administration
ventilation standards and other resources and subject links
www.osha.gov/SLTC/ventilation/index.html

Chapter 15
Activating Power Management Features in Different Types of
Computers (How To)
*www.energystar.gov/index.cfm?c=power_mgt.pr_power_mgt_users
www.energystar.gov/
index.cfm?c=power_mgt.pr_power_mgt_implementation_res#tech_assistance*
Directory of Power Management Software
*www.energystar.gov/
index.cfm?c=power_mgt.pr_power_mgt_comm_packages*
Find ENERGY STAR–Qualified Office Equipment
*www.energystar.gov/
index.cfm?fuseaction=find_a_product.showProductCategory&pcw_code=OEF*
DC Pro Software Tool for Managing Data Center Energy Use
dcpro.ppc.com/
Greenpeace *Guide to Greener Electronics.*
Updated regularly.
*www.greenpeace.org/international/campaigns/toxics/electronics/how-
the-companies-line-up*

Chapter 17
American Council for an Energy Efficient Economy
www.aceee.org/pubsmeetings/index.htm
Consortium for Energy Efficiency
www.cee1.org/
Industrial Efficiency Alliance—Resource Page
www.industrialefficiencyalliance.org/resources.html#Pumps
U.S. Department of Energy, Industrial Technologies Program
Software Tools
www1.eere.energy.gov/industry/bestpractices/software.html#psat
U.S. Department of Energy, Focused Industry Energy Efficiency
Guides
*www.energystar.gov/
index.cfm?c=in_focus.bus_industries_focus#plant*

Chapter 18
American Council for an Energy Efficient Economy
www.aceee.org/pubsmeetings/index.htm
Compressed Air Challenge
www.compressedairchallenge.org/library/index.html#Best_Practices
Consortium for Energy Efficiency
www.cee1.org/
Industrial Efficiency Alliance—Resource Page
www.industrialefficiencyalliance.org/resources.html#Pumps
U.S. Department of Energy, Industrial Technologies Program
Software Tools
www1.eere.energy.gov/industry/bestpractices/software.html#psat
U.S. Department of Energy, Focused Industry Energy Efficiency
Guides
*www.energystar.gov/
index.cfm?c=in_focus.bus_industries_focus#plant*

Chapter 19

Find a Professional Solar Installer (includes contact information, experience, certifications)
www.findsolar.com/

Green Power Purchasing

Green-e
www.green-e.org
U.S. Department of Energy, *Buying Green Power*
apps3.eere.energy.gov/greenpower/buying/index.shtml
U.S. Department of Energy's Green Power Search Engine
www.dsireusa.org/index.cfm?EE=1&RE=1

Solar Assessment

Clean Power Estimator™ for California
www.consumerenergycenter.org/renewables/estimator/
Solar Assessment (Roof Ray) in Beta
www.roofray.com/
U.S. National Renewable Energy Laboratory PV WATTS Calculator
rredc.nrel.gov/solar/codes_algs/PVWATTS/

Chapter 20

Battery University (Don't let the name fool you. There's a lot of solid content here.)
www.batteryuniversity.com/index.htm

Chapter 21

Carpools, Vanpools, Ride-Matching Databases
www.erideshare.com/
www.rideshareonline.com/
www.carsharing.net/where.html
U.S. Environmental Protection Agency SmartWay℠ Transport Partnership
A voluntary collaboration between U.S. EPA and the freight industry designed to increase energy efficiency while significantly reducing greenhouse gases and air pollution.
www.epa.gov/smartway/
SmartWay℠—EPA's Program to Control Freight Energy, Greenhouse Gas Emissions and Air Pollution
www.epa.gov/oms/smartway/idlingtechnologies.htm#truck-mobile-sdsu
An Overview of the Applications Addressed by the Federal Intelligent Transportation Systems (ITS) Program
www.itsoverview.its.dot.gov/default.asp

Fuels

The Alternative Fueling Station Locator
afdcmap2.nrel.gov/locator/FindPane.asp
Gasoline and Diesel Fuel Update
Posted weekly by the Energy Information Agency.
tonto.eia.doe.gov/oog/info/gdu/gasdiesel.asp
U.S. Dept of Energy *Clean Cities Alternative Fuels Price Report*
Published semi-annually by the Dept. of Energy.
www.eere.energy.gov/afdc/price_report.html
EPA's Gas Saving and Aftermarket Retrofit Device Evaluation Program
www.epa.gov/oms/consumer/reports.htm

Hybrid Tax Incentives
www.cleancarcampaign.org/hybridstate.shtml
Hybrid Trucks Financial Incentives
Identifies incentive programs to support the purchase of hybrid trucks. *www.edf.org/page.cfm?tagID=1124*

Public Transit

American Public Transportation Association (APTA)
www.apta.com
Public Transportation Database for Locating Public Transit
publictransportation.org/
www.commuterchoice.com/

Telecommuting

Desktop Video Conferencing Best Practices
www.wiredred.com/video-conferencing/desktop-video-conferencing.html
Excellent Comprehensive Resource Directory From AT&T
www.kn.pacbell.com/wired/vidconf/links.html
Multiple Articles and Resources
www.hr-guide.com/data/011.htm
The Telework Coalition
www.telcoa.org/index.htm
"The Psychology of Effective Business Communications in Geographically Dispersed Teams" from the U.S. Department of Health and Human Services Telecommuting Program Policy
www.hhs.gov/ohr/telework/policy.html

Transportation Statistics

Center for Transportation Excellence
www.cfte.org

Vehicle Efficiency

ACEEE's Green Book Online
A full listing of green cars and trucks.
www.greenercars.org/
California Air Resources Board's *The Buyer's Guide to Clean Cars*
www.arb.ca.gov/msprog/ccbg/ccbg.html
Future Cars
www.futurecars.com
Fuel Cells
fuelcells.org
Hybrid Cars
www.hybridcars.com
Union of Concerned Scientists' Comparison Website
www.hybridcenter.org/
U.S. Department of Energy's Vehicle Gas Mileage and Emissions Guide
www.fueleconomy.gov
U.S. Department of Energy's Vehicle Efficiency
apps1.eere.energy.gov/consumer/your_vehicle/
U.S. Environmental Protection Agency's *Green Vehicle Guide*
www.epa.gov/greenvehicles/Index.do
Transportation Software Directory
www.google.com/Top/Business/Transportation_and_Logistics/Trucking/Software

Chapter 22

Global Environmental Management Initiative, Connecting the Drops Toward Creative Water Strategies: A Water Sustainability Tool. An excellent resource on business risks and opportunities, setting goals and strategic direction.
www.gemi.org/waterplanner/

Water Librarians' Home Page
A portal for information on a broad range of water-related topics.
www.interleaves.org/~ rteeter/waterlib.html

WaterWiser
The American Water Works Association's Web-based clearinghouse of resources on water conservation, efficiency, and demand management for conservation professionals and the larger water supply community.
www.awwa.org/Resources/Waterwiser.cfm?navItemNumber=1561

Irrigation and Landscaping

American Society of Irrigation Consultants
www.asic.org

The Irrigation Association
www.irrigation.org/

The Irrigation Water Management Society
Offers watering calculators and real-time weather information for irrigation systems based on their locations.
www.iwms.org/

Xeriscape Colorado
www.xeriscape.org

Fixtures, Products, and Consultants

The American Water Works Association
Maintains a list of equipment, products, and consultants in their sourcebook.
www.awwa.org/awwa/sourcebook/

The California Urban Water Conservation Council
Has an excellent Product News directory.
www.cuwcc.org/products_tech.lasso

Composting Toilet World (Envirolet)
www.compostingtoilet.org

Composting Toilet Systems—Descriptions
oikos.com/library/compostingtoilet

The Environmentally Preferable Purchasing Guide
Assembled by Minnesota's Solid Waste Management Coordinating Board to help direct purchasing decisions and includes a section on water-efficient products.
www.greenguardian.com/government/eppg

Rebates

Kohler
Maintains a searchable database for rebates.
www.us.kohler.com/onlinecatalog/waterconservation-rebates.jsp

Chapter 23

Searchable Noise Control Idea Base (Enter Equipment/Tool and Industry)
www.lni.wa.gov/Safety/Topics/ReduceHazards/NoiseBank/search.asp

Noise Pollution Clearinghouse
www.nonoise.org

NIOSH Hearing Protection Device Compendium
www2a.cdc.gov/hp-devices/hp_srchpg01.asp

Chapter 24

U.S. Environmental Protection Agency's National Environmental Compliance Assistance Clearinghouse
cfpub.epa.gov/clearinghouse/index.cfm?TopicID=C:10:700:AIR:

U.S. Environmental Protection Agency's RACT/BACT/LAER Clearinghouse (RBLC)
cfpub.epa.gov/rblc/htm/bl02.cfm

U.S. Environmental Protection Agency's Map of Radon Zones
www.epa.gov/radon/zonemap.html

U.S. Environmental Protection Agency's Indoor Air Quality Building Education and Assessment Model (I-BEAM).
www.epa.gov/iaq/largebldgs/i-beam/index.html

U.S. Environmental Protection Agency's GHG calculator
www.epa.gov/cleanenergy/energy-resources/calculator.html

Chapter 25

Ecospecifier
A database of sustainable products most useful in green building but also helpful in identifying substitute materials.
www.ecospecifier.org/

freecycle™
A worldwide gifting movement: post a description of the item you no longer want.
www.freecycle.org/

Global Recycling Network
www.grn.com/

Institute of Scrap Recycling Industries, Inc.
www.isri.org

National and Regional Listings of Material Exchanges
www.epa.gov/jtr/comm/exchstat.htm#ma
www.recycle.net/
www.wastexchange.org/

Product Stewardship Institute, Inc.
www.productstewardship.us/

California Integrated Waste Management Board's Recycled Content Products Directory
www.ciwmb.ca.gov/RCP/Product.asp?VW=CAT&CATID=258

U.S. Environmental Protection Agency, *Waste Reduction Model* software for calculating GHG emissions.
www.epa.gov/climatechange/wycd/waste/calculators/Warm_home.html

Batteries

Rechargeable Battery Recycling Corporation
www.rbrc.org/

Composting

Resource Database, Including Large Scale
www.howtocompost.org/

Construction and Demolition

Building Material Reuse Association Directory
www.buildingreuse.org/directory/

Construction Materials Recycling Association Directory
See also their companion pages on concrete, shingles, and drywall recycling.
www.cdrecycling.org/find.html#ri
The Association of Postconsumer Plastic Recyclers
www.plasticsrecycling.org/
Grass Roots Recycling Network
www.grrn.org/
National Association for PET Container Resources
www.napcor.org/

E-Waste
Purchasing ENERGY STAR–Rated Office Equipment
www.energystar.gov/
index.cfm?fuseaction=find_a_product.showProductCategory&pcw_code=OEF
Purchasing Office Equipment
www.betterbuys.com
Green Electronics Council's *Environmental Product Environmental Assessment Tool* (EPEAT)'s Product Registry
www.epeat.net/Search.aspx
International Association of Electronics Recyclers' Certified Electronics Recycler® Certified Companies
www.iaer.org/communications/cer-list.htm
Purchasing Guidelines for Environmentally Preferable Computers
www.noharm.org/details.cfm?type=document&id=1634
Electronics Environmental Benefits Calculator (EEBC)
eerc.ra.utk.edu/ccpct/eebc/eebc.html
National Center for Electronics Recycling
www.electronicsrecycling.org/public/
techsoup's "Keeping Old Computers Alive"
www.techsoup.org/learningcenter/hardware/archives/page9667.cfm
ecyclingtools.com
www.ecyclingtools.com
EPA's "Where Can I Donate or Recycle My Old Computer and Other Electronic Products?" Web Page Directory
www.epa.gov/epaoswer/hazwaste/recycle/ecycling/donate.htm
My Green Electronics™ Directory
www.mygreenelectronics.org/
Telecommunication Industry Association
www.eiae.org/
Earth911
earth911.org/electronics/
Donating Equipment
www.cristina.org
computersforlearning.gov/
Cell Phones Donation Directory
www.recellular.com/recycling/donatePhones.asp
Electronics Take-Back Campaigns
www.computertakeback.com/
Securing Data From Computers: "Do the 'PC' Thing: Donate Computers"
www.ecyclingtools.com/_documents/DataSecBusiness.pdf
Companies That Have Signed the "Electronic Recycler's Pledge of True Stewardship"
www.ban.org/pledge/Locations.html

Trade-Ins, Auctions, Marketplace
www.dealtree.com/services.cfm
Free Cell Phone Data Erasing
www.recellular.com/recycling/data_eraser/default.asp

Food
America's Second Harvest—Food Bank Locator
www.secondharvest.org/zip_code.jsp

Local Foods
USDA Farmers Markets database
apps.ams.usda.gov/FarmersMarkets/
Eat Local Challenge
eatlocalchallenge.com
Slow Food USA
www.slowfoodusa.org/index.html
Food Routes
www.foodroutes.org
Healthy Seafood Watch, Monterey Aquarium
www.mbayaq.org/cr/SeafoodWatch.asp

Rendering
Check Yellow Pages for "Rendering" or "Grease Traps."
"Shopper's Guide to Pesticides in Produce"
Download from Environmental Working Group's Food News Site
www.foodnews.org/

Glass
Secondary Market Directories
www.ecoglass.net/
www.recycle.net/Glass/index.html

Metals
Steel Recycling Institute
www.recycle-steel.org/index.html
Scrap Metal Purchasers, Searchable Directories
www.metalworld.com/a/0100.html
www.recycle.net/
earth911.org/recycling/

Oil
Filter Manufacturers Council
Sponsored Used Filter Recycling Hotline.
(800) 993-4583

Plastics
Biodegradable Plastics Institute
Compostable products certification directory.
www.bpiworld.org/BPI-Public/Approved/1.html
Plastic Loose Fill Council
Directory for packing peanuts.
www.loosefillpackaging.com/search/default.asp

Tires
State Regulatory Database
www.epa.gov/epaoswer/non-hw/muncpl/tires/live.htm
Scrap Tire Disposal and Recycling Exchange
www.rubber.com/rubber/a/rb8001.html?affilid=100034

Chapter 26
Stop Mailings
EcoLogical Mail Coalition
(800) 620–3975
www.ecologicalmail.org/index.html
"Stop Sending"/"Correct Information" Postcard Template to Send
to Mailers
www.metrokc.gov/dnrp/swd/nwpc/MailCard.pdf

Forestry Practices
Forestry Stewardship Council
U.S. and international Websites.
www.fscus.org
www.fscoax.org
Certified Paper, Printers, Pulp Suppliers, Merchants, and
Manufacturers
www.fscus.org/paper/
Time, Inc. Supplier Environmental Performance Scorecard
research.yale.edu/gisf/assets/pdf/tfd/Time_Inc.pdf
Forest Certification Resource Center
Certified wood supply database and tracking services.
www.certifiedwood.org
Green Press Initiative
Evaluation of forest certification options in Toolkit for
Responsible Paper Use.
www.greenpressinitiative.org/documents/PrinterToolkit.pdf

Paper
Conservatree
Comprehensive directory of papers.
www.conservatree.org/paper/PaperMasterList.shtml
www.conservatree.com/public/localsources/copypaper.html

Printing
Green Press Initiative
Directories of papers and printers.
www.greenpressinitiative.org/action/suppliers.htm
Printers' National Environmental Assistance Center's Pollution
Prevention Self-Assessment Checklist for Commercial Printing
www.pneac.org/sheets/all/checklist.cfm

Chapter 27
Natural Marketing Institute
www.nmisolutions.com/index.html

Chapter 28
Canada's EcoLogo^{CM} Program
www.ecologo.org/en/abouttheprogram/
Consumers Reports' Greener Choices^{SM} Eco-labels Center
www.greenerchoices.org/eco-labels/eco-home.cfm?redirect=1
European Union Eco-label
ec.europa.eu/environment/ecolabel/index_en.htm
Fairtrade Labelling Organizations International
www.fairtrade.net/
Global Ecolabelling Network (GEN)
A global, non-profit association of ecolabeling organizations.
www.gen.gr.jp/
International Organization for Standardization (ISO)
www.iso.org/iso/iso_catalogue.htm

Chapter 30
Corporate Register's directory of corporate responsibility
reports:*www.corporateregister.com/*
Global Reporting Initiative
www.globalreporting.org

Index

GLENN BACHMAN is a Certified Management Consultant and Certified Planner who has consulted with businesses, government agencies, and educational institutions for more than 30 years.

During his first 15 years of consulting, Glenn focused on energy and environmental planning projects, ranging from cost-benefit studies of electric generating facilities for the Bonneville Power Administration, to studies of landfill operations, light rail, and office towers.

For the past 15 years Glenn has been a consultant to management, specializing in strategic planning, and alignment and creating performance breakthroughs. He has assisted growing organizations in strategic thinking, planning and plan implementation, capitalization, and project management.

Glenn's company, Raven Business Group, LLC, focuses on sustainability consulting: assisting organizations in becoming more ecologically and socially responsible, while improving their profitability and ability to compete. He works well with clients in the preparation of business cases, environmental audits, energy management plans, and sustainability reports.

Glenn is well-respected for his colorful presentations on topics related to sustainability, transforming businesses into green enterprises, green as strategy, and green economic development.

For more information visit: *www.ravenbusiness.com.*